2019 AALSO Field Guide

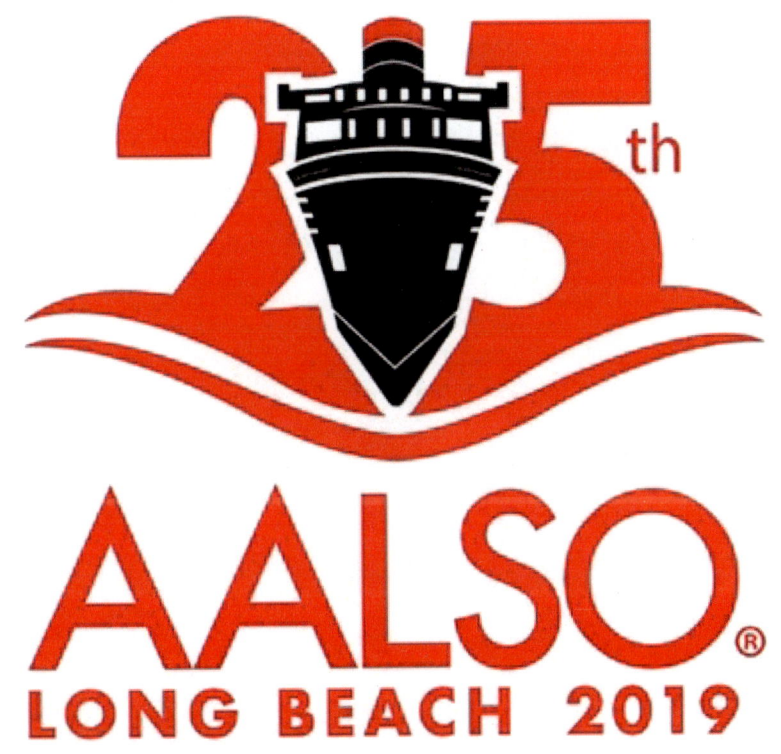

A Field Guide to Water Quality Practices, Common System Components, and Practical Mathematics

2019 Field Guide Committee

AALSO
Aquatic Animal Life Support Operators
312 Crosstown Road #353
Peachtree City, GA 30269
info@aalso.org
www.aalso.org

Editors, Authors, Illustrators, and Industry Reviewers

Editors

Micah Buster 2019 - Wonders of Wildlife
Laurie Patel 2016-2019 - California Academy of Sciences
Karen Tuttle Stearns 2016-2019 - Aquarium of the Pacific

Authors

2019 Authors

Micah Buster 2017-2019 - Wonders of Wildlife
Andrew Bywater 2019 - Saint Louis Zoo
Trevor Erdmann 2019 - Oregon Coast Community College
Elizabeth Fisher 2016-2019 - Walt Disney Parks and Resorts
Johnny May 2018 - OdySea Aquarium, 2019 - Merlin Entertainments plc
Laurie Patel 2016-2019 - California Academy of Sciences
Jason Steinmetz 2016-2019 - Walt Disney Parks and Resorts
Karen Tuttle Stearns 2016-2019 - Aquarium of the Pacific

Field Guide Committee and Past Contributors

Ajua Ampadu 2017 - New York Aquarium
Arnel Bautista 2016-2018 - California Academy of Sciences
Mike Bajek 2014-2015 - Landry's Golden Nugget, 2016-2019 - Wonders of Wildlife
Remy Corner 2011-2015 - Six Flags Discovery Kingdom
Jeff Gibula 2016-2019 - Newport Aquarium
Matt Hoard 2016-2018 - The Marine Mammal Center
Steve Massar 2016-2019 - Vancouver Aquarium
John Masson 2017 - Georgia Aquarium
Matthew Regensburger, Editor 2016-2018 - Georgia Aquarium
Jeff Sedon 2016-2017 - Walt Disney Parks and Resorts
Byron Waller 2016-2019 - Virginia Aquarium
Susan Walsh (formerly Susan Goodridge) 2017 - Georgia Aquarium

Illustrators

Micah Buster 2017-2019 - Wonders of Wildlife
Alex Hirota 2017-2019 - Wonders of Wildlife
Richard Prince 2017-2019 - Wonders of Wildlife

Industry Reviewers

Chris Andrews, PhD 2017-2018 - Merlin Entertainment
Jill Arnold 2017-2018 - National Aquarium
Ethan Barr 2018 - Seattle Aquarium
Chris Carr - 2018 - Aquarium of the Pacific
Ray Davis 2017 - New York Aquarium
Nina Fisher 2017, 2019 - New England Aquarium
Robert Frazier 2017 - Georgia Aquarium
Evan Jamison 2019 - Loveland Living Planet Aquarium
David Lo 2017-2019 - New York Aquarium, 2019 Audubon Aquarium of the Americas
Chris Manley 2017, 2019 - California Academy of Sciences
Blayk Michaels 2017 - Bass Pro Shops
Roger Phillips 2019 - Monterey Bay Aquarium
Kasie Regnier 2017-2019 - Monterey Bay Aquarium
Steve Ritchie 2018 - Aquarium of the Pacific
Kent Semmen 2017-2018 - Walt Disney Parks and Resorts
Joel Skaggs 2017 - The Marine Mammal Center
Matt Wandell 2017 - Monterey Bay Aquarium
Joel Yankie 2017 - Columbus Public Health Division of Environmental Health
Mark Fisher 2019 - Cincinnati Zoo

Table of Contents

Foreward

In 1994, approximately 30 zoo and aquarium Life Support System (LSS) professionals met in Las Vegas to discuss water filtration systems. By sharing ideas and pooling their knowledge, the attendees hoped to benefit individual operators and entire facilities. What started as a meeting for a few individuals turned into an annual symposium attended by over 400 life support operators, water quality technicians, curators, aquarists, researchers, managers, and equipment manufacturers. Aquatic Animal Life Support Operators (AALSO) has expanded greatly in the last 25 years. The organization now has over 1,300 members, 850 certified operators, and roughly 450 vendor members. These vendor members supply the zoo and aquarium industry with pumps, valves, filters, heat exchangers, sensors, and every other piece of equipment that keep animals and their habitats healthy.

This field guide has been created by AALSO members for AALSO members. Drafted specifically for the zoo and aquarium industry, it is a critical tool of the AALSO Education Program, which is dedicated to disseminating technical information on the care of aquatic animals. AALSO provides education opportunities at the annual symposium and as onsite training as part of the Education and Training Program. This program partners with universities to train students in preparation for a career in aquatic animal care. By reaching out to educational institutions, and the national and international zoo and aquarium community, AALSO hopes to further enrich the life support knowledge base, understanding that different ideas and solutions from different places help improve our industry.

The AALSO Symposium is an annual five day idea exchange. Members share their successes and failures, facilities describe their new projects and system retrofits, and vendors conduct equipment specific training and display their latest products. In addition, AALSO has created three levels of Life Support Operator and Water Quality Technician Certification. The Certified Pool Operator (CPO) course, Occupational Safety and Health Administration (OSHA) 10-hour training, and PVC/CPVC Pipe Bonding Certification are a few of the programs offered at AALSO. At the symposium, members are able to rebuild pumps, size chillers, calibrate sensors, fuse pipes, and operate ozone systems on an automated 5,000 gallon aquatic system. Information on discussion forums, job postings, scholarship opportunities (including paid trips to the symposium), college programs, study material, and details on past and future symposiums, are available through the website, www.aalso.org.

An organization like AALSO, which thrives on information exchange and new ideas, is only as good as its membership is diverse. Along these lines, AALSO has open enrollment for zoo and aquarium facilities, institutions, and companies interested in learning and sharing information with other industry professionals. Take advantage of the amazing opportunity to collaborate with aquatic experts from around the globe and access a wealth of knowledge by joining AALSO for a small membership fee. Thus far, the symposium has captivated worldwide interest, drawing in attendees from countries such as: England, Portugal, Australia, Mexico, Spain, China, Hong Kong, Canada, Italy, Bahamas, Cayman Islands, South Africa, Japan, United Arab Emirates, and Russia. Since its inception, AALSO has established itself as a leading organization and network for anyone who works with zoo and aquarium water systems, and we're only getting started. Start planning now to attend the next AALSO Symposium. See you there! For more information on AALSO, please visit: www.aalso.org

We hope you enjoy this Field Guide as much as we have enjoyed putting it together,

The 2019 AALSO Board of Directors

Laura Patel
AALSO Executive Board – President
Steinhart Aquarium
San Francisco, CA   USA

Dennis Ethier
AALSO Executive Board – Vice President
New York Aquarium
New York, NY   USA

Karen Tuttle Stearns
AALSO Executive Board – Secretary
Aquarium of the Pacific
Long Beach, CA   USA

Matt Regensburger
AALSO Executive Board – Treasurer
Georgia Aquarium
Atlanta, GA   USA

Ryan Leasure
AALSO Board of Directors
Cleveland Metroparks Zoo
Aurora, OH   USA

Steve Massar
AALSO Board of Directors
Mississippi River Aquarium
Gulfport, MS   USA

Joel Yankie
AALSO Board of Directors
Columbus Zoo and Aquarium
Columbus, OH   USA

Ben Ashe
AALSO Board of Directors
MDM Pumps
Colorado Springs, CO   USA

John Hale
AALSO Board of Directors
RCK Controls
San Diego, CA   USA

Adrian Megay
AALSO Board of Directors
RK2 Systems
Gilbertsville, PA   USA

1 Diversity found in Aquatic Exhibitry

Aquatic exhibits are diverse, like the animals they display. There are thousands of zoological facilities with aquatic exhibits and each exhibit is unique. There is no one-size-fits-all aquatic exhibit; each system is designed according to specific animal welfare needs, staffing, resources, and guest engagement. An ideal exhibit design will meet all of these needs.

1.1 History

No single person can lay claim to creating the first aquarium. Adaptations and supplemental components led to what is known as a modern day aquarium. In 1852, Madame Jeanette Power used the "Water Cage," a glass case filled with water, to study marine animals. Nathaniel Bagshaw Ward published a book in 1842, called *On the Growth of Plants in Closely Glazed Cases* (Ward, 1842), that discussed the "Wardian Case," which held both plants and animals, where oxygen and carbon dioxide were exchanged. Anna Thynne introduced plants into the water cage with the aim to help preserve the purity of the seawater in 1846. All of these innovations lead to what was then known as a "Balanced Aquarium." Philip Henry Gosse's 1854 Victorian best-seller *The Aquarium: An Unveiling of the Wonders of the Deep Sea* (Gosse, 1854) sparked the popularity of the modern aquarium displays that is known today.

Before Gosse's ground breaking publication, he was given the opportunity to display his "vases" of aquatic life at the Regent's Park zoo in 1851. In 1853, the zoo opened new enlarged aquatic exhibits within the complex called the Aquavivarium. These were the first aquarium displays on record and sparked a new trend for aquatic display at zoological gardens and public museums. Similar displays popped up throughout Europe over the following 20 years. In 1871, the first aquarium, called the Crystal Palace Aquarium, opened and housed sixty large display tanks containing 200,000 gallons of seawater exhibits and another 100,000 in storage. Another even larger aquarium opened a year later, called the Brighton Aquarium, which exhibited 300,000 gallons of seawater with another 500,000 in storage that was pumped directly from the sea. Philip Henry Gosse helped again with the challenge of getting clean seawater to inland aquariums. He devised a way of mixing sea salts with fresh water to make artificial seawater (McCosker, 1999).

In New York City, P. T. Barnum started adding aquarium attractions to his museums in

1856. He purchased the Aquarial and Zoological Gardens in Boston and moved the collection to New York and continued to acquire more animals and build new displays. This lead to the establishment of the New York Aquarium which opened in 1896. By 1930, America had aquariums in New York, Detroit, Philadelphia, Waikiki, San Francisco, and Chicago (McCosker, 1999).

1.2 Size: One Size Doesn't Fit All

An aquatic display can be as small as a tabletop fish bowl or as large as a 5 million gallon exhibit; they come in all sizes. The size of an aquatic display is dependent on the goal or purpose of the exhibit and the needs of the animals. Large exhibits are typically representative of the natural ecosystem of the geographic area being displayed and are usually dynamic, mixed species exhibits. Multi-taxa exhibits can have a mix of fish, invertebrates, and in some cases plants or macroalgae; however, large mammals and reptiles are typically exhibited in large single species exhibits.

Not all animals can thrive in a large mixed species exhibit. These large exhibits can be surrounded by smaller displays that focus on one or a few key species. This gives the visitors the opportunity to get up close to smaller animals that would be missed in the larger exhibits. Smaller exhibits are also good for species that do better by themselves, like an octopus or a mantis shrimp.

1.3 Exhibit Style: Pools to Ecosystems

Modern aquaria exhibits are trending more towards a more natural and dynamic design, in order to better educate guests on ecosystems and provide an environment for the animals that resembles their natural habitat. Such exhibits may include live or artificial corals or kelp, rockwork, and even water movement features, such as a wave surge. These features work together to create the illusion of peering into a snapshot of the ocean to the guests, and provide many of the aquatic inhabitants the comforts of home.

While these exhibits are engaging and provide good enrichment to the animals, they can pose challenges for cleaning, maintenance, and the ability to observe animals. For some animals, like sea jellies, rockwork and other obstacles could actually cause harm to the animals. A pool style exhibit looks much like a swimming pool, with limited decor and smooth walls and floor. These pools offer less enrichment to the animals and do not represent their natural habitat. In some circumstances, such as during medical quarantine, it is actually desirable to house animals in a pool style of exhibit, so they can be more closely monitored by veterinary and husbandry staff. Pool-style exhibits can be cleaned easily, require much less maintenance, and have a lower operating cost, making them ideal for facilities engaged in animal rehabilitation.

1.4 Filtration Type: From Dump and Fill to Robust Filtration System

Throughout the history of life support systems, improvements have been made for many reasons. One of the primary driving forces for life support progression has been animal welfare. Different animals have varying water quality requirements that must be satisfied to keep them healthy, requiring more robust systems to house a larger variety of animals safely. Filtration systems have been refined to provide clear water, which makes for better presentation to the public. Water conservation has been another factor that has been optimized by using modern life support systems, saving water from being used once and then dumped down a drain to the public sanitary system; many sanitary systems limit the amount of saltwater that can be dumped down the drain at a given time.

It is important to choose a filtration system that provides animal health needs, balances exhibition aesthetics, and water use. Dump and fill exhibits still exist but reside mainly as small pools in a zoo setting, where clarity or animal health will not be compromised and water is not scarce. This style is mainly wading pools for small mammals, such as capybara or water fowl in an outdoor setting. Wading pools for larger animals are usually older, antiquated systems that are still in use and have not yet been updated. Systems ramp up complexity from these basic dump and fill pools in varying degrees, depending on size of exhibit, salinity requirements, clarity demands, ability of staffing, and ability of the facility to afford such a system.

As exhibits grow larger and larger, the LSS grows with it. Filtration expansion demands more time from staff to maintain the equipment; a way to counter staffing needs is to automate the system as much as possible. Automation reduces the hands on tasks such as constant juggling of balancing flows; however, it creates a need to have specialized personnel on staff to maintain the automated control system and the life support system components.

1.5 Water: Fresh or Salt, Hot or Cold

The purpose of aquatic animal life support is to maintain water quality targets for aquatic exhibitry. Good water quality is not universal and depends upon factors such as the climate of the animal's point of origin, their ability to adapt to change, and how they breathe and osmoregulate.

Water has been termed the "universal solvent", which is mostly attributed to its polarity. The oxygen atom, being electrochemically negative, is repelled by the hydrogen atoms, which are electrochemically positive. Salts dissolve readily in water due to its positive and negative dipoles. Water in aquatic exhibits may be described as freshwater, brackish, and saline.

Euryhaline animals are species that tolerate a wide range of salinity. Euryhaline animals are often found in brackish conditions such as estuaries. Stenohaline animals need a tight range of salinity to survive. The salt concentration of the exhibit water should reflect levels that are safe and the animals are adapted to live in. For euryhaline animals, changes in salinity need to be made gradually, to allow the animal's body to adjust gill and kidney functions. For stenohaline animals, salinity should be kept within a narrow target and monitored often for changes due to evaporation or water changes. Saline water can be labor intensive and high quality salt can be expensive to prepare so it is often desirable to keep the salinity lower than natural seawater for euryhaline animals. In the case of air-breathing aquatic animals, they can survive in water with lower salinity found in their natural habitats; however, this may cause other health problems. Marine birds and marine mammals are adapted to consuming high levels of salt. The United States Department of Agriculture (USDA) requires that salinity values for marine mammal pools must be maintained between 15-36 ppt (Coakley & Crawford, 1998).

Salinity is not the only concern for water living animals. Temperature can have as big of an impact on the animals as salinity. Animals that tolerate a wide temperature range are called eurythermic and animals that can only tolerate a narrow temperature range are called stenothermic. The temperature set points in exhibits can vary dramatically, because aquatic animals have adapted to live in a wide range of temperatures. Water is mainly heated by the sun, and the extent of the energy added to the water depends upon the position of the sun relative to the latitude and tilt of the earth. Water found near the surface of the ocean is much warmer than water found in deep waters and water found near the equator will be much warmer than water found in polar regions. Water, under standard atmospheric pressure at sea level, has a freezing/melting point of 32°F (0°C) and a boiling point of 212°F (100°C). Although there are extremophiles that can exist in the upper and lower temperature ranges of liquid water, aquatic exhibits have much more moderate temperature set points.

When water or any substance is heated, the molecules begin moving at a higher rate. When dissolving solid or liquid substances in water, this increased movement of molecules creates better conditions for the substance to be dissolved. When dissolving gases in water, less movement between the molecules is desired. Oxygen and carbon dioxide, for example, stay in solution much better when the temperature of the water is lower. Exhibit water temperature influences solubility, system pH, reaction rates, and system equilibrium.

2 Safety

Water Quality testing and Life Support operations may involve hazardous chemicals, confined spaces and specialized equipment. It is a priority to ensure that staff has the training and knowledge needed to perform their job safely and responsibly before work is performed.

2.1 OSHA Standards

The *Occupational Safety and Health Act* of 1970 created a set of US federal standards that apply to many aspects of facility operations. The *AALSO Field Guide* presents safety standards required by the Occupational Safety and Health Administration (OSHA), which is part of the United States Department of Labor, and the laws pertain to all 50 states and US territories. It is beyond the scope of the *AALSO Field Guide* to detail every safety requirement for each state and for every country; therefore, it is a facility's management's responsibility to ensure that all applicable safety laws are being observed, and that the workplace has the right programs and documentation in place.

Title 29 CFR (Code of Federal Regulation) section 1910 addresses workplace standards. The regulation and standards can be viewed on the OSHA website by going to www.osha.gov and searching for "1910."

In Canada, access the *WORKSAFE* site for the province where the facility is located. For example, in British Columbia go to www.worksafebc.com and search for "ohs regulations" or "OHSR".

2.1.1 Water Quality OSHA Safety Operations

In 1990, OSHA issued the *Occupational Exposure to Hazardous Chemicals in Laboratories Standard* [29 CFR 1910.1450]. This is commonly known as the *Laboratory Standard*, developed to address workplaces where small quantities of hazardous chemicals are used in a non-production basis. In 2011, OSHA developed the *Laboratory Safety Guidance* [OSHA 3404-11R, 2011] which provides an overview of recommendations as well as descriptions of mandatory safety and health standards. This *Laboratory Standard* applies to all individuals engaged in laboratory use of any hazardous chemicals.

The five major elements in the *Laboratory Standard* are Hazard Identification, Chemical Hygiene Plan, Information and Training, Exposure Monitoring, and Medical Consultation and Examinations. Each laboratory must appoint a Chemical Hygiene Officer (CHO) to develop and implement the Chemical Hygiene Plan.

For the element of Hazard Identification, each laboratory must identify which hazardous chemicals will be encountered by its workers. All containers of chemicals must have a label that identifies the contents and relevant hazard warning(s) and be stored properly as described in the Safety Data Sheet (SDS). An SDS sheet received by the laboratory must be readily available to laboratory workers at all times.

The Chemical Hygiene Plan must contain the following information: Standard Operating Procedures (SOPs), Criteria for Exposure Control Measures, Adequacy and Proper Functioning Fume Hoods and other Protective Equipment, Information and Training, Requirement of Prior Approval of Laboratory Procedures, Medical Consultations and Examinations, Chemical Hygiene Officer Designation, and Particularly Hazardous Substances. The plan is maintained by the Chemical Hygiene Officer, a person whose training or experience qualifies them for the role and who is designated to assume it.

In regards to Information and Training for the *Laboratory Standard*, laboratory staff must be provided with training and information relevant to the hazards of the chemicals present in their laboratory. Training must be provided at the time of initial assignment and must include the following: the content of the OSHA *Laboratory Standard*, the location of the Chemical Hygiene Plan, Permissible Exposure Limits (PELs) for OSHA-regulated substances, signs and symptoms associated with exposure to hazardous chemicals in the laboratory, and the location and availability of reference materials such as the SDS.

For the element of Exposure Determination in the Laboratory Standard, OSHA has determined the permissible exposure limits (PELs) for hundreds of chemical substances. The PEL is the chemical-specific concentration in inhaled air that is intended to represent what the average, healthy worker may be exposed to daily for a lifetime of work without significant adverse health effects. Employers must conduct exposure monitoring through air sampling if there is reason to believe that workers may be exposed to chemicals above the action level (a concentration, generally lower than the PEL) that initiates certain required activities such as exposure monitoring and medical surveillance. Periodic exposure monitoring is also recommended.

The Medical Consultations and Examinations section requires that employers must provide all exposed workers with an opportunity to receive medical attention by a licensed physician whenever the following instances occur: a spill, leak, or explosion; the employee develops signs or symptoms associated with a hazardous chemical; or the employee has been exposed to levels routinely exceeding the OSHA action level or

PEL. These medical examinations are to be free to the employee, without loss of pay, and at a reasonable time and place.

2.1.2 LSS OSHA Safety Operations

Since LSS or mechanical departments will have varying areas of responsibilities and tasks, managers and operators should familiarize themselves with the regulations so they can determine which subparts and standards apply to their specific operations. A facility's safety and operational policies must meet the minimum requirements of the applicable OSHA standards or exceed them. It should be noted that company policies, SOPs, and equipment manufacturer's manuals can be considered mandatory rules by the "incorporation by reference" provision. This is especially relevant if an incident or accident occurs. Below is a partial list of the subparts that can apply to LSS operations:

Subpart D - Walking and Working Surfaces
This subpart covers ladders and scaffolding.

Subpart F - Powered Platforms and Man-lifts
This subpart covers personal fall arrest systems, man-lifts (scissor lifts, aerial boom lifts).

Subpart G - Occupational Health & Environmental Control
This subpart covers ventilation related to grinding and cutting of materials as well as the handling of silica and other media. Handling of dry filter sand can generate dust requiring ventilation as well as the use of proper personal protective equipment (refer to subpart J) by the operator. This subpart also covers occupational noise exposure. This includes Table G-16 *PERMISSIBLE NOISE EXPOSURES*, which defines the duration per day of exposure for specific decibel levels.

Subpart J - Personal Protective Equipment
This subpart covers the use of head, eye and face, respiratory, hearing, foot and hand protection.

Subpart O - Machine Guarding
This subpart covers guard requirements for many types of equipment.

Subpart T - Commercial Diving Operation
This subpart covers a variety of diving operations, including guidelines for scientific diving.

2.1.3 Injury and Illness Prevention Program

An *Injury and Illness Prevention Program* (IIPP) is a proactive process that allows employers to identify hazards in the workplace before workers get hurt (OSHA, 2012). An IIPP requires management, employee and volunteer participation for hazard identification, assessment, prevention and control. It will also include education, training and program review. Incidents, injuries and illnesses should be investigated to determine the cause and prevent further occurrences. Investigations should include clear documentation of the event, witnesses, causes, how this might be prevented in the future, and an action plan. Serious injuries or fatalities must be reported to the nearest office of the Division of Occupational Safety and Health within 8 hours [8 CCR, Section 342].

2.1.4 Emergency Action Plan

Facilities should have a written *Emergency Action Plan* (EAP) to provide an organized and managed system to minimize disruption of operations, reduce injuries, and protect property. In the United States, an EAP is required by OSHA; similar documents may be required in other countries. An EAP should describe how the organization prepares for emergencies and actions to be taken during and following an emergency. All potential emergencies should be considered, such as fires, explosions, floods, hurricanes, tornadoes, toxic substance releases, workplace violence, and acts of terrorism. Facilities should take into account their surrounding environment when developing a site-specific plan. Continually review the surrounding area and assess potential hazards and potential risks. Ensure that staff know safe emergency exit routes and predetermine a safe refuge location. Know what resources are available and how to access them. Determine methods of communication to be used during an emergency. The EAP should include contact information for key personnel and a chain of command. The plan should also include information on training and drills.

2.1.5 Hazard Communication Plan

Employees have the right to know about the potential hazards they may encounter in their workplace. Facilities should have a written *Hazard Communication Plan*, which includes policy guidelines and procedures for implementing and maintaining the program; and information about container labeling, safety data sheets, employee training, storage requirements for hazardous materials and personal protective equipment necessary to handle these materials safely. In the United States, the Hazard Communication Standard (HCS) [29 CFR 1910.1200] requires workplaces to have a written *Hazard Communication Plan*.

2.2 Globally Harmonized System (GHS)

The United Nations (UN) adopted the Globally Harmonized System (GHS) in 2003, which includes criteria for the classification of health, physical and environmental hazards and specifies what information should be included on chemical labels and on safety data sheets (United Nations, 2003). Many countries have developed their own labeling and hazard communication requirements, leading to inconsistent information for users and a burden for manufacturers. GHS is not a regulation or a standard; it is program designed to meet the standard of any hazard communication program, and has been adopted and integrated into existing programs by regulatory authorities in a number of countries. GHS covers all hazardous materials and classifies them into different hazard classes: physical hazards, health hazards, and environmental hazards.

2.2.1 Safety Data Sheets (SDS)

Safety Data Sheets (SDS) replaced Material Safety Data Sheets (MSDS) when GHS was implemented. SDS's are standardized, informational guides that contain the following information for a chemical: Product or chemical identifier, Hazard(s) Identification, Composition/Information on Ingredients, First-Aid Measures, Fire-Fighting Measures, Accidental Release Measures, Handling and Storage, Exposure Controls/Personal Protection, Physical and Chemical Properties, Stability and Reactivity, Toxicological Information, Ecological Information (non-mandatory), Disposal Considerations (non-mandatory), Transport Information (non-mandatory), Regulatory Information (non-mandatory), and Other Information (OSHA, 2012). All chemicals used in a facility must have an SDS readily available either in hard copy or an online index of all chemicals in the facility. Each employee should be familiar with the SDS prior to using a chemical for the first time. As a best practice, laboratory policy should require that an employee read, understand, and follow the SDS.

2.2.2 Chemical Labeling

Chemical manufacturers must include standardized label elements as part of GHS. These elements are intended to let the user know important safety information. Each GHS chemical label must include the following:

- Pictogram(s)
- Signal Word
- Hazard Statements
- Precautionary Statements
- Product Identifier (ingredients)
- Supplier information (name, address, telephone number)
- Supplemental information

Pictograms include the harmonized hazard symbols that include black symbols on a white background with red diamond shaped borders. See Figure 2.1 for a list of GHS pictograms and the associated hazards.

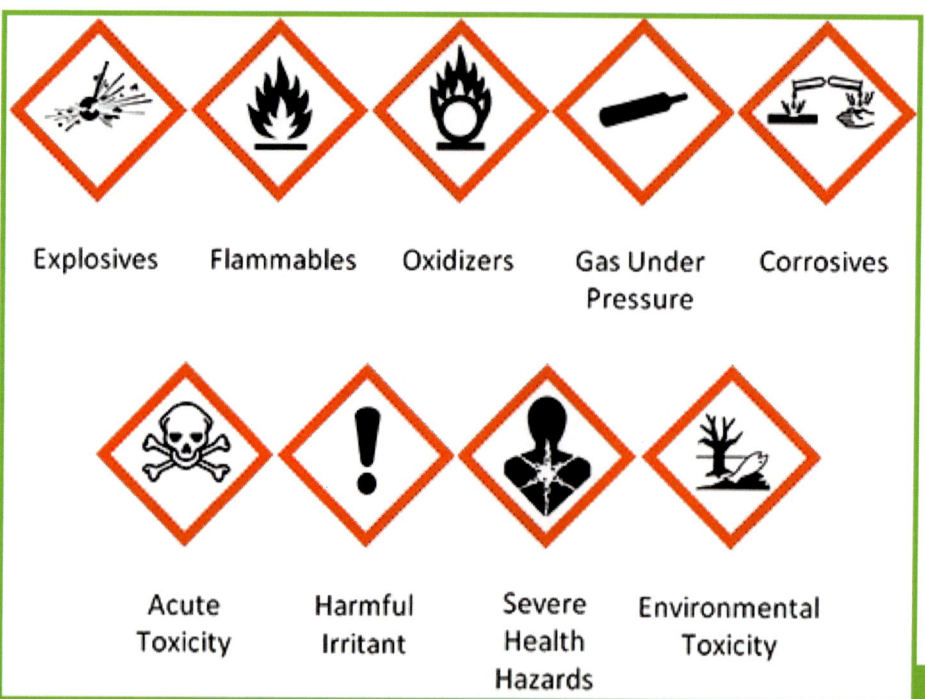

Figure 2.1 - GHS Pictograms and Hazards

Signal words are used in GHS labels to relay severity of a hazard. Chemicals will either have the signal word "Danger" for more severe hazards or "Warning" for less severe hazards.

Hazard Statements are standardized and assigned phrases that describe the hazard(s). A statement for each hazard should be included on the label.

Precautionary Statements provide information on ways to prevent or minimize exposure from physical, health or environmental hazards, for example, appropriate responses in the event of an accident, first aid, storage considerations, ventilation controls, personal protective equipment, and environmental considerations.

Product Identifiers may include the chemical name, ingredients in a mixture, product name, CAS number, and may even include batch number.

Supplier Information must include the name of the supplier, address and telephone number, so in the event of an emergency they can be easily contacted.

It is important to note that chemical labels from a manufacturer will include these elements; however, when transferring chemicals out of their original container or creating mixtures, all of these elements must be included on a new label to ensure clear hazard communication and compliance. See Figure 2.2 for an example of a GHS compliant label.

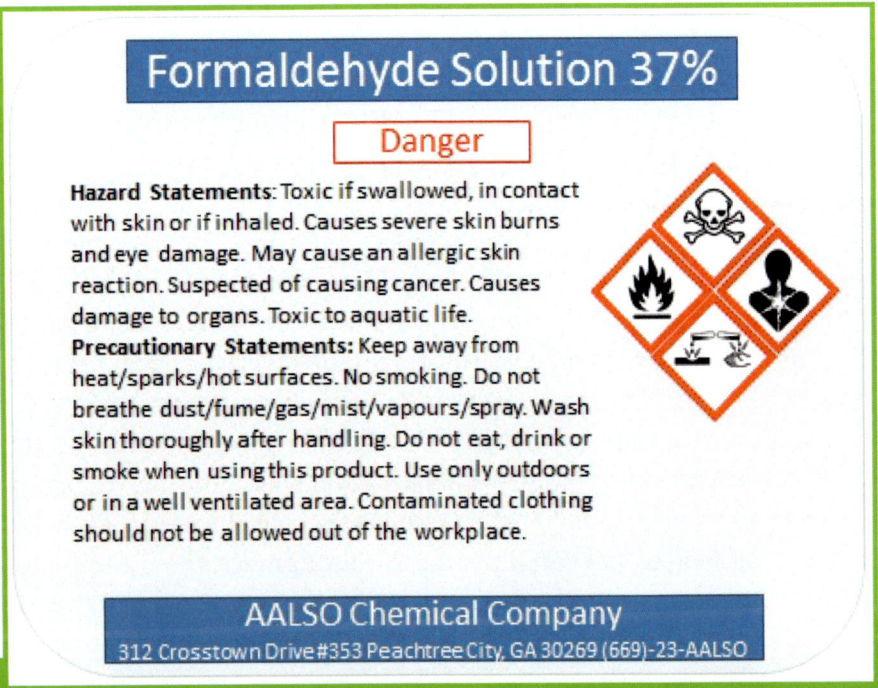

Figure 2. 2 - GHS Label Elements

2.3 Chemical Storage and Compatibility

Proper chemical storage is crucial for the safety of all employees who enter an environment where chemicals are used. One of the most important safety precautions for proper chemical storage is that all chemicals are properly and clearly labeled. This information included on the label ensures that anyone who comes in contact with the chemical can identify it properly and easily find the SDS. Other information that is helpful, but not necessary for safety, is the date received, date opened and expiration date.

Compatible chemicals may be stored together. Incompatible chemicals should never be stored in the same cabinet or container where they or their vapors could mix if the containers were compromised. For example, corrosives, such as muriatic acid, should never be stored with oxidizers, such as bleach, and reactive chemicals should never be stored with flammable ones. Flammable chemicals must be labeled as flammable and can only be stored in approved flammable storage cabinets; failure to do so can create a major safety hazard.

2.3.1 Toxic Substances

There are many types of toxic substances that may be present while working in a laboratory: irritants, corrosives, allergens, asphyxiants, neurotoxins, reproductive and developmental toxins, and carcinogens (National Research Council, 2011). Risks associated with toxic substances depend on both the extent of exposure and the toxicity of a chemical. Routes of exposure may include inhalation, ingestion, and/or absorption (through the skin). Even low exposure to a highly toxic substance can cause adverse health effects. An acutely toxic substance causes damage after a single exposure, whereas chronically toxic substances, such as carcinogens, cause damage after repeated or long-term exposure. Chronic toxins are particularly dangerous because their effects are not immediately apparent. When working with toxic substances, staff must acquire the knowledge, skill, and discipline to carry out safe laboratory practices consistently through training and experience. It is important to remember that many substances used in research have not been tested for carcinogenicity; therefore, it is prudent to treat all substances used in the laboratory as if they were hazardous unless otherwise known. When working with toxic substances, use engineering controls (such as fume hoods) as the primary line of defense, as well as personal protective equipment (PPE), indicated by the safety data sheet (SDS), in order to keep exposure below permissible exposure limits (PELs).

2.3.2 Flammable Substances

A flammable liquid is defined as having a flash point under 199.4°F (93°C) (OSHA, n.d.). A flash point is the lowest temperature that the vapors of a substance will ignite, given an ignition source. It is determined by heating the liquid and measuring the temperature at which a flash is obtained when a small flame is introduced. There are different categories for flammable liquids, based on their flash points. A flash point is different than the ignition temperature, which is the minimum temperature required to initiate self-sustained combustion (National Research Council, 2011). Flammable liquids are dangerous not just because of their ease of ignition, but because they also pose an explosion risk. Flammable materials must not be stored with acids, bases, or oxidizers due to the risk of mixing during a catastrophic event, such as an earthquake or hurricane. There are a number of storage considerations for flammable liquids. They must be stored in a yellow flammable cabinet designed to keep the temperature below 325°F during a standard 10 minute fire test (OSHA, n.d.). These cabinets have specific requirements for ventilation, electrical wiring, clearance, and volume of flammable substances based upon their hazard category. Fires require an ignition source (such as sparks, flame, or motors), fuel and an oxidizer (air) to be present. By containing and segregating storage of oxidizers, fuels and ignition sources, fire risks can be reduced.

2.3.3 Reactive and Explosive Hazards

An explosion occurs when there is a violent release of energy when a material undergoes a reaction. An explosive chemical is a chemical that causes sudden and almost instantaneous release of pressure, gas and heat when subjected to sudden shock, pressure or high temperature (OSHA, 2012). Reactive substances can cause bodily harm due to the release of gases that will burn, explode or produce high pressure.

Mixing incompatible chemicals can create a reactive hazard, such as strong acids and bases, or reactions between oxidizers and reducing agents, or oxidizers and metals. An oxidizer is a chemical (other than a blasting agent or explosive) that initiates or promotes combustion in other materials, thereby causing fire of either itself or through the release of oxygen or other gases (OSHA, 2012). An oxidizing agent brings about an oxidation reaction, where a substance either provides oxygen to the substance being oxidized (for example, ozone), or a substance receives electrons from the substance undergoing oxidation (for example, chlorine).

2.3.4 Compressed Gases

All compressed gasses are potentially hazardous because they are under great pressure, including SCUBA tanks. The rapid release of gases under pressure can cause damage through the great force exerted and can cause the container to propel a long distance. If the compressed gas has other hazards, such as being flammable or toxic, there are more hazards associated with accidental release. Pressurized gas cylinders must be stored properly to prevent leakage and/or a sudden and dangerous release of pressure. Cylinders must be properly labeled. The label must identify the contained gas and its hazards. Do not rely solely upon the manufacturer's color code identification scheme. All gas cylinders must be either securely strapped or chained to a wall or a permanent benchtop. Do not store gas cylinders with other chemicals, especially corrosives. Vapors from some corrosives can affect the integrity of the gas cylinder and regulator. It is also important to remember basic chemical storage safety practices such as keeping corrosives away from oxidizers and flammables away from reactive chemicals, even when storing gas cylinders. Conduct monthly inspections to ensure that gas cylinders that are stored onsite for extended periods of time have current cylinder inspections and hydrotesting stamps. Finally, it is also a best laboratory practice not to store empty cylinders with full cylinders (National Research Council, 2011).

2.3.5 Biohazards

Biohazards are substances that pose a threat to the health of humans and other living organisms, and include pathogenic microorganisms, viruses, toxins, spores, and fungi. Biohazards are a concern in laboratories in which microorganisms are handled (National Research Council, 2011). While the majority of biohazards at the workplace usually come from human body sources, biohazards from animal feces and laboratory cultures pose a significant risk to water quality technicians and life support operators. There are four levels of controls for working with biohazards, referred to as biosafety levels. Generally, Biosafety level 1 or 2 are the highest levels needed in zoo and aquarium labs. Biosafety levels 3 and 4 require special air filtration and at least two doors separation from regular building traffic, and use of biological safety cabinets (National Research Council, 2011). When working with biohazards, use good personal hygiene (see section 2.4.5), wear protective clothing, and disinfect/sterilize work surfaces and equipment after use.

2.4 Chemical Handling

It is essential to exercise caution and prudence when working with hazardous chemicals. While it is not possible to eliminate all risks associated with hazardous chemicals, it is possible to greatly enhance safety when working with chemicals through training, risk management and prevention.

2.4.1 Acquisition and Inventory

When purchasing chemicals, it is important to consider the chemical's life cycle at the facility, from acquisition to storage to use and, ultimately, to disposal. It is advised that an institution limits the number of staff authorized to purchase chemicals. This allows the facility to keep track of inventory and prevent redundant purchases. When purchasing a new chemical, it is important to note the minimum quantity needed for its current use. It is advised to purchase at most the amount of chemicals than can be used within one calendar year. Another consideration for the acquisition of new chemicals is whether the size of the container is permissible in the areas where it will be stored; this is especially important for flammable materials. Review the SDS and determine if the chemical can be managed safely upon arrival, including the availability of appropriate PPE and storage options. It is critical to have a copy of the SDS, review it before receipt of a new chemical, and ensure that all persons who may be exposed to the chemical understand the hazards and required precautions. Transportation of the chemical from delivery to the designated storage area must be performed and managed safely, using suitable carts, carriers and secondary containment with the capacity to contain all of the material in case of a spill or failure of the primary container.

Chemical tracking and an updated inventory is essential for safe chemical management. It is important to track the identity of the chemical, manufacturer, storage location and any other safety considerations needed for handling. An accurate inventory is needed not only for a facility to prevent over-purchasing supplies, but also to minimize the risk of theft, releases and exposures during emergencies, and waste disposal. Ensure that chemical labels are complete and legible, and that storage containers are in good condition. Periodically inspect labels and containers for damage or deterioration.

2.4.2 Right to Know

Right to Know refers to a law in the United States; many countries have similiar laws, such as Canada, Australia and the European Union. This law dictates that individuals have the right to know about the chemicals that they are exposed to. Workers must be given information about the potential hazards in the workplace and their effects, including access to safety data sheets, records of monitoring exposure to chemicals, and chemical inventories. Workers must be trained on hazard communication and understand the hazards they face in the workplace so they can understand the protective measures to be taken to minimize risk and exposure.

2.4.3 Minimizing Exposure

When working with hazardous chemicals, take precautions to avoid exposure by contact with skin and eyes, inhalation, and ingestion (National Research Council, 2011). Methods for minimizing exposure (in order of preference) include substituting less hazardous materials or processes; reducing the amount of toxic material in use and storage as much as practicable; using engineering controls; and using personal protective equipment. It is critical that staff follow basic safety rules and policies, (such as not eating or drinking in the lab, and washing hands), use engineering controls and PPE as directed by the SDS, keep workspaces tidy, and maintain situational awareness.

2.4.4 Chemical Selection

When possible, it is best to select the methods or chemicals that eliminate or reduce the use and generation of hazardous substances. Consider working with smaller volumes and using microscale techniques. Choose laboratory equipment that requires the least amount of reagents or uses materials that are least hazardous (National Research Council, 2011). For example, substitute mercury-free thermometers in the laboratory, and substitute alternative methods for nitrate testing other than those using cadmium.

2.4.5 Personal Hygiene

When working with hazardous chemicals, good personal hygiene is required for staff to remain safe. To avoid contact with skin and eyes, wear gloves and eye protection and refrain from touching the eyes or face. Contact lenses should not be worn when chemical vapors are present or a chemical splash is possible. If a staff member chooses to wear contact lenses, then chemical splash goggles must be worn (National Research Council, 2011). Eating, drinking, smoking, gum chewing and applying cosmetics must be strictly prohibited in a laboratory or where hazardous chemicals are used or stored. Do not store cups or utensils in areas where hazardous materials are stored, or store food in refrigerators used for chemical storage. Do not wear lab coats or gloves outside of the laboratory. Always wash hands with soap and water after working with chemicals, even if gloves were worn.

2.4.6 Transportation

Transport of hazardous materials by mail, roads, or air, is regulated by local, national and international laws. When transporting chemicals within a facility, do not use motorized vehicles. Secondary containment should always be used for carrying bottled chemicals (National Research Council, 2011). The secondary containment should be sized to contain all of the material in the event that the primary container fails. In addition to GHS elements, chemical labels should also include the date and contact information of both the originator and receiver.

2.4.7 Waste Disposal

It is important to have a management strategy in place for the ultimate disposal of waste that may present chemical or biological hazards. No activity should begin unless a plan for the disposal of nonhazardous and hazardous waste has been formulated (National Research Council, 2011). Planning ahead ensures that regulatory requirements are met and the facility is able to handle the materials safely. Before disposal through incineration or land disposal (burial in a landfill), consider alternatives that minimize environmental impact when possible: pollution prevention, source reduction, reuse or redistribution of unwanted materials, treatment, reclamation and recycling materials within the water (National Research Council, 2011). Choose methods that produce less hazardous waste, use micro-scale techniques to minimize hazardous waste, and purchase no more materials than are needed. Although landfills for hazardous materials disposal have been designed to contain waste, there is always a risk of eventual leaking into the environment.

Hazardous waste generally refers to materials having one or more of the following characteristics: ignitability, corrosivity (pH <2 or >12.5), reactivity, and toxicity. Do not allow waste to accumulate longer than twelve months; check with local and national disposal requirements and make a list of common materials that can be disposed of in the trash, sanitary sewer, or after neutralization. Take care not to mix incompatible wastes, and keep wastes segregated by their characteristics. Collect waste in containers that are made of materials suitable for storage, which will keep contents secure. Glass containers may break, so it is recommended to use plastic containers with a wide opening, such as a polyethylene jerry can. Use secondary containment to protect from spills or leakage. Ensure that the hazardous waste is clearly and fully labeled: never just write "waste" on a container. For empty containers that once held hazardous chemicals, it is suggested to triple rinse the containers (the rinsate must be disposed of properly), remove the labels, and label the container "empty and clean" before disposing in the trash or recycling.

2.4.8 Chemicals of Unknown Composition

Unidentified chemicals pose a problem because hazards must be identified for disposal facilities to safely transport the chemicals and to manage hazardous waste safely. If a chemical has an unknown composition, analysis and identification by an outside laboratory can be very expensive. While there are methods for in-house characterization, they do not meet regulatory requirement for waste management. Also, testing requires highly trained laboratory personnel, and is not recommended for the water quality laboratory in a zoo or aquarium. Characteristics of unknown chemicals for waste disposal that can be determined are physical description, water reactivity, water solubility, pH, ignitability (flammability), presence of an oxidizer, and presence of peroxides, sulfides, cyanides, and halogens (National Research Council, 2011).

2.5 Zoonotic Diseases

A zoonotic disease is any virus, bacteria, fungi or parasite which is transmitted by an animal to a human. There are simple actions that can be taken to reduce the risk of transfer of zoonotic diseases such as reduced exposure, handwashing, effective cleaning, and the use of disinfectants. In a zoo or aquarium setting, the route of disease transfer can vary. Diseases can be transmitted through the air, contact with skin, ingestion of contaminated water, or an animal bite. All facilities should have a *Zoonotic Disease Policy* that outlines the risks associated with the facility's living collection and preventive measures taken to reduce risk to staff exposure. Staff training on this policy should be provided to all staff and volunteers when they start at the facility and on an annual basis.

2.5.1 Hand Washing

Hand washing is the easiest way to protect against the transfer of zoonotic diseases. When appropriate, the use of gloves can help add an additional protective layer to skin contact but should not replace the act of hand washing. Wash hands with soap and hot water before and after handling animals, enclosures, equipment, feed and bedding.

2.5.2 Cleaning and Disinfectants

Cleaning an animal enclosure can present one the greatest risks of zoonotic disease transfer. Collecting and disposing of large bulky material such as bedding or fecal matter should be done prior to using a hose. Using a high pressure hose can aerosolize contaminants and increase the risk of inhalation exposure and cross contamination of other exhibits. Care should be taken when hosing to prevent any unnecessary splashing or excess contamination into exhibit water. When performing partial or full body immersion, such as diving in exhibit water, there is the risk of transfer to skin and exposed mucous membranes like the mouth. Exhibits that require staff to be submerged should be tested routinely for bacteria and evaluated for risk to staff exposure. For more information on bacteria testing see Section 5.10. Disinfectants can range from the use of ozone in the water to bleach on surfaces. Facilities should make available to staff a range of disinfection products that are effective against the diseases found in the living collection. Chlorine, iodine, chlorhexidine, and ozone are a few of the common disinfectants in use in zoos and aquariums.

2.5.3 Zoonoses

Zoonotic exposure will vary with the animals found in each collection. The identification of any zoonotic disease at a facility should be noted and shared with the staff at the annual zoonotic disease training. There are some common risks associated with mammals, birds, reptiles, amphibians and fish.

The following are examples of possible zoonotic diseases associated with each group listed from high exposure risk to lower risk (Amand, 1993):

Mammals: Salmonella sp., Campylobacter sp., Giardia sp., Dermatophytes (ringworm), Cryptosporidia, Mycobacteria, Rabies

Birds: Salmonella sp., Campylobacter, Cryptosporidia, Mycobacteria, Pentastomiasis, *Chlamydia psittaci*

Reptiles: Salmonella sp., Campylobacter, Cryptosporidia, Mycobacteria, Pentastomiasis

Amphibians: Salmonella sp., Campylobacter, Yersinia, Cryptosporidia, Mycobacteria
Fish: *Plesiomonas shigelloides*, Cryptosporidia, Mycobacteria

2.6 Engineering and Environmental Controls

The first line of defense in protecting workers from chemical exposure are engineering and environmental controls. These controls provide a barrier between the workers and hazardous materials. Engineering and environmental controls should be employed where possible. Personal protective equipment (PPE) may provide protection in addition to engineering controls but should not be used as substitutes for engineering controls where the latter are practicable. Engineering controls require maintenance and monitoring to ensure they are providing adequate protection.

2.6.1 Laboratory Chemical Hoods

Laboratory chemical hoods (fume hoods) are a type of safety device commonly found in laboratories or facilities where hazardous chemicals are used. Laboratory chemical hoods physically protect a person using a hazardous chemical and are fire and chemical resistant. Laboratory chemical hoods have one large opening (the face) in the front of the hood which also has a movable window (the sash) which allows the user access inside the hood to perform work. The way in which a laboratory chemical hood works is that air is pulled from the inside of the room in which the hood is located through the face of the hood and then is removed through an exhaust duct to an area outside the facility (typically, the roof). This air flow removes any contaminants or hazards from inside the hood and safely sends them out to the atmosphere. Proper design and planning must be taken into account when laboratory chemical hoods are deemed necessary for a facility.

Prior to using a laboratory chemical hood, understand how the hood operates and also verify that it is the correct type of hood for the intended use. This can be verified by looking at the instruction manual of the chemical hood. To verify that a hood is performing properly prior to use, check that the face velocity meets the specified criteria, verify the absence of turbulence, and ensure a continuous performance monitoring device is present and in working order. Operators must never put their head into a hood while in operation to check on an experiment.

Maximize efficiency and keep electrical costs down when operating a chemical hood by opening and closing the sash slowly; placing equipment as far to the back of the hood as practical without blocking the bottom baffle; and refraining from storing hazardous chemicals in a chemical hood (National Research Council, 2011).

2.6.2 Ambient Ozone Monitors

An ambient ozone monitor, also known as a low concentration ozone monitor, is a device that continuously samples the air and tests for low levels of ozone which could indicate the presence of a leak in the ozone system or that ozone gas may be accumulating in an area, creating an environment unsafe for staff and animals. Ozone monitors are used in areas where ozone is generated or injected into life support systems. If low levels of ozone are detected, an audible and visual alarm can notify staff before they enter an unsafe area. Low concentration ozone monitors may be able to send a signal to disable ozone generation when in alarm. Low concentration ozone monitors typically have a self-test feature to verify functionality of audible and visual alarms. All monitors of this type require regular testing and calibration.

2.7 Personal Protective Equipment (PPE)

Every laboratory should be fully stocked with a variety of PPE in different sizes and available to staff as needed. This equipment should be stored in an easily accessible area, preferably by the door to the laboratory. Staff should be trained how to properly use this equipment when they first start working in the laboratory, annually as a refresher, and any time a new chemical or procedure is introduced. The manufacturer's SDS should be referenced prior to purchasing any chemical to ensure that the laboratory has all the necessary PPE in stock before the chemical arrives.

2.7.1 Gloves

Most of the activities performed in the laboratory are done with the hands, so gloves are a primary form of PPE used. Gloves are available in a range of thicknesses and materials with unique properties. Widely available material types include latex, nitrile, polyvinyl chloride (PVC) dipped, vinyl, butyl, insulated, and blends of neoprene, nitrile and/or natural rubber. For daily activities, every laboratory should provide latex or nitrile gloves for staff working in the laboratory. When working with highly corrosive chemicals, such as hydrochloric acid, thicker acid-resistant gloves, like butyl gloves, should also be worn.

2.7.2 Laboratory Coats and Footwear

Another primary PPE item used in the laboratory is the lab coat. Lab coats should be available in a variety of sizes to meet the needs of the staff. They should be hung by the door for staff to don as they enter the laboratory. Lab coats should not be worn outside of the laboratory. The use of the lab coat adds a layer of protection to the clothing and skin. They should be easy to remove if a chemical is spilled on them. Another clothing requirement is closed-toe shoes. Sandals are not to be worn in the laboratory.

2.7.3 Eye Protection

While there are many options available for eye protection, safety goggles are the preferred standard for daily laboratory use. Goggles provide better protection than safety glasses because they reduce the risk of eye injury due to chemicals splashing from the side, top or bottom of the eye. For chemical vapor or caustic dust hazards, the minimum recommended eye protection consists of well-fitted non-vented goggles or full-facepiece respirators. Safety goggles may be worn over corrective glasses without disturbing the adjustment of the glasses. Contact lenses do not provide eye protection. When working with highly hazardous materials, the addition of a face shield adds an additional layer of protection.

2.7.4 Safety Shields

A safety shield is an additional barrier that can be used to protect the face from splash or impact. A safety shield does not eliminate the need for chemical splash goggles. Shields are commonly made of a transparent material such as acrylic or glass. Some safety shields have cutouts at the base to allow the technician to wrap their hands around the shield to work. Some fume hoods have a sash that will open from the sides allowing the front sash to act as a safety shield when ventilation is adequate.

2.7.5 Respiratory Protection

In a laboratory setting, engineered local exhaust systems, such as fume hoods, are recommended as the primary form of respiratory protection; however, there are some situations where a fume hood is not practical. When this is the case, a personal respirator is the next best option. They are available in half and full masks with replaceable cartridges. Masks are available in different sizes and must be fitted to the user's face. Each staff member using a respirator must be issued their own respirator (they cannot be shared) and must complete an annual fit test while wearing their respirator. Respirator cartridges come in different types and provide protection against specific gas or vapor hazards. It is important to purchase the right cartridge for the work being performed and note the maximum time the cartridge should be used before it needs to be replaced. This varies from 2 hours to 1 year.

2.8 Emergency Response Equipment

Equipment should be made available for staff to use to respond to an emergency. Safety showers, eyewash stations, spill kits and fire extinguishers are some of the equipment commonly found in laboratories. All emergency equipment should be checked regularly to ensure that it is functioning properly. Safety showers and eyewash stations should be activated monthly to ensure proper functioning. Fire extinguishers should be checked monthly and refilled if used. Spill kits should be refreshed after each use.

2.8.1 Safety Shower and Eyewash Stations

Safety showers and eyewash stations (known as emergency fixtures) should be available in facilities where chemicals are used. Requirements for the installation and maintenance of safety showers and eyewashes are set by the American National Standards Institute (ANSI). According to ANSI, emergency fixtures should be located within 10 seconds or 55 feet from the potential hazard and be unobstructed. Any safety fixture should be able to run with a continuous flow for 15 minutes. Each type of safety fixture has a minimum flow rate that must be maintained for that 15 minute period. An eyewash must have a minimum flow rate of 0.4 gpm, while a safety shower must have a minimum flow rate of 20 gpm. This means that there should also be adequate drains installed where safety showers are placed, because one could easily have 300 gallons of water on the floor of the facility very quickly if a safety shower is used. Another important standard for emergency fixtures is the temperature of the water that is deployed from a fixture. The water temperature must be tepid (between 60°F and 100°F). This temperature encourages the injured party to complete the full 15-minute flush. Also, the pressure of the water delivered by a safety fixture should result in a flow that is non-injurious to the user. Emergency fixtures should be constructed of non-corrosive materials and protected from airborne contaminants [ANSI Z358.1-2014].

2.8.2 Spill Kits

It is important to use safe work practices when working with hazardous materials to avoid accidental release of chemicals; however, accidents can happen and it is important to have a plan in place to respond to any potential safety hazards. When working with chemicals, it is safest to work with the smallest volumes possible. Large containers of chemicals should never be stored on the bench; use approved storage cabinets. Secondary containment should be used when storing or transporting chemicals in case of spillage or container breakage.

Laboratories should invest in spill control kits, which may contain absorbent pillows or pads, absorbent powder or clay, neutralizing agents for acidic or basic spills, mats to block drains to the sewer, PPE to use while cleaning the spill, and signage to warn others who may enter the area. The spill kits should be kept in the area where potential spills may occur. The majority of spills in a water quality laboratory are small in volume and of chemicals that are not highly toxic, flammable or volatile. Such spills may be cleaned by laboratory staff using items in a spill control kit. Acidic or basic waste can be neutralized; chemicals can be absorbed and then disposed of accordingly. Broken glassware should be swept up to avoid cuts and disposed of in specially labeled containers, not in a regular trash can. If the glassware has hazardous chemicals on it, it should be sealed up and disposed of as hazardous waste; do not try to rinse off or clean broken glass.

If the quantity of spilled hazardous substances exceed the US Environmental Protection Agency's (EPA's) established "reportable quantities," emergency responders must handle the spill. It may be necessary for emergency responders to clean up spills of substances that are not especially hazardous if the volume spilled is large. It is important that staff has the knowledge and training to assess the situation, perform the spill cleanup or, if necessary, contact emergency responders, and ensure proper disposal. Never jeopardize the health of anyone while addressing a chemical spill.

There are specific spill cleanup procedures for mercury, flammable solvents and highly toxic substances, but such procedures are beyond the scope of this manual.

2.8.3 Fire Extinguishers

Fire extinguishers are a standard piece of fire protection for all buildings and should be distributed in numerous locations. They are a small handheld device that can discharge an agent used to put out small fires. They are designed to be simple to use. There are 5 classes of fire extinguishers. Most common building fire extinguishers are A-B-C class. These will extinguish fires from combustibles, liquids, gases and electrical fires. Class D are intended for combustible metals. Class K are commonly found in commercial kitchens are appropriate for oil and fat fires.

2.9 Training and Records

All safety protocols should be reviewed with staff and volunteers when they first start working at a facility and then again each year. If a procedure or responsibility changes to include new hazards then additional training should occur before starting the new task and again each year. A designated safety person should ensure that all trainings occur for each protocol.

A record should be kept of all safety training. This should be stored in a safety training binder in a central location, preferably with the department's SDS binder. Having the SDS binder, safety protocols and safety training records in one location will make it easy for staff and inspectors to reference them. A record should also be kept of any drills, staff injuries, accidental exposures, and chemical spills, and the responses to such events, including any follow up training that occurred.

Periodic unannounced in-house inspections should be completed for all safety protocols. These inspections are to make sure that all safety protocols are functioning properly. Check that chemicals are stored properly, SDS's are up to date and available, fume hoods are functional, and safety showers are being activated monthly - these are but a few examples of how a facility can prepare for an actual inspection by a safety official.

There are many options for water quality testing equipment, from low-tech to state-of-the-art instrumentation. Selection will depend on budget, staff ability and knowledge, needed turnaround times and needed levels of accuracy and precision. It is important to be familiar with the spectrum of water quality testing equipment to make informed decisions regarding testing methodologies.

3.1 Spectrophotometers

Absorption spectroscopy is one of the most useful tools available for quantitative analysis, especially in water quality testing. Although some chemicals, such as organic compounds, absorb ultraviolet (UV) light on their own, many non-absorbing species can be analyzed after a reaction with a color-changing reagent. Species that can be analyzed using this method include chlorine, copper, ammonia, nitrite, nitrate, phosphate and many more.

Spectrophotometers are instruments that can measure the absorbance or transmittance of a sample. Absorbance is the amount of incident light that is absorbed while traveling through a sample. Transmittance is how much light passes through a sample. The two are inversely related as follows:

$$\textbf{Absorbance = -log(Transmittance)}$$

Beer's law states that absorbance is directly proportional to concentration, for example, absorbance measurements will increase with increasing concentration, with a straight line going through the origin. Many spectrophotometers have the calibration curves built into their software, but it is important to make sure that the sample is within the range of the curve, it is not safe to assume the linear relationship past the scope of the calibration curve.

Derivations to Beer's law may be caused by mismatched sample cells (Skoog et al., 2007). It is important that sample cells (or cuvettes) are matched and have the same pathlength. Many times, it is possible to use the same cell for the blank and the sample, eliminating mismatched cell problems. For example, 1-inch square cells have a different path length than 1-inch round cells and substation will introduce a bias to the reading (HACH, 2008). Sample cells come in a variety of materials and vary in cost and durability: plastic, glass and quartz. Sample cell selection depends on the test method, the instrument and analysis wavelength. It is also important to orient the cells the same way during measurements to reduce variability. Clean sample cells carefully: fingerprints and other deposits can alter readings. Ensure that colored solutions are not left in the cells for extended periods of time and be careful not to scratch the cells, especially if using a brush.

A spectrophotometer looks at the absorbance of a sample at a particular wavelength. The wavelength is usually selected at the point corresponding to the absorption maximum. The most common light source in a spectrophotometer is a tungsten filament lamp, capable of measuring in the visible and near-infrared spectrum (350 nm - 2500 nm). Deuterium lamps allow measurements in the ultraviolet (UV) region of the spectrum (190 nm - 400 nm) (Skoog et al., 2007), but are not present on all spectrophotometers.

3.1.1 Calibration Curves

A calibration curve indicates the relationship between the concentration of the analyte (the parameter being measured) and the analytical response (such as absorbance). A calibration curve is usually determined by running chemical standards that bracket the expected range of the samples. The data is generally plotted with the concentration of the analyte as the x axis and the absorbance as the y axis. An external standard calibration with a linear curve (such as those following Beer's Law) is the most commonly used method for calibration, but other mathematical relationships may occur, such as exponential or polynomial functions. This model (called linear regression) assumes that the relationship between the measured response and the standard concentration is linear, where the calibration curve is represented as

$$y = mx + b$$

where *b* is the y intercept (the value of y when x is zero) and *m* is the slope of the line (Skoog et al., 2007). In Figure 3.1, the equation of the line indicates a slope of 0.0118 and a y intercept of 0.0016.

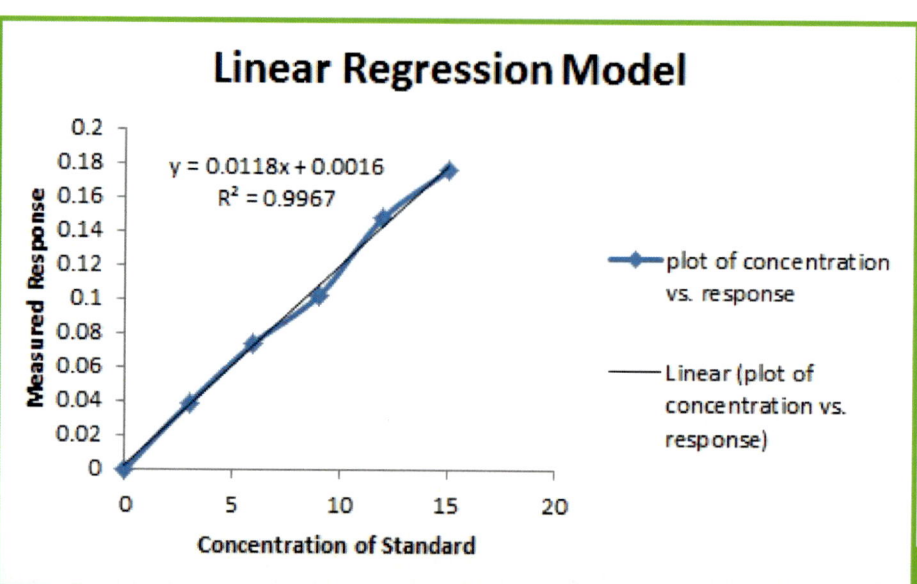

Figure 3.1
Linear Calibration Curve with Equation
of the Line and R² Value Displayed

The coefficient of determination is commonly referred to as R^2. Simply put, an R^2 value demonstrates the variance from linearity of a calibration curve. As R^2 approaches 1, the regression points better fit the data. A value of 0.99 indicates a good fit and a value of 0.30 would indicate a poor fit.

External standard calibrations assume that the same responses will be measured when the same concentration is present in the sample as in the standards, but this is not always true. Blank corrections help with this derivation, but many times matrix effects can cause samples to give different responses. Matrix effects arise from other species in the sample (such as high salt content in seawater), that can alter the accuracy and recovery of known standards in a test, causing the sample to respond differently than the calibration standards. When performing a new method, check the listed interferences. Saltwater may have interfering ions or too high of a pH for the analysis.

A standard additions calibration is useful when working with samples that exhibit high matrix interference, because the sample matrix remains relatively unchanged and the calibration is sample specific. Typically, samples containing identical volumes are *spiked* with one or more increments of a standard or they can be carried out using successive increments of standard to a single sample aliquot (Skoog et al., 2007). A least squares analysis can be used to determine the slope, *m* and the y intercept, *b*. The concentration of the analyte in the original sample can be extrapolated using the formula for a line, and corresponds to the x intercept, where the x axis is the volume added to the sample, as seen in Figure 3.2.

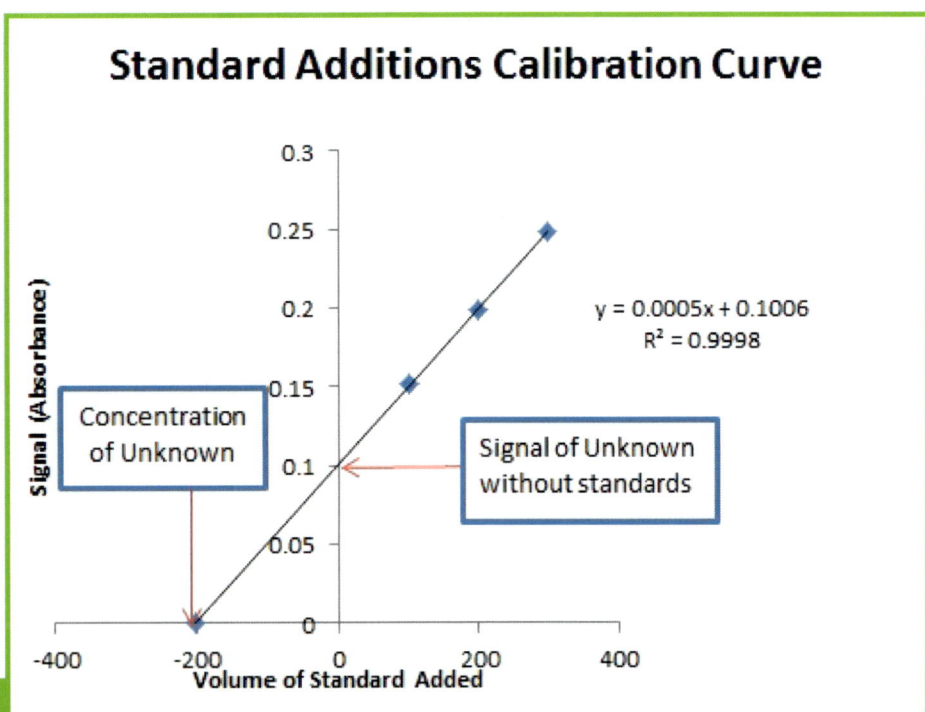

Figure 3.2
Standard Additions Calibration Curve with
Equation of the Line and R² Value Displayed

Many Spectrophotometers are preloaded with commonly used methods for water quality testing, so the operator does not need to perform the calibration; however, it is important for an analyst to understand and interpret calibration curves.

3.2 Colorimeters

The terms colorimeter, photometer and filter photometer are often used interchangeably. These refer to a relatively simple and inexpensive device that performs absorption measurements at a limited set of wavelengths, corresponding to colors such as blue, green, red, etc. A colorimeter is similar to a spectrophotometer in that both measure the absorbance of a solution at a set wavelength, and follow Beer's law (absorbance readings are directly proportional to concentration).

A spectrophotometer can be set to any wavelength within its range, whereas a colorimeter can be set to only a limited number of wavelengths. Some colorimeters are designed to operate at only one fixed wavelength; however, for some colorimeters, wavelengths of 420 nm, 450 nm, 476 nm, 500 nm, 550 nm, 580 nm, 600 nm, and 650 nm are available (Skoog et al., 2007) and correspond to different colors of light in the visible spectrum. With some colorimeters, the wavelength is automatically changed by changing the light emitting diode (LED) or a filter. Using a light source that is the complementary color of the solution to be analyzed gives the best detection limit. For example, if a solution pink in color (such as a nitrite or chlorine test), a wavelength in the green region should be selected because the solution absorbs mostly green light.

For most colorimeters, before a measurement can be made, it is necessary to run a blank. The 0% Transmittance reading is obtained by blocking the light beam with a shutter (Skoog et al., 2007). The 100% transmittance reading is measured by using a solvent or reagent blank that takes into account light being absorbed by the solvent and by the walls of the sample cell.

Colorimeters tend to be much more inexpensive than spectrophotometers and can even be portable, but lack the higher level of accuracy and diversity of testing methods that spectrophotometers provide.

3.3 Meters and Electrodes

Potentiometry is an analytical methodology that is based on measurement of an electrochemical cell's potential (measured in millivolts). The equipment used for potentiometry is relatively inexpensive and simple, containing three key components: an indicator electrode, a reference electrode, and a potential measuring device (meter). Electrodes (also called probes) can be used to measure a wide variety of water quality parameters, but are usually designed for testing a single parameter. Sometimes it is possible to combine multiple electrodes into a single apparatus, such as a pH and salinity combination electrode. Although convenient, as combination electrodes gain more components, they become more expensive, more difficult to troubleshoot and have a greater likelihood of failure.

3.3.1 Temperature

Temperature can be described as the kinetic energy (energy of motion) of the molecules of a substance. When water is heated, for example, the molecules become more and more excited. They begin to move more rapidly until the point at which they begin to change state (into steam) as they escape the vessel containing them. Heat is simply a byproduct of those movements. As the molecules collide and vibrate and rub against one another, the friction causes heat to be released (similar to warmth obtained by rubbing hands together on a cold day). When water molecules are moving very rapidly, the distance between molecules is great. This relationship can be viewed in the form of water vapor. When the molecules are severely slowed, they group together to form ice.

When temperature is tested in a laboratory setting, it can be done using a standard liquid thermometer which measures the temperature-pressure relationship of the liquid inside the thermometer, or by use of a probe. Although mercury-filled thermometers are more accurate, they should not be used due to the toxic characteristics of mercury. Other liquid thermometers are available and can have higher levels of accuracy compared to temperature probes. It is important to look at the specifications when selecting temperature measuring equipment and choose according to the application. A temperature probe most typically measures the resistance of a known material using a thermistor or thermocouple and converts the signal into temperature units based on a proportional relationship using software calculation or analog circuitry to adjust the slope (Skoog et al., 2007). Many electrodes use automatic temperature compensation (ATC) to account for drift in potentiometric measurements caused by temperature differences, such as most pH electrodes. It is not usually necessary to re-calibrate an ATC probe, since the measurements taken during calibration for the target analyte (such as pH) accounts for the temperature bias.

3.3.2 pH

The pH of a substance is the measurement of the activity of the hydrogen ions present in the substance (not to be confused with the actual concentration of hydrogen ions). The use of the letter "p" has no known original reference, but is modernly referred to as the "power" or "potential" of hydrogen in the solution. pH can be mathematically expressed as the inverse logarithm of the hydrogen activity in a compound, whose scale runs from 0 – 14.

At the low end of the pH scale are strong acids, whose hydrogen activity is very high. Acids such as hydrochloric and sulfuric acid are strong acids, which references their ability to "donate" hydrogen ions to other substances. At the high of the pH scale are strong bases, whose hydrogen activity is very low. Bases such as sodium hydroxide (lye) and potassium hydroxide are strong bases, which references their ability to "accept" hydrogen ions. Acids when mixed with water will form hydronium ions (H_3O^+) whereas bases will reduce the level of hydronium ions in the water. Figure 3.3 demonstrates the pH of many well-known substances.

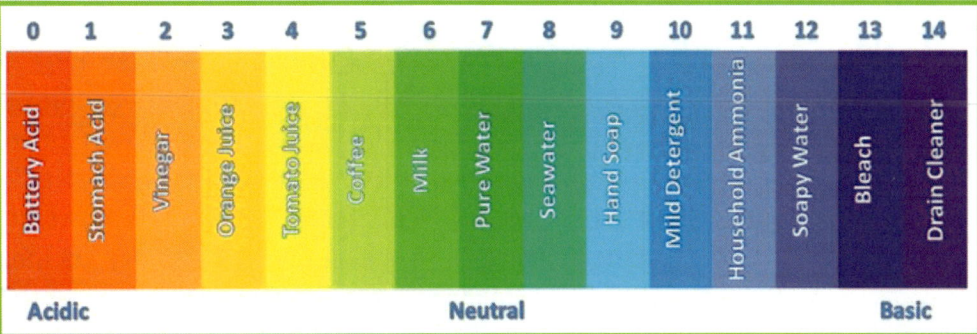

Figure 3.3 - The pH Scale

Pure water theoretically sits at the middle of the pH scale with a value of 7 at 25°C; however, it is important to note that deionized water tends to be acidic, as a result of the ion exchange resins. At a pH of 7, a substance is considered neither an acid nor a base but rather a neutral substance. Seawater; however, is not pure and ranges in pH from 7.5 to 8.4 (Chester & Jickells, 2012). Many compounds affect the pH of seawater including carbon dioxide in the air above and minerals in the ocean, such as carbonates and bicarbonates, alkaline earth metals.

pH measurements are one of the most important and frequently used tests in water chemistry (Rice et al., 2012). pH is most often tested using a direct calibration of the meter with a specific set of pH buffers. pH buffers are color coded for easy identification; for example, pH 4 buffer is pink, pH 7 buffer is yellow and pH 10 buffer is blue. Frequency of calibration required may vary, but for the most accurate measurements calibration should be performed daily, shortly before measurement with fresh buffers. Most pH probes use a glass electrode but it is possible to measure pH less accurately by a chemical substance with known reactions to pH, such as litmus or phenolphthalein.

A pH electrode generally consists of a glass indicator electrode combined with a reference electrode, temperature probe, and an internal electrolyte solution. Measurement errors can arise from measurements in low ionic strength solutions and dehydration of the membrane. It is important for pH electrode performance that the sensing bulb is not allowed to dry out and most electrodes should be stored in a 3 M potassium chloride solution, but it is important to check the user manual.

3.3.3 Salinity

Salinity is an indirect, temperature dependent measurement of salt ion concentration in water and for seawater is preferably expressed in parts-per-thousand (ppt or °/oo). Salinity may be determined by measuring properties such as conductivity, density, or refractive index (Rice et al., 2012). The methods for testing salinity in an aquarium environment are usually by use of the refractive index (with a refractometer) or by conductivity (with an electrode).

Salts are typically composed of a cation (an electropositive ion) and an anion (an electronegative ion). An example of this would be sodium chloride, or table salt. Sodium (Na^+) is a cation and chloride (Cl^-) is an anion. When salts are dissolved in water, they dissociate into their respective ions. The equation $NaCl$ (s) → Na^+ (aq) + Cl^- (aq) expresses this relationship. This separation forms electrolytes (substances that conduct electricity in water), which allows the ability to measure salinity as conductivity. The electrode measures the specific conductance of the water, which is the ability of the water to carry an electrical charge. Conductivity and temperature measurements are usually converted to salinity using mathematical relationships based on the Practical Salinity Scale (Lewis, 1980) automatically by the probe or meter. Many meters will automatically convert results between salinity, conductivity, resistivity, and total dissolved solids (TDS), but these can be manually calculated using mathematical relationships.

Measurement errors can arise from bubbles on the electrode, temperature changes (if the electrode does not have an ATC probe), and mineral build up on the electrode from dried samples. It is important to ensure the electrode is stored clean and dry, after being rinsed off with distilled or deionized water to make sure dried salts do not adhere to the electrode.

Although salinity determinations based on conductivity measurements are more accurate, a portable refractometer is a quick and easy way to measure salinity. The USDA regulates that salinity values for marine mammal pools must be maintained between 15 ppt - 36 ppt (Coakley & Crawford, 1998).

Concentration	Percentage
Chloride (Cl^-)	55.03%
Sodium (Na^+)	30.59%
Sulfate (SO_4^{2-})	7.68%
Magnesium (Mg^{2+})	3.68%
Calcium (Ca^{2+})	1.18%
Potassium (K^+)	1.11%
Bicarbonate (HCO_3^-)	0.41%
Bromide (Br^-)	0.19%
Borate (BO_3^{3-})	0.08%
Strontium (Sr^{2+})	0.04%
Miscellaneous Constituents	0.01%

Figure 3.4
The Major Salt Ion Concentrations of Seawater by Percentage

3.3.4 Dissolved Oxygen

Dissolved oxygen is simply defined as the amount of oxygen currently dissolved in a body of water. Adequate and constant dissolved oxygen concentration is a vital component for almost all aquatic organisms, including aerobic bacteria. In natural bodies of water, oxygen is constantly entering water from two main sources: the atmosphere and via photosynthesis. In an aquarium setting, this is often supplemented with additional aeration or diffusion of one or many types (bubblers, air stones, air curtains, uplifts, etc.) as exchange is further promoted through exchange of carbon dioxide (produced by respiration) with atmospheric oxygen, with additions of trickle towers (deaeration towers), waterfalls, fountains, surface agitation etc.

There are three methods available for measuring dissolved oxygen concentrations. It can be measured by titration, colorimetric methods, or a probe sensor with a meter. The traditional method is sometimes referred to as the Winkler titration. While this method was considered the most accurate and precise for many years, it is also subject to human error and is more difficult to execute than the other methods. The Winkler method now exists in seven modified versions which are still used today (Rice et al, 2012).The colorimetric method offers a basic approximation of dissolved oxygen concentrations in a sample. There are two methods designed for high-range and low-range dissolved oxygen concentrations. These methods are quick and inexpensive for basic projects, but limited in scope and subject to error due to other oxidizing agents (chlorine, bromine, ozone) that may be present in the water. Modern, rapid techniques involve either an electrochemical or optical sensor. The dissolved oxygen sensor is attached to a meter for spot sampling and laboratory applications or to a data logger, process monitor or transmitter for deployed measurements and process control.

The maximum dissolved oxygen carrying capacity of water varies greatly depending on temperature and to a much lesser degree water depth, pressure and salinity. Dissolved oxygen concentrations may change dramatically with depth. Oxygen production occurs in the top portion of a water column. Oxygen consumption is greatest near the bottom of the column, where sunken organic matter accumulates and decomposes. In deeper, stratified systems (lakes, ponds, etc.), this difference may be dramatic - plenty of oxygen near the top but practically none near the bottom. In most systems this is counteracted by good water movement or aeration that helps mix any striation.

Both temperature and salinity correlate with dissolved oxygen in a reverse proportion. In other words if temperature goes up, the carrying capacity decreases. As the temperature goes down, the carrying capacity increases. It is necessary and wise to know what the animal's natural life history dictates as a norm for them. To ensure their health, measurements of dissolved oxygen in (mg/L), should be simultaneously quantified with percent saturation (%), and temperature (degrees F or C).

It is suggested that regular routine monitoring of dissolved oxygen levels (mg/L, [%] and temperature) be recorded and trended on all systems. This will ensure proper concentration for animal safety and promote a healthy overall system.

3.3.5 Total Gas Pressure (TGP) and Supersaturation

Total Gas Pressure (TGP) is the sum of the partial pressures of all dissolved gases and the vapor pressure of water (Rogers, 2005). In the absence of variations in barometric pressure and any physical introduction of gases into water, the partial pressures of dissolved gases in a well-mixed body of water should be in equilibrium with the partial pressures of the same gases above the surface of the water (Rogers, 2005). The total gas pressure in mm Hg is the sum of the partial pressures in mm Hg, as seen in the equation below:

$$TGP = pN_2 + pO_2 + pCO_2 + pH_2O + pTrace$$

The total dissolved gas concentration in a body of water is a function of the salinity, temperature, barometric pressure, and gas composition (Colt, 1984). As pressure increases, the solubility of a gas in a specific volume of water will increase; in other words, water under higher pressure conditions is capable of holding more dissolved gas than water under lower pressure conditions. As salinity increases, the solubility of a gas in a specific volume of water will decrease; water with lower salinity is capable of holding more dissolved gas than is water of higher salinity. As the temperature of a specific volume of water increases, the solubility of a gas within this volume of water will decrease; warm water is capable of holding less dissolved gas than is cold water.

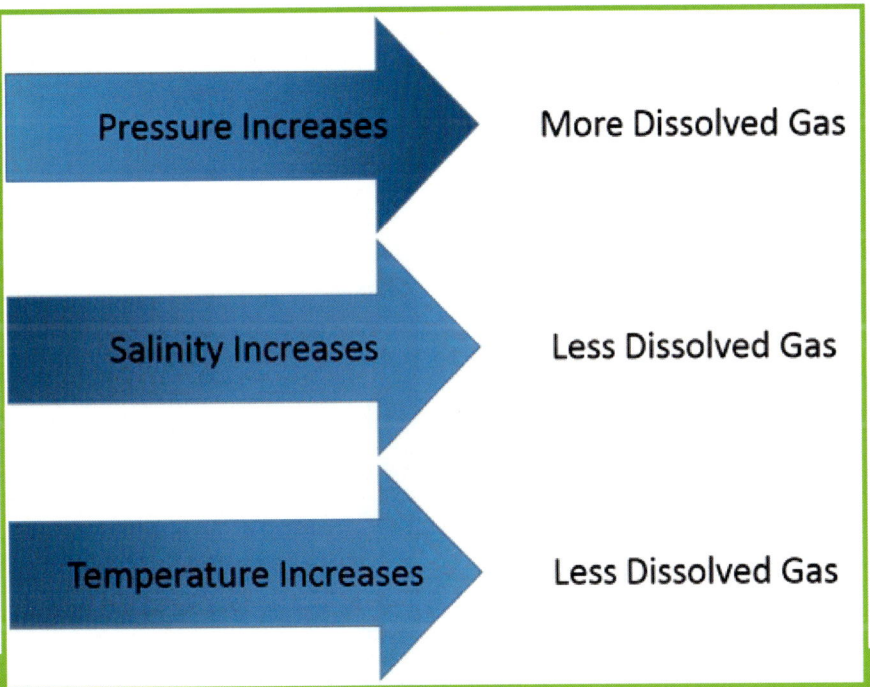

Figure 3.5 - Effects on Dissolved Gas from an Increase of Pressure, Salinity, and Temperature

TGP can be determined using chemical titration, volumetric tests, mass spectrometry, gas chromatography, manometry, and by headspace partial pressures (Rogers, 2005). The use of a handheld device called a saturometer is the most commonly used method to measure TGP in an aquaculture or aquarium setting. A saturometer measures TGP and barometric pressure (BP) in units of mm Hg and temperature. It can take many minutes and sometimes hours to obtain a stable TGP measurement in a system. Measurements should be taken at the same depth and location each time in order to provide accurate trending in an exhibit over time. Ideally, the depth of measurement should be below the compensation depth, or the point in the water column below which dissolved gases do not bubble out of solution, either in the water or in tissues (Colt, 1984). This point can be difficult to determine in an aquarium setting; it can be calculated using relationships between measured TGP, barometric pressure, and water depth. Slight water flow around or agitation of the instrument is useful for accurate stabilization and to prevent bubble formation on tubing in the event the measurement is occurring above the compensation depth. It also is important to set salinity compensation on the total gas meter or use a calculation to account for the contribution from salinity. Percent saturation is then derived by the following formula (D'Aoust, 2016):

$$\% \text{ Saturation} = \left(\frac{\text{TGP}}{\text{BP}}\right) \times 100\%$$

The following equation can be used to calculate the percent saturation of nitrogen gas when the percent of dissolved oxygen and the TGP percentage are known. This equation assumes the levels of dissolved CO_2 and Ar are insignificant (D'Aoust, 2016) and that the atmosphere above the water body has normal composition of 20.95% O_2 and 78.08% N_2.

$$N_2 \text{ (\% sat)} = \left(\frac{\text{TGP\%} - (0.2095 \times \text{DO\%})}{0.7807}\right)$$

Supersaturation of water bodies with dissolved gases can be caused by mixing of waters of different temperatures, heating of a body of water, ice formation, decreasing hydrostatic pressure, aircraft transport, airlift aeration, gas injection systems, photosynthesis, waterfalls, air entering the inlet of a pump from a leak in piping, the inlet of a sump, and vortex formations in sumps and exhibits (Carlson, 2005; Rogers, 2005). Supersaturation can sometimes be rectified by locating and correcting the source of the problem. Additionally, carefully increasing aeration or installing degassing columns or vacuum degassers into the life support of closed systems can help reduce TGP to acceptable levels.

Gas Bubble Disease (GBD) is a term commonly used to describe the effects of supersaturation on aquatic organisms. Symptoms of GBD include gas bubble formation along the lateral line of fishes, air emboli in the gill vasculature or other tissues, swollen eyes, buoyancy problems, and sudden abnormal behavior (Carlson, 2005). These conditions occur when dissolved gas (usually nitrogen) emerges from solution within the blood or tissues of an organism; similar to the cause of the "bends" in divers. Although supersaturation is technically occurring anytime TGP of a water body exceeds 100%, the level at which health issues will appear varies with animal species (syngnathids are particularly susceptible to supersaturation), exhibit depth, duration of supersaturation, depth changes when an animal moves, dissolved oxygen level, and overall health of the animals. In general, supersaturated conditions can lead to fish mortalities; in serious cases, entire exhibit populations have been lost, especially in shallow exhibits. Understanding the theory behind TGP and how to accurately measure it is critical for life support operators and water quality technicians.

3.3.6 BOD and COD

The demand for oxygen in water is usually expressed in the terms of biological or biochemical oxygen demand (BOD) and chemical oxygen demand (COD). Both BOD and COD are assessments of the overall workings and the ongoing balance of oxygen debt within an exhibit.

BOD is the amount of dissolved oxygen needed by aerobic biological organisms to oxidize the readily decomposable organic matter. BOD is tested by filling a bottle of sample water, measuring the initial DO, then sealing it in a glass bottle with a glass stopper and flared mouth and incubating it in the dark at 68°F (20°C) for 5 days. The measured loss of DO in milligrams per liter is used to calculate the BOD. BOD measurements are used in calculating the carrying capacity of an aquatic system (Spotte, 1992).

COD is used in aquaculture primarily as an index of organic matter concentrations. It is the measure of the amount of oxygen needed to degrade the organic matter. The COD is expressed in milligrams of oxygen per liter; however, COD is less specific, since it measures everything that can be chemically oxidized, rather than just levels of biodegradable organic matter.

In different ways, these measure the organic constituents in water and provide an estimate of dissolved organic substances. Understanding dissolved organic compounds and how they affect aquariums will help sustain an enriching environment for aquatic plants, aquatic invertebrates and fish. In general, the lower the BOD or COD value, the better the overall water quality. Imbalances stemming from higher BOD or COD can cause excessive algae formation, water yellowing, and in extreme cases major drops in dissolved oxygen.

3.4 Measuring and Dispensing Equipment

Laboratory equipment used to measure and dispense chemicals are very important tools for the Laboratory Technician. But just like any tool, some perform better at specific tasks than others. The following is a list of equipment commonly found in laboratories and the primary function of each (Kerri et al., 2008).

3.4.1 Erlenmeyer Flask

This container is wide at the base and narrow at the mouth. It is available in thin or thick wall options and wide or narrow mouth openings. The wide mouth option is best used for mixing chemicals and the narrow mouth opening is best used for titrations. With a flat wide base and tapered narrow opening, the Erlenmeyer flask is the best flask to use when mixing a liquid solution on a spinner plate.

Photo 3.1 - Erlenmeyer Flask

3.4.2 Graduated Cylinder

This container is tall and round with a molded spout for easy pouring. It is available in sizes ranging from 5 mL to 4,000 mL and is more accurate for measuring the volume of a liquid than a beaker. When selecting a graduated cylinder to use, it is best to select the smallest one that can fit the volume being measured. A more accurate volume will be obtained if a 10 mL graduated cylinder is used rather than a 100 mL graduated cylinder to measure 8 mL of a solution.

Photo 3.2 - Graduated Cylinder

3.4.3 Volumetric Flask

This container has a round base and a long narrow neck with a calibrated line to mark the volume of the flask. This flask is to be used for measuring and diluting but not for heating or storage. This is the most accurate measurement of a fixed liquid volume and the preferred flask to use when performing a dilution.

Photo 3.3 - Volumetric Flask

3.4.4 Beaker

This container is a round mouth, straight sided glass with a molded spout for easy pouring. It is available in thin or thick wall options. The thick wall is more durable in a mechanical dishwasher but less able to withstand rapid temperature changes (Smith, et al., 1995). This general use all-purpose glassware is the perfect container for mixing solutions and weighing dry chemicals.

Photo 3.4 - Beaker

39

3.4.5 Titration Equipment

Burets, also known as burettes, come in two basic options: one is a calibrated glass hollow rod with a stopcock plug for dispensing, the other is a bottle top dispensing burette where the burette can quickly refill for continuous titrations. The main difference between these two is where the titrant is held.

The standard glass burette is the more economical option of the two. This burette type does not have a space to store the titrant other than the body of the burette and it is required to fill the burette with titrant from the top with a funnel frequently. This type of burette is better suited for fewer tests as it is inefficient to have to continually refill the burette for additional titrations. Using the stopcock plug for titrating is a skill and is only as accurate as the technician's hands are steady. With this burette, the current volume of titrant is noted and the titration is performed. Once completed, the new volume is noted and the difference is the amount of titrant used. This type of burette presents the risk of spilled titrant while refilling and the risk of errors with reading the meniscus at different heights.

The bottle top dispensing burette is the preferred option as it allows the technician to perform multiple titrations or measurements in a row utilizing the bottle it is attached to for a continuous supply of titrant chemical. The bottletop burette is designed to pull titrant into a storage chamber and then dispense it slowly while accurately measuring the volume of the titrant used. The burette can easily switch between filling and dispensing and there is little risk of spillage. Bottletop burettes come in many styles: digital, manual, plunger, roller wheel, fixed, variable or measurable volume options. In Photo 3.5, the two bottletop burettes on the left are for titrating and the one on the right is for dispensing.

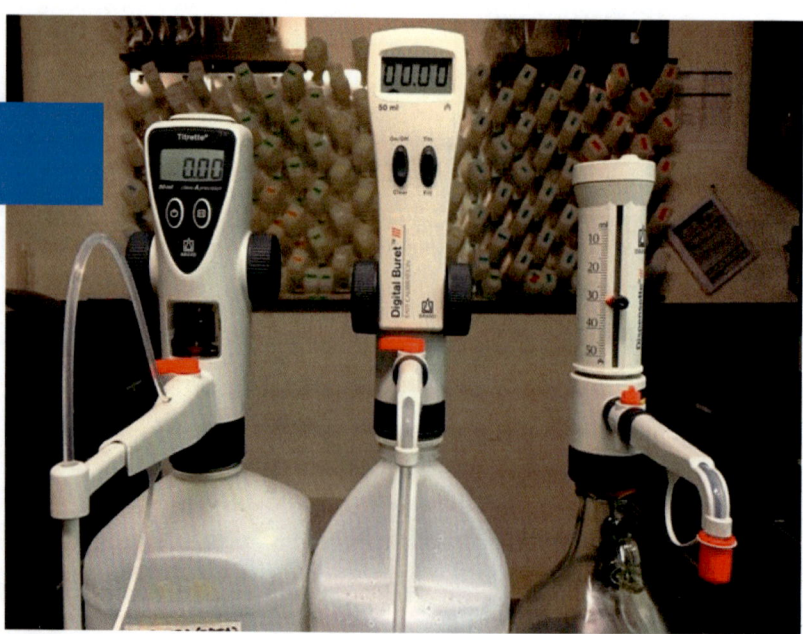

Photo 3.5 - Bottle Top and Dispensing Buret

3.4.6 Pipettes: Transfer, Serological, Volumetric, Micropipettes

Pipettes are an ideal tool for both measuring and dispensing a small amount of liquid accurately. They come in a variety of styles to meet the need of the technician. Pipettes can be made of glass or plastic. They can be inexpensive and disposable, or an expensive laboratory measuring device. The range of options for pipettes is so broad that a laboratory can have many pipette options for a variety of needs, such as manual, automated, ergonomic, high volume, and multi tipped. There are four main types of pipettes used in the Water Quality Laboratory: transfer, serological, volumetric, and micropipettes, described below.

Transfer Pipettes

The most economical type is a disposable plastic transfer pipette. These are useful when sterility and accuracy are not important. An example of this use would be adding drops of sample water to a vessel where the measurement is being taken from the bottom of the meniscus. The accuracy of the pipette is irrelevant as is the sterility.

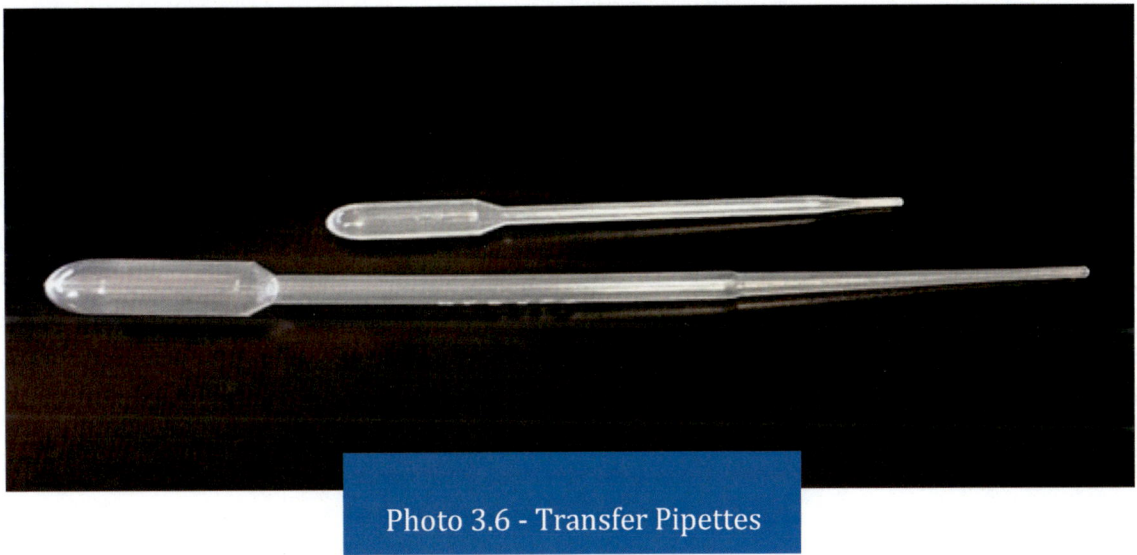

Photo 3.6 - Transfer Pipettes

Serological Pipettes

A serological pipette is one that is often individually wrapped, preventing contamination of the other unused pipettes when handling. This type of pipette is used for larger unfixed volumes from 1 mL - 25 mL and when there is room for a small margin of error in the measurement. These pipettes usually have ascending and descending measurements on the pipette for easy measuring and dispensing of liquids. This type of pipette can be inserted into a variety of pipettors for use. Pipettor options for this type of pipette are a silicone bulb, pipette pump, or a pipette controller. The best option for pipettor selection depends on the repetition of the required task and the required budget. A silicone bulb type is sufficient for a limited number of measurements and a pipette controller is best for multiple.

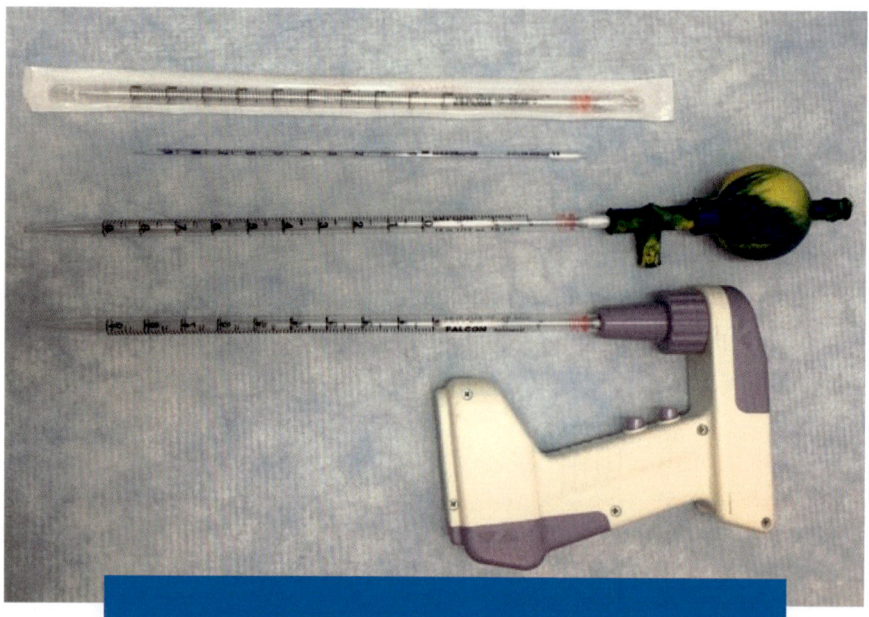

Photo 3.7 - Serological Pipettes with Pipettors

Volumetric Pipettes

A volumetric pipette is made of glass and used to measure a fixed amount of liquid. Because it can only be used to measure one volume, like a volumetric flask, many volumes should be made available to meet different needs. Volumetric pipettes come in standard volumes such as 0.5, 1, 2, 3, 4, 5, 10, 20, 25, 50, 75, 100, and 200 mL. This pipette is calibrated to a specific measurement which makes it one of the most accurate type of pipette options described. Like the serological pipette, it can be used with a variety of pipettors best suited for the number of times the task is to be repeated.

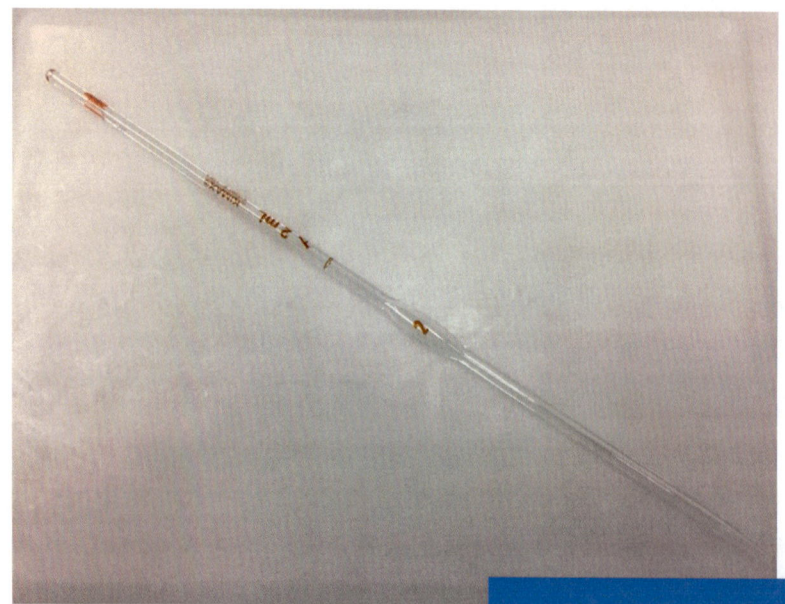

Photo 3.8 - Volumetric Pipette

Micropipettes

A micropipette is used for measuring the smallest amount of liquid with accuracy. A micropipette tip is a small, plastic, single use pipette that is attached to a larger plunger type pipettor that is of high quality, calibrated, and deliver volume with known accuracy and precision (Curtis, 1999). These pipettors can be purchased individually or as a set for a range of measurable volumes. Each pipettor can be adjusted to measure a fixed volume within the range of that particular pipettor such as 0.2 µL - 2.0 µL or 100 µL - 1000 µL. Micropipette pipettors are available in a multi-channel option, allowing the technician to pipette 8, 12, or 16 samples at one time.

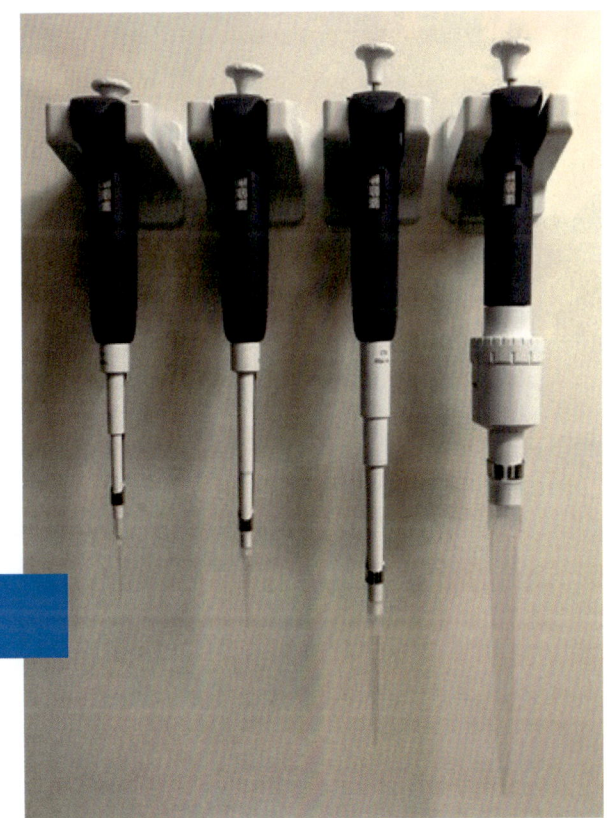

Photo 3.9 - Micropipettes

3.5 Laboratory Temperature Control Devices

Temperature has a major effect on a number of properties of laboratory samples, such as liquid density, reaction rates, bacterial growth rates and method holding times. The majority of water quality testing is performed at room temperature (68 - 77°F, 20 - 25°C), but it is not uncommon to require a more controlled temperature range.

3.5.1 Refrigerator

In a water quality laboratory, a refrigerator is typically used to store samples between collection and analysis, store temperature sensitive reagents or cultures, and occasionally storage of flammable materials. Do not store food or beverages in a refrigerator if it is located in a laboratory, used for animal food storage, used for chemical storage, or contains deceased animals, media or cultures. The laboratory refrigerator should be maintained at a temperature between 2 and 8°C (Rice et al., 2012). For non-flammable materials storage, a general purpose refrigerator may be used. For flammable storage, a refrigerator must be designed to prevent ignition of flammable materials. Even a small amount of flammable materials in a conventional refrigerator may cause an explosion due to electrical sparks from the thermostat, light switch, fans, etc. In rare circumstances, the hazards may require an explosion-proof refrigerator. Use secondary containment to separate incompatible chemicals and to provide spill containment.

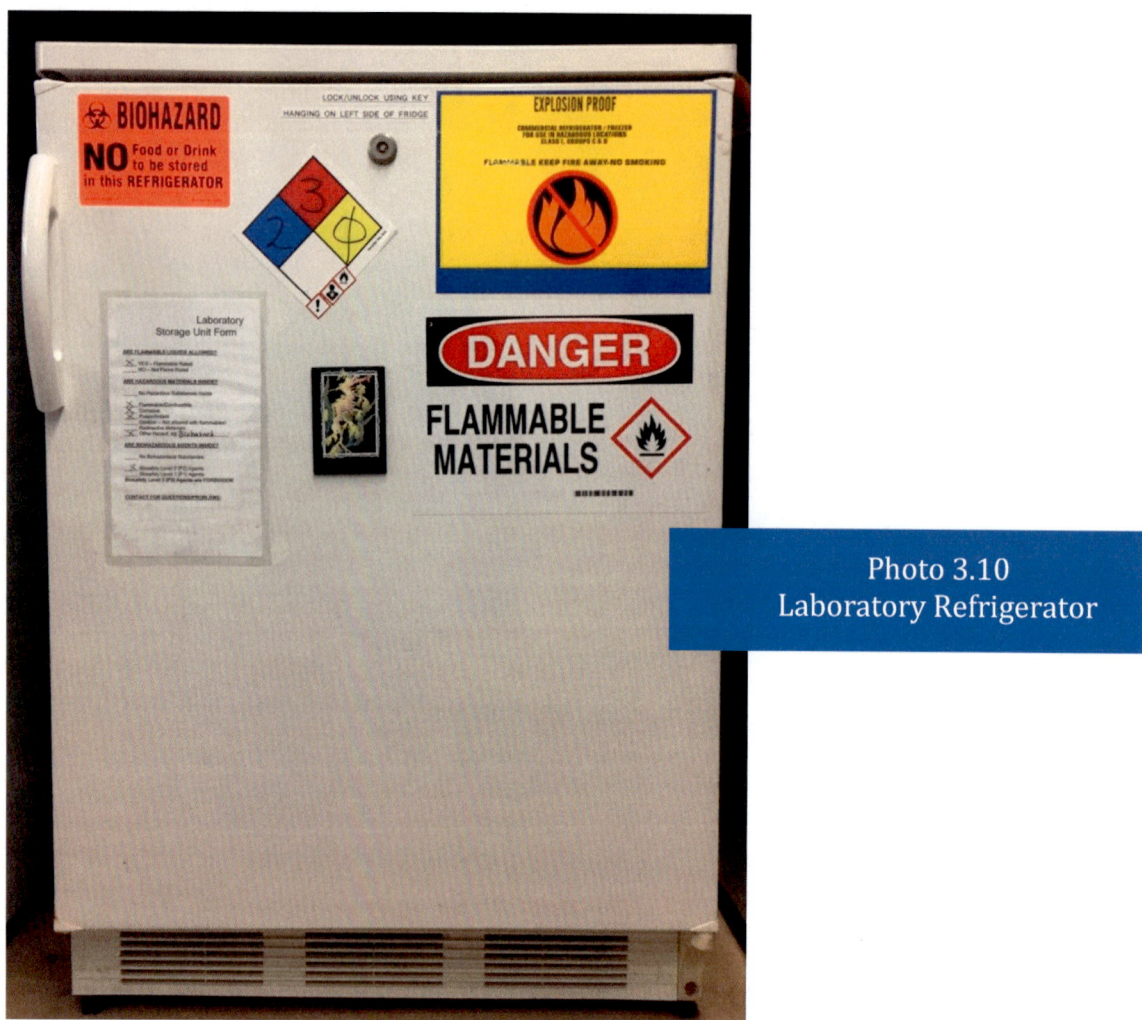

Photo 3.10
Laboratory Refrigerator

3.5.2 Freezer

Freezer temperatures vary depending on the application. A standard freezer typically ranges from -10 to -20°C (Rice et al., 2012). Some specialty freezers can go to -80°C or lower for cryogenic applications. Freezers may be used to store samples, cultures or media, but it is important to note that most water quality samples should not be frozen, they should be refrigerated. Check method specific requirements for sample storage temperature. All laboratory freezers must have a label indicating that they are not for storage of food or drink. Freezer ice buildup must be quickly corrected to ensure upright storage and for access. Use secondary containment to separate incompatible chemicals and to provide spill containment.

3.5.3 Incubator

An incubator is chamber designed to maintain a set temperature, providing a warm, stable environment. Incubators are commonly used for a variety of applications, such as warming eggs in animal husbandry, and for growth and storage of bacterial cultures in water quality applications. Incubators come in a variety of sizes, features and specialty functions, such as maintaining a set temperature, humidity, or carbon dioxide level. It is important that an incubator is of sufficient size to maintain constant and uniform temperatures (Rice et al., 2012). Check temperatures daily using a NIST-traceable thermometer and calibrate annually.

Photo 3.11
Laboratory Incubator

3.5.4 Water Bath

A water bath is also used as an incubation tool; heated water provides a uniform temperature for samples. Water baths can heat samples more quickly and evenly than an air incubator, because water offers better contact surface and heat transfer; however, water bath incubators may be subject to more contamination and growth of microorganisms. Proper maintenance and a regular disinfection process may be required.

3.5.5 Autoclave

An autoclave (also referred to as a steam sterilizer) is a chamber designed to sterilize its contents through high heat and pressure. It is necessary to verify the temperature and pressure achieved for each run, as well as use heat-sensitive tape to ensure temperature was achieved. It is recommended to use a biological indicator monthly as further confirmation of the sterilization process. A biological indicator contains viable microorganisms that have a proven resistance to the sterilization process. Successful sterilization of these organisms, such as *Geobacillus stearothemophilus*, gives confidence in the sterilization process. It is important to incubate both a sterilized indicator and an unaltered biological indicator to prove that the sterilized indicator was viable prior to autoclaving. Ensure that the autoclave is filled with clean, distilled water. Contaminants in the water may cause the autoclave to not reach the set temperature. Follow scheduled maintenance as directed by the user manual to ensure it is functioning properly. Ensure that all bags, containers, bottles, lids, and materials are autoclavable and will not melt or break when subjected to high heat and pressure. Generally, the autoclave must reach and maintain a temperature of 121°C for at least 15 minutes by using saturated steam under at least 15 psi (100 kPa) of pressure to effectively sterilize its contents.

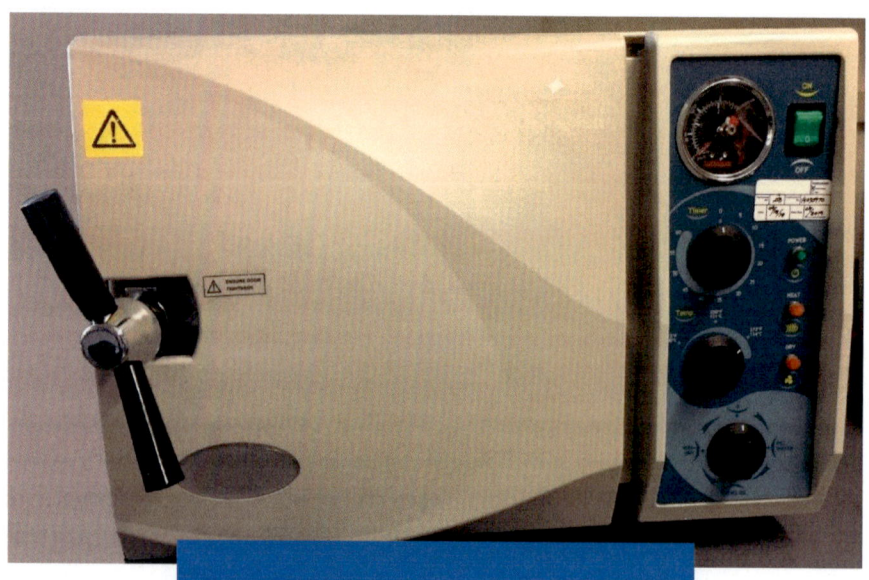

Photo 3.12 – Benchtop Autoclave

3.6 Chromatography

Chromatography is a useful technique that allows separation of components on a complex sample to quantify a compound of interest (analyte) at low concentration. Analytes can be ions, or organic molecules (such as pharmaceuticals) and can be separated and quantified with various forms of chromatography, which makes these techniques very important in science, research, and even to the animal care industry. There are many applications of chromatography beyond the scope of this Field Guide.

Chromatography consists of a few different components. The first is the mobile phase, which is responsible for 'carrying' or 'pushing' the sample through the chromatographic system usually via a pumping system. The mobile phase can either be a gas, liquid such as an organic solvent or buffer system to name a few. Next is the sample injection, which allows the user to either inject the sample manually into the mobile phase, or automatically (usually with an autosampler that is controlled by a computer). The samples sit in a carousel. The separation of the analyte occurs in the stationary phase or analytical column. Depending on the type of chromatography being employed, the column is either packed with bead-like particles coated with a resin or unpacked, where the walls of the column are coated with the resin (for example, silica gel is used commonly in organic chemistry). Regardless of the type of column that is used, the analyte must interact with the stationary phase in a reversible manner, meaning that the compound only adsorbs and can desorb from the resin (Kellner, 2004). Lastly, the separated analyte in the mobile phase enters the detector, which quantifies the amount of the analyte present in the sample. These components are the basis of any chromatographic system; however, applications such as Thin Layer Chromatography (TLC) do not use a detector and use UV light or a stain to view separations. Depending on the type of chromatography or compound being separated, there may be additional components. The composition of the mobile and stationary phases will also differ between the different types of chromatography.

Chromatographic systems are much more sensitive and selective than colorimetry, titrations, or drop test kits; however, they are also much more expensive both in analyte extraction process and instrument operation. Many facilities opt to use less expensive equipment for detection of similar analytes.

3.6.1 Ion Chromatography

Ion-Exchange or Ion Chromatography (IC) is a method of separation and quantification of ions or polar molecules found in a sample. IC is a method of liquid chromatography that uses the principle of ion-exchange. In the Zoo & Aquarium industry, nitrite and nitrate are the more common ions quantified by this method. IC can also be used for the quantification of other anions (negatively charged species) such as chloride, bromide, fluoride, sulfate and sulfite, to name a few as well as cations (positively charged species) such as lithium, magnesium, calcium, strontium, and barium, among others (Skoog, 2007).

Anionic IC typically uses bicarbonate and carbonate buffered water as the mobile phase (also called eluent). The sample is injected into the mobile phase and is carried to the analytical column, which is packed with an ion exchange resin. The anions interact with the resin within the column in different manners, depending on their overall charge, type of resin, pH and ionic strength of the mobile phase, which causes the separation (Kellner, 2004). Cationic IC typically uses methane sulfonic acid as the mobile phase, and involves similar, but oppositely charged reactions within the analytical column. IC systems also use suppressors after the analytical column. This helps to not overload the detector with too many ions by 'removing' the ionic forms of the compounds in the mobile phase and not affecting the compound of interest. Suppressors have to be 'regenerated' periodically, as to not lose their exchange properties. Traditional IC systems employ conductivity detectors, as salt ions are the analytes; however, recently UV detection methods are being used more frequently, as they are more sensitive and selective, especially for nitrate detection, because there is little interference from the mobile phase.

For nitrate, many other non-chromatographic methods of quantification do not distinguish between nitrite and nitrate and just report the results as total nitrite plus nitrate as nitrogen. Separation and detection by IC allows for the separation and separate quantification of nitrite and nitrate individually (Standard Methods, 2012). Some methods also experience other interferences such as high organic levels, which would not be an interference in IC.

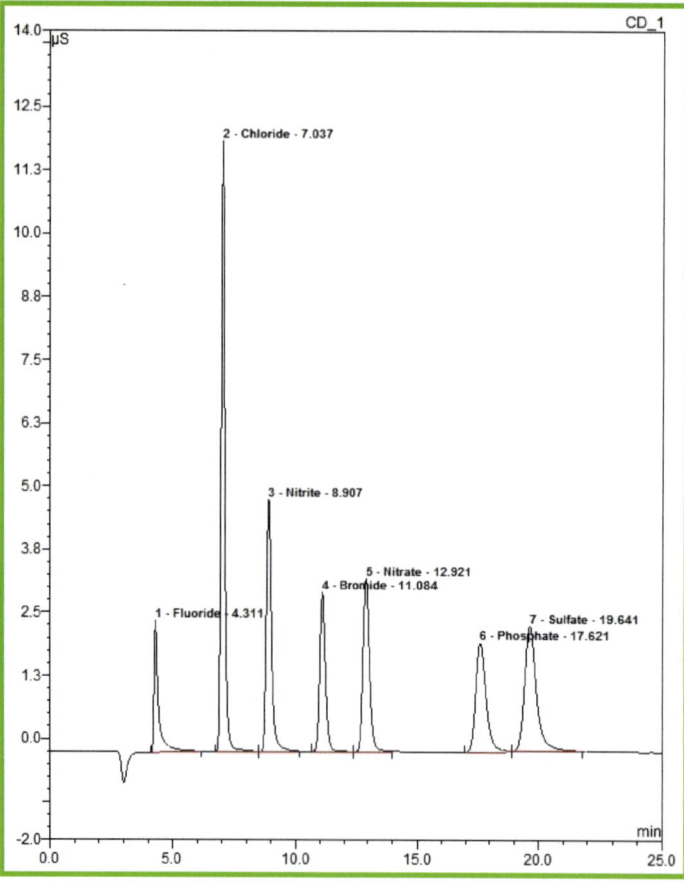

Figure 3.6
Anionic Chromatograph

3.6.2 High Performance Liquid Chromatography

High-Performance Liquid Chromatography (HPLC) is a very powerful and efficient method of separation and analysis of various samples at very low concentrations. In traditional HPLC, the mobile phase consists of an organic solvent or mixture of organic solvents at either a constant composition (isocratic) or varying concentration (gradient), which is dependent on the method being employed and the complex nature of the sample. The stationary phase is a packed column of beads with various particle diameters ranging from 3-10μm (Skoog, 2007). High pressure flow 'pushes' the analyte through the packed column to initiate separation. The packed column contains various functional groups, which interact with the analyte resulting in the separation. Different molecules interact differently with the functional groups in the stationary phase, which is what makes HPLC so powerful. The exact composition of both the mobile and stationary phases depend on the analyte in question. HPLC can be used to test for pharmaceuticals such as praziquantel (Crowder, 2004), polycyclic aromatic hydrocarbons and many more. Once the separation occurs in the column, a detector (often a UV detector) is primarily used to quantify the analyte(s). An HPLC system is very robust and flexible and allows the user to develop custom methods to determine the concentration of various compounds. These custom methods can use different types of analytical columns, mobile phase solvent systems and detectors, making HPLC a very powerful, selective and flexible instrument.

3.7 Total Organic Carbon Analyzer

Total Carbon can be broken into two main components; Total Inorganic Carbon (TIC) and Total Organic Carbon (TOC). TIC refers to compounds such as carbonates, bicarbonates and any dissolved carbon dioxide, and TOC is all other carbon-containing compounds, which could be a multitude of different molecules. As discussed in Section 5.7, TOC is an important parameter to measure in an aquatic system. A build-up of TOC in an aquatic environment can cause decreases in dissolved oxygen, decrease in visibility through the water column and other issues that could negatively impact aquatic life. Regularly measuring TOC can assist with monitoring the concentration and making sure that an export mechanism is readily available or is working properly (physical removal, protein skimmer).

A Total Organic Carbon Analyzer, quantifies the amount of organic carbon found in the water sample. There are a couple of different methods that TOC Analyzers use to accomplish this; however, their overall process is similar. From the sample, inorganic carbon, such as carbonates and carbon dioxide, are removed by acidifying the sample, which converts the carbonates and bicarbonates to carbon dioxide, then purging the sample with the carrier gas, which can be high-purity air, oxygen or nitrogen to expel the carbon dioxide. During the process, Volatile Organic Carbon (VOC), also known as Purgeable Organic Carbon (POC) is expelled as well, which is a component of TOC;

therefore, making the process a measurement of Non-Purgeable Organic Carbon (NPOC) and not a 'true' measure of TOC. In most aquariums, is can be assumed that there is little POC input and that the measurement of NPOC is essentially a measurement of TOC. The remaining organic carbon (NPOC) is converted to carbon dioxide, which is then quantified, representing the total amount of organic carbon. The method of conversion and detection of the carbon dioxide produced is what differentiates the types of TOC Analyzers. Analyzers can use high temperature combustion, UV light, chemical oxidants, or a combination of these methods to determine the amount of NPOC. The resulting carbon dioxide is quantified using a non-dispersive infrared detector (NDIR), which is the most common method of detection.

Proper laboratory techniques and procedures are essential for performing water quality testing. Whether the testing includes drop test kits, chromatography, or other analytical methods, it is important to have a quality assurance plan and to regularly assess the performance of the testing methods and technicians.

4.1 Quality Assurance

Quality Assurance (QA) refers to the practices and principles employed to produce highly accurate and defensible data that is essential to animal husbandry and life support functions. Basic husbandry functions (tank cycling, water changes), medical treatments (copper, chloroquine), and a variety of corrective actions (disinfection, pH adjustment) are dependent upon the laboratory analytical results. A QA plan should include all necessary actions and documentation to support the laboratory's and the technician's competence and reliability.

4.1.1 Staff Organization and Responsibilities

Having clearly defined roles and responsibilities is essential to assert the level of control necessary to ensure the laboratory's effectiveness and reliability. In larger, accredited laboratories, a QA officer is typically employed to monitor all aspects of laboratory processes including SOPs, QA/QC, among others. Within the zoo and aquarium industry; however, where data are produced and used solely in-house, the analysts themselves are usually responsible for assuring data quality. This might lead to a conflict of interest. To eliminate potential bias, data verification should be done by someone other than the principal analyst such as the lab manager or other technicians. A good QA plan ensures data and method validation, lab and technician competence, and application of necessary corrective actions.

4.1.2 Analyst Training Requirements

The analyst should be adequately trained to perform any assigned testing procedure. To eliminate bias and other systematic errors, data should be reproducible between analysts. Consistent training methods will ensure consistent results, despite a change in analyst. Training records should be well documented and filed by supervisors for greater accountability. Any analyst performing a new method should satisfactorily pass an Initial Demonstration of Capability (IDC).

4.1.3 Laboratory Facilities

A QA plan should be employed regardless of the amount of space and staffing available. The space should be dedicated for specific tasks and needs to be kept organized and clean to reduce cross contamination risks or other variability caused by sharing a space and resources with other departments and tasks. Having dedicated laboratory staff to properly perform tasks and analyses ensures the laboratory is running efficiently and reduces mistakes that could compromise the quality of data being produced.

4.1.4 Instrument Maintenance Procedures

Regular and preventative maintenance ensures the consistent operation of equipment and reproducible results. The laboratory's responsibility is to follow all recommended maintenance procedures as directed by the manufacturer. These routine procedures also help to reduce instrument downtimes and malfunctions that lead to poor data production. Instrument maintenance varies from simple cleaning procedures to professional servicing such as calibration checks on analytical balances, pipettes and other instrumentation. A calibration and maintenance log should be kept for each piece of equipment. Keeping these logs up-to-date often helps to diagnose and troubleshoot problems that may arise.

4.1.5 Instrument Calibration and Verification Procedures

An important part of quality assurance is routine instrument calibration and verification. Although most spectrophotometers and colorimeters are factory calibrated, instrument drifts from environmental, physical, and chemical changes may occur. Some instruments with stored factory made programs, a simple one point calibration adjustment or verification of a known standard may be used to monitor for the drift from the factory calibration. It is more desirable; however, that a new calibration be performed routinely using certified standards. Generally, three or more standard points covering the expected range of the analysis are analyzed to generate a new calibration curve. Refer to the particular method for specific requirements for calibration points, frequency, and other pertinent information. The instrument manual should be consulted as guidance on how to perform calibration and verification procedures.

4.1.6 Standard Operating Procedures

A standard operating procedure (SOP) is a written document that describes a procedure with enough detail that an experienced technician, though unfamiliar, can follow to produce the expected end result. A SOP should be available for every procedure in the laboratory. These include sampling, analysis, operation of equipment, calibration and maintenance of equipment, and reporting of results. SOPs are used to standardize and streamline the processes for better quality assurance and data validity. They may reference other SOPs or expand upon related aspects from another SOP. A well written SOP is clear enough to remove all potential deviations and misunderstandings. SOPs are specific to the laboratory, the instrument, and their intended use. SOPs should contain more than line-by-line instructions on how to perform the tasks. Manufacturer's guide, instruction manual, or other published articles/methods do not eliminate the need for individual SOPs. SOPs should be reviewed annually or as changes in a procedure are made, to ensure accuracy. See Appendix 19.4 for sample SOPs.

4.1.7 Sampling Techniques

It is important for all staff to be consistently trained and to follow a proper sampling standard operating procedure. Variations such as when, where, and how a sample is collected can have noticeable effects on the results. All samples must be stored and handled consistently. Many water quality tests have a "holding time" or the time in which analysis should be completed before the sample degrades. It is important that the analysis takes place within the method's holding time to ensure deviations of results are not due to time lapsed before analysis. See Appendix 19.3.4 for a list of commonly tested parameters, required container type, preservation, and holding times.

4.1.8 Reporting

Data reports are the culmination of all the daily work performed and completed by the laboratory. The reports are used to make husbandry, veterinary, and life support decisions that can impact animal and overall exhibit health. It is important that the data is presented accurately and completely. Refer to Appendix 19.6 for an example of a water quality data sheet. For better interpretation of results, the accompanying quality control data for a given batch should be reported to assess accuracy and precision (see Section 4.2.1). Data qualifiers are notes to the end user regarding nearly any issue they should be aware of that may affect the quality of the data, may also be used. Data qualifiers can be used to identify issues such as improper collection techniques or that a sample was analyzed outside of holding time. They can also be used to express data quality issues such as estimated results below the reporting limit, samples analyzed outside of their method holding time, improper collection techniques, low or high recovery of standards, method blank contamination and poor duplicate precision. When qualifiers are used, the associated corrective actions should also be presented. These qualifiers and quality control data allow the end user to interpret the overall usefulness and usability of the data.

4.1.9 Mistakes vs. Unethical Behavior

Water quality data should be trustworthy, dependable, and defensible because the interpretation might impact the quality of animal or exhibit care. Mistakes do happen. Following established SOPs would reduce such errors. Laboratory fraud or scientific misconduct; however, is not a simple mistake but rather intended to manipulate. Laboratory fraud is the deliberate falsification during reporting of analytical and quality assurance results that failed method and contractual requirements to make them appear to have passed requirements (USEPA, 2014). This can include procedural deceptions (calibration or analysis short cuts) and measurement deceptions (changing results, data creation, data/peak manipulation). Examples include manipulating calibration curves to get a better QC recovery or to avoid rerunning under or over diluted samples and falsifying documents, holding times, or analysis time stamp. Laboratory staff must understand that data quality and reliability are foremost important, despite pressure of meeting specific deadlines that might not be feasible due to both procedural and staffing requirements. It is acceptable to make an occasional mistake, but unacceptable to hide the mistake.

4.1.10 Resampling and Retesting

Samples should be recollected if contaminated or if not analyzed within the specified holding time. Samples should be retested and reanalyzed when the results exceed the maximum concentration on the calibration curve. Do not dilute processed samples after the fact. The reagents used to perform the analysis are limited to specific maximum concentration and volume. Samples should also be reanalyzed when samples are over-diluted, meaning the specific analyte under investigation is diluted far beyond the lower limit of the calibration curve. Should any concern arise during analysis, it's best to repeat the procedure. It is also recommended to retest when results are outside the target range or are significantly different than what is normally found. Errors in data may be caused by a variety of issues such as mixing up samples, procedural mistakes, and errors made while recording results.

4.1.11 Precision and Accuracy

All measurements contain a level of error, which arise from a combination of systematic error (bias) and random error. Systematic error refers to errors that are predictable and repeatable; meaning they are consistent across a number of measurements and do not average out. Systematic errors can be attributed to faulty equipment, calibration errors, incorrect use, or even from flaws in experimental design. Random error refers to unpredictable errors that average out, have a varying magnitude and are unpredictable. An example of systematic error is the incorrect calibration of a refractometer, which will cause all results to be either biased high or biased low. An example of random error is measuring the mass of an object three times and getting slightly different values. Gross errors are attributed to analyst carelessness or broken equipment. Generally, these errors are so large in magnitude that they can be eliminated from a data set as an "outlier", through statistical analysis, such as a "Q test".

Precision indicates how closely repeated measurements agree (random error) and accuracy refers to how close a measurement is to the true value; a bias in the data (systematic error) will affect the accuracy of the measurement.

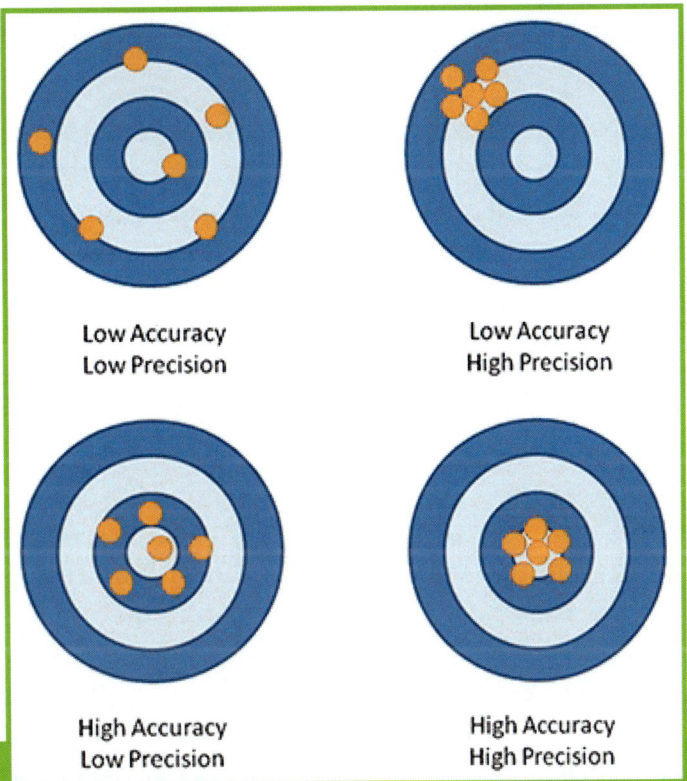

Figure 4.1 - Accuracy and Precision

4.2 Quality Assessment

Quality Assessment is a process used to determine the quality of data provided by the laboratory (Rice et al., 2012), taking into account both internal quality control practices and external quality control practices. Internal quality control practices include recovery of known additions, analysis of known standards, and the analysis of duplicate samples. External quality control includes performance audits and performance evaluation (PE) samples. Recognizing trends is also a valuable assessment tool. The ability to assure the quality of the data produced is essential to prove lab performance and its overall value to a facility.

4.2.1 Internal Quality Control Samples

Internal quality control samples are an extremely valuable tool and demonstration of performance for laboratory work. It is recommended to analyze a set of QC samples for every batch of samples tested. A batch should consist of 20 samples; however, if more samples must be analyzed simultaneously, additional QC samples should be considered. At minimum, QC samples should be tested for water chemistry parameters daily. All water quality analysts should be able to prepare (from a secondary source) and interpret QC samples.

Sample Blank

A sample blank is a solution free of the analyte(s) of interest and is usually the solution used in instrument calibration and to zero a spectrophotometer before reading sample results. The sample blank corrects for color or turbidity in the sample before any reagents are added. Zeroing to a sample blank ensures that the color measured by a spectrophotometer or colorimeter is attributed only to the colorimetric reaction taking place (HACH, 2008). In some methods, the sample blank may be seawater that is free of the target analyte.

Reagent Blank

A reagent blank refers to the positive error of the test results that is attributed by the reagents used in the analysis (HACH, 2008). The reagent blank monitors purity of reagents and the overall procedural blank (Rice et al., 2012). The reagent blank should be processed in exactly the same manner as regular samples. The reagent blank is used to assess contamination resulting from the entire analytical process, including reagent purity, sample handling techniques, and carry-over. The reagent blank is especially important in analysis of low-level samples, since a small positive error comprises a larger percentage of the result, thus a higher loss in accuracy. The reagent blank can be subtracted from the sample results in some circumstances. It is important to analyze a reagent blank with every testing batch or lot of reagents.

Laboratory Fortified Blank

A laboratory fortified blank (LFB), sometimes called a blank spike, is a solution of analyte-free water with known amount of target analyte, usually half of the maximum detection limit. LFB is used to show that sample preparation procedures do not contribute to loss of analyte(s). A secondary source standard should be used to determine accuracy of the stock standard used to make new curve and as LFBs. Typically, the second source should be from a different manufacturer or a different lot number from the same manufacturer. It should be processed as a laboratory fortified blank. Consult the particular method for specific requirements regarding the use of a second source.

Laboratory Fortified Matrix

A laboratory fortified matrix (LFM), sometimes called a matrix spike, is an aliquot of sample with the addition of known amount of target analyte prior to sample preparation and analysis. A matrix spike is used to assess the bias of a method in a given sample matrix.

Laboratory Fortified Matrix Duplicate

A matrix spike duplicate is a duplicate of the matrix spike also used to assess the precision and bias of a method in a given sample matrix.

Matrix Duplicate

A matrix duplicate is a split sample used to assess the precision of a method in a given sample matrix.

4.2.2 Performance Evaluation Samples

Performance Evaluation (PE) samples contain target analyte(s) with unknown concentration for a particular analysis. They are usually obtained from a third party or manufacturer. Analysis of PE samples is a great way to ensure that the analysis is performed accurately and that analyst bias does not come into play. This external quality control of an unknown also helps in method validation, overall method performance, and sometimes in determining the accuracy of laboratory instruments. Routine evaluations of PE samples allow the tracking of the laboratory's and its technicians' performance.

4.2.3 Performance Audits

Most professional laboratories in other industries are regulated and must be accredited. Performance audits are performed by national and/or state accrediting institutions to give their stamp of approval on analyses performed by the applying laboratory. Performance audits are a great tool for these laboratories to get a third party perspective into the overall operations of the laboratory and completeness of their quality assurance. Laboratories within the zoo and aquarium industry are generally unregulated, so there is no rigorous external auditing process. Performing in-house performance audits can help in assessing the lab's effectiveness. An in-house performance audit should involve an objective review of all procedures from start to finish and ensure that all steps of standard operating procedures are followed, and that all appropriate maintenance of equipment is being addressed and documented. Important insights can be gained when taking a formal approach instead of trying to assess compliance while the laboratory is operating business as usual. The performance audit should be done by a supervisor and/or other technicians familiar with the methods and not by the technicians who routinely perform the methods.

4.2.4 Corrective Actions

The validity of a data set relies on the batch quality control data. When quality control samples are found to be inaccurate or out of control, the entire procedure should be evaluated. Review calculations and records for transposition and computational errors. Check reagents and standard solutions used for calibration of equipment for their shelf life, storage conditions, and any errors that could have occurred during preparation. Review equipment calibration and maintenance records for laboratory equipment such as spectrophotometers, pipettes, analytical balances, etc. Re-calibrate laboratory equipment as needed and ensure proper operation. The resulting data from a batch with failed QC is not valid. Re-analyze or use qualifiers to note that the quality control samples failed and the results may or may not be reliable. Recommended corrective actions for unacceptable QC data are as follows (Rice et al., 2012):

- Check data for calculation or transcription error. Correct results if error occurred.
- Determine whether sample was prepared and analyzed according to the approved method and SOP. If not, prepare and/or analyze again.
- Check calibration standards against an independent standard or reference material. If calibration standards fail, re-prepare calibration standards and/or recalibrate instrument and re-analyze affected sample(s).
- If an LFB fails, analyze another LFB.
- If a second LFB fails, check an independent reference material. If the second source is acceptable, re-prepare and re-analyze affected sample(s).
- If an LFM fails, check LFB. If LFB is acceptable, then qualify the data for the LFM sample, use another method, or use the method of standard additions.
- If an LFM and associated LFB fail, re-prepare and re-analyze affected samples.
- If reagent blank fails, analyze another reagent blank.
- If second reagent blank fails, re-prepare and re-analyze affected sample(s).
- If surrogate or internal standard know addition fails and there are no calculation or reporting errors, re-prepare and re-analyze affected sample(s).

4.2.5 Method Development

All methods, whether they are based upon entirely new research, or whether they are pre-established methods or simple test kits, need to be validated by the water quality laboratory. Method development involves determination of bias and precision, analysis and recovery of unknown samples and determination of the method's "ruggedness."

The first step to evaluating a method is to verify the accuracy (bias and precision of the method). The bias of the method can also be thought of as the systematic error (Rice et al., 2012). Check the precision using a single operator to determine the random error associated with the method. This check eliminates the differences that arise from technician to technician or instrument to instrument (Rice et al., 2012).

A Method Detection Limit (MDL) study is performed by analyzing at least seven standards that are at or slightly above the expected detection limit and at least seven blanks. A good place to start regarding the seven standards is to prepare them at a concentration that is slightly above the manufacturer's detection limit claims, since those values are determined in a best-case scenario. The seven standards and seven blanks are analyzed and the standard deviation is calculated (s). The standard deviation is then multiplied by the Student's t value for 6 degrees of freedom at the 99% confidence level, which is 3.143.

$$MDL = (s)(3.143)$$

Compare the MDL calculated from the low level standards with the MDL calculated from the blanks. The larger of the two should be selected as the MDL.

To verify the MDL from the standards, ensure that the following are observed:

Spike Level: Verify MDL x 10 > Spike Level and verify MDL < Spike Level

Signal to Noise Ratio: Average/standard deviation should be between 2 and 10

Average Percent Recovery: Should be within an acceptable range of 80% to 120%, although this can change depending upon the analysis type.

The method detection limit should not be confused with a practical quantitation limit (PQL). The PQL represents the detection level where data is practically and routinely achievable with a good certainty and reliability. The PQL is generally about five times higher than the MDL (Rice et al., 2012). Results obtained between the MDL and PQL should be considered estimates.

The next step to method validation is to analyze independently prepared standards with a concentration unknown to the analyst. The mean should be within three standard deviations (s) of the mean value. The percent recovery should be within an acceptable range and the reproducibility and repeatability of the method should be ensured.

Finally, the ruggedness of the method should be determined. The method ruggedness is the degree of reproducibility of test results obtained under a variety of testing conditions, such as different analysts, different lots of reagents, different laboratory temperatures, etc. It is important to determine any potential changes in the conditions that may occur while using the method and ensuring that the results are not affected by these changes. It is also prudent to perform equivalency testing to compare results obtained using another established method, especially if the method in question is based on new research.

4.2.6 Quantitative Limits

Determination and familiarization of quantitative limits for a test method ensure that results reported are within the applicable range for that method. Both the minimum and the maximum detection limits are equally important. Report only results within the range of the calibration. If a result is below the lowest point in a calibration curve, the sample should be reported as having a concentration less than that minimum detection limit. Even if there is a number produced, that is just an estimate. If a result is above the highest point in a calibration curve, the sample should be diluted with reagent water that is free of the target analyte, so that the result will fit within the range of the test. Remember to multiply the result by the dilution factor when reporting the result. The MDL and PQL also must be multiplied by the dilution factor, since low-level sensitivity is reduced by dilution. The dilution should be made prior to analysis, because testing reagents only contain a specified amount of chemicals to react with the target analyte(s). Typically, the maximum reaction is the method's maximum detection limit so if the sample were to contain higher analyte concentration above that limit, no additional reaction would occur. Dilutions performed after the reaction is complete give an estimate that may or may not be even close to the true value.

5 Water Quality Theory and Testing

Unfortunately, there is not a probe or electrode that can measure every constituent of concern in water. The majority of water quality laboratories rely on basic wet chemistry methods. Wet chemistry employs the use of scientific glassware and liquid solutions and doesn't generally use complicated analytical instrumentation. Methods include colorimetric determinations, titrations, potentiometry and use of electrodes, and other simple tests that take place on the laboratory bench.

5.1 Nitrogen

Nitrogen is an extremely abundant element on earth and its existence extends from its prevalence in our atmosphere to the makeup of animal DNA. Understanding its role in an aquatic environment is integral to the animals' lives we preserve. Total ammonia nitrogen (TAN), is a combination of ammonia (NH_3) and ammonium (NH_4^+), with the relative quantities being dependent on the pH of the system. Ammonia and its various forms are the result of the microbiological decay of animal and plant proteins and waste products from animals. It is most prevalently excreted by mammals through their urine; however in the case of fish, through the gill membranes. The primary concern with ammonia is its toxicity to fish, especially at higher pH levels. Animals range in their specific sensitivity to ammonia, but in general the overall goal for our systems is to have sustained, long term levels of as close to 0 mg/L as possible. At lower pH levels, ammonia is ionized to ammonium (NH_4^+) whose toxicity is less of a concern. Controlling ammonia levels in a fish system can present a challenge; however, the nitrogen cycle is a process that removes the ammonia naturally.

5.1.1 The Nitrogen Cycle

The breakdown of ammonia into less toxic compounds of nitrogen is a bacterial process known as nitrification (Figure 5.1). Nitrogenous toxins in the water are oxidized by nitrifying bacteria. While academia has proven that the exact species doing the work changes according to the several water parameters, in most of our controlled environments, the nitrifying bacteria oxidize highly toxic ammonia to moderately toxic nitrite (NO_2), which is further oxidized by nitrifying bacteria to the least toxic of the group, nitrate (NO_3).

In natural water systems, animals secrete toxic nitrogen, ultimately found in the system as ammonia. Decomposing biological materials, such as plants, will also release ammonia. Nitrifying bacteria found in natural environments, will use the ammonia for energy and convert the ammonia into nitrite through the following formula (Spotte, 1992):

$$NH_4^+ + 3O_2 \rightarrow NO_2^- + H_2O + 2H^+$$

Nitrite, like ammonia, is toxic to fish. It can enter a fish's bloodstream through the gills and impair the transport of oxygen by red blood cells, a condition known as brown blood disease (Chappell, 2008); however, another kind of nitrifying bacteria, will use the nitrite as an energy source and convert the nitrite into harmless nitrate through the following formula (Spotte, 1992):

$$NO_2^- + 12O_2 \rightarrow NO_3^- + 2H^+ + 4e^-$$

Nitrate is less toxic to aquatic life. Nitrate may be assimilated into plant life in the environment, or it may be off-gassed from the water in the form of nitrogen gas (N_2). The nitrate that is accumulated by plants which may be eaten by fish then will undergo this process again. This recurring process is called the nitrogen cycle.

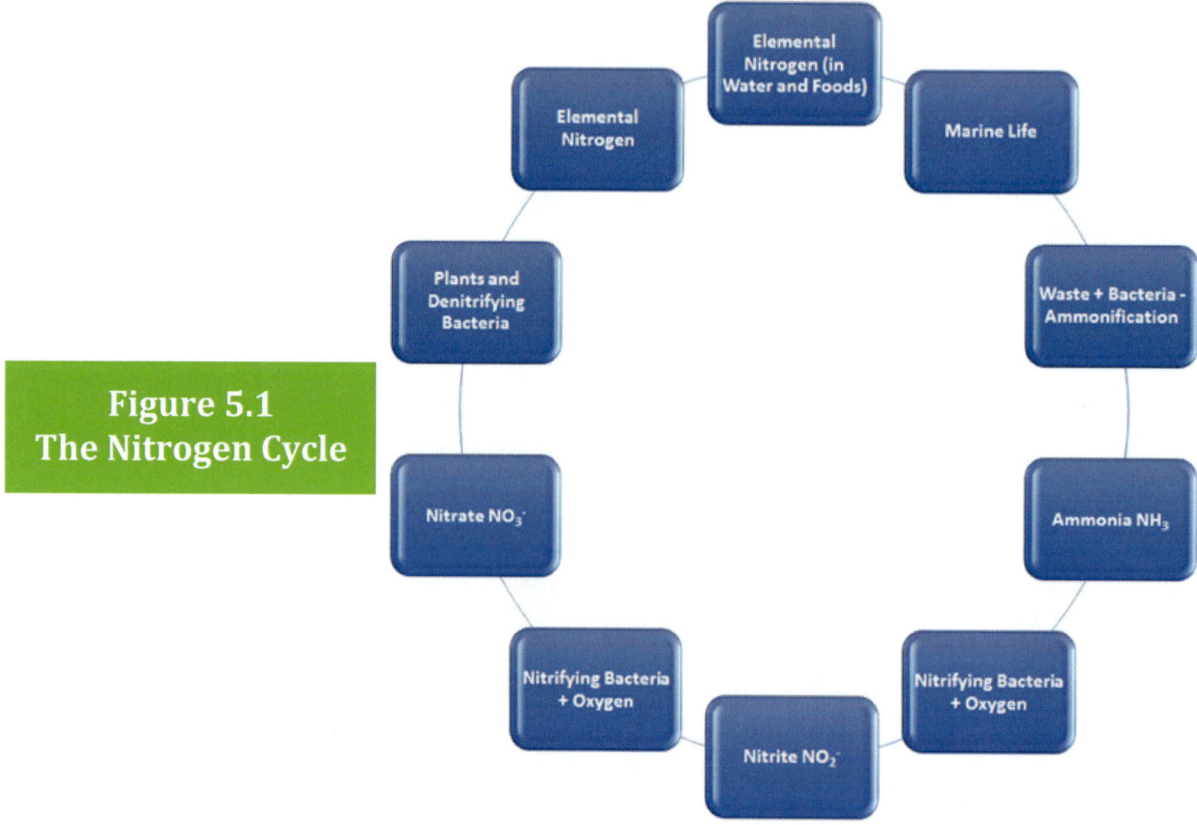

**Figure 5.1
The Nitrogen Cycle**

The nitrogen cycle can be forced in aquaria but it will occur naturally. It is important when starting a new fish system that the water be left to cycle for several weeks to allow the bacteria to colonize the surfaces of the system. Nitrifying bacteria are sustained by ammonia or urea, so it is important to provide a source of ammonium chloride or urea to new or empty exhibits as a food source. Keep in mind that just as fish need oxygen in the water to breath, nitrifying these bacteria need oxygen to complete these processes as well. Frequent monitoring of these nitrogen levels is fundamental.

It is critical to understand that colorimetric nitrate tests will have positive interference from nitrite present in the sample. In a cycled exhibit, the contribution from nitrite will be nearly negligible, but if nitrite levels are high, interferences from nitrite can be significant and must be subtracted. It is recommended to report nitrate levels directly from a spectrophotometer as NO_x because of the contribution from both Nitrate (NO_3) and Nitrite (NO_2). The following calculation can be used to convert units of NO_x-N to NO_3-N, if Nitrite results are known:

$$NO_3\text{-}N = NO_x\text{-}N - NO_2\text{-}N$$

5.1.2 Ammonia, Nitrite, and Nitrate Ranges and Limits

The ranges in Figure 5.2 clarify the acceptable limits for each parameter and quantify the actions to take when parameters are out of normal range. By following these ranges, data driven responses can be used to keep water quality parameters at appropriate levels while minimizing unnecessary water usage. These ranges are appropriate for a standard teleost exhibit and are based upon the authors' collective experience. Many facilities will have ranges that differ from these based upon availability of water exchanges, animal species exhibited, staff availability and other factors. Nothing is an absolute and systems vary due to different species specific requirements. For example, a coral reef aquarium may reach a toxic level of NO_3^- at 20 mg/L and an amphibian exhibit would be considered toxic at 30 mg/L.

Water change per week	5% to 15% a week	15% to 30% a week	50% or more as needed
Parameter	Normal	Almost Out of Range	Out of Range
Ammonia NH_3	< 0.05 mg/L	0.05 - 0.09 mg/L	0.1 mg/L
Nitrite NO_2^-	< 0.5 mg/L	0.5 - 0.9 mg/L	1 mg/L
Nitrate NO_3^-	< 50 mg/L	50 - 99 mg/L	100 mg/L
Water change per week	5% to 15% a week	15% to 30% a week	50% or more as needed
Parameter	Normal	Almost Out of Range	Out of Range
Ammonia NH_3-N	< 0.04 mg/L	0.04 - 0.07 mg/L	0.08 mg/L
Nitrite NO_2^--N	< 0.15 mg/L	0.15 - 0.29 mg/L	0.3 mg/L
Nitrate NO_3^--N	< 11 mg/L	11 - 22 mg/L	23 mg/L

Figure 5.2 – Suggested Nitrogen Parameters in Aquarium Systems

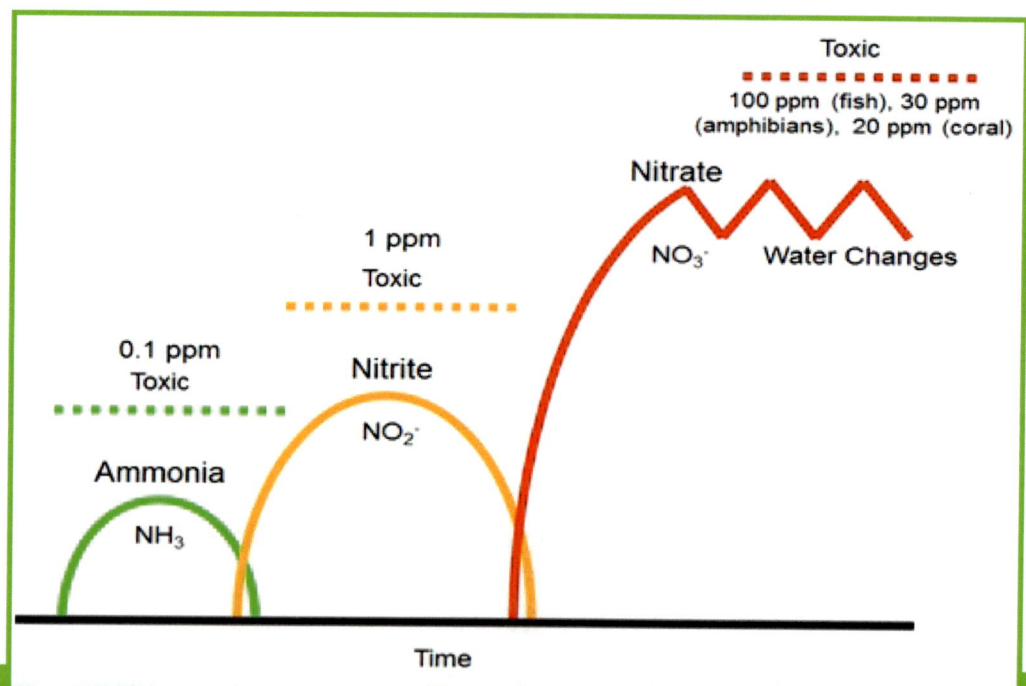

Figure 5.3 - Nitrogen Cycle Concentration Over Time

In a stable biologically mature system, the nitrifying bacteria are able to process the system's bioload so that there is little to no ammonia or nitrite detected. The nitrate levels will gradually rise but can be kept at safe levels with water changes or denitrification. This is demonstrated in Figure 5.3.

"New Tank Syndrome" is a term that is used to refer to a new system that has not had time to become established. The bacteria have not reached a population level large enough to process the available ammonia or nitrite produced. An example of this is a quarantine system that has been bleached, neutralized, and filled with new water and dosed with ammonium chloride. This new immature system will have high levels of ammonia and nitrite until the bacteria is stable enough to process the bioload of the system. This can take 3-4 weeks for a tropical aquarium and 6-8 weeks for a temperate aquarium. If nitrifying bacteria is introduced to the system, this maturing process will be faster.

"Old Tank Syndrome" is a term that is use to refer to an old or established system that is at risk for producing high levels of nitrates. This is due to the buildup of residual nitrate necessitating larger water changes to dilute the waste out of the system. This can be avoided by monitoring the nitrate levels weekly and being proactive on water changes before it is a problem.

5.1.3 Nitrogen Species Units and Conversions

It is important to ensure that the units of the measurements are understood, especially when referring to ionic species. For example, there are two ways to represent Nitrate: NO_3 (Nitrate molecule) and NO_3-N (Nitrate-Nitrogen). Nitrate-Nitrogen is also commonly referred to as Nitrate as N or Nitrate-N. It is important to understand that there are many ways that operators may refer to the sample being reported as Nitrogen. The NO_3-N form uses the molecular weight of only the nitrogen atom. The NO_3 form uses the molecular weight of the entire nitrate ion, 1 nitrogen atom and 3 oxygen atoms (HACH, 2018). For nitrate, the difference in results reported as NO_3-N versus as NO_3 is very significant, because 3 oxygen atoms have a large contribution to the molecular weight. For ammonia, the difference in results reported as NH_3-N versus as NH_3 is less because the contribution of three hydrogen atoms to the overall molecular weight is much smaller. A simple conversion between these units can be made, as seen in Figure 5.4. Reporting values as N is helpful when evaluating the nitrogen cycle because it relates ammonia-N to other nitrogen compounds such as nitrite-N (NO_2-N) and nitrate-N (NO_3-N).

Ammonium	mg/L NH_4-N	mg/L NH_4
1 mg/L NH_4-N	1	1.29
1 mg/L NH_4	0.776	1
Ammonia	mg/L NH_3-N	mg/L NH_3
1 mg/L NH_3-N	1	1.21
1 mg/L NH_3	0.822	1
Nitrite	mg/L NO_2-N	mg/L NO_2
1 mg/L NO_2-N	1	3.28
1 mg/L NO_2	0.304	1
Nitrate	mg/L NO_3-N	mg/L NO_3
1 mg/L NO_3-N	1	4.43
1 mg/L NO_3	0.226	1

Figure 5.4 – Conversions Between Nitrogen Species

Both ammonia (NH_3) and ammonium (NH_4^+) can be reported as N, in which case the units are interchangeable, since only the molecular weight of nitrogen is used. When ammonia and ammonium are not reported as N, a conversion factor must be applied to account for the extra hydrogen atom. Some instruments are capable of doing this conversion automatically and the preferred units can be selected by the user.

Ammonium/Ammonia	mg/L NH_3	mg/L NH_4
1 mg/L NH_4	0.944	1
1 mg/L NH_3	1	1.06

Figure 5.5 – Conversion Between Ammonium and Ammonia

The terms ammonia and ammonium are often used interchangeably in the zoo and aquarium industry; leading to some confusion when comparing data from one institution to another. It is important to remember that 1 mg/L NH_4-N is equal to 1 mg/L NH$_3$-N, but 1 mg/L NH$_4$ is not equal to 1 mg/L NH$_3$. Water quality tests will usually report results as either total ammonia or total ammonium, even though both ammonia and ammonium are typically present in the sample. Typical water quality tests (such as phenate and salicylate) actually measure Total Ammonia Nitrogen (TAN), which is comprised of both NH$_4^+$-N and NH$_3$-N. To avoid confusion, it is recommended to report ammonia results as TAN, since both ammonia and ammonium are present in aquatic samples.

5.1.4 Ammonia Toxicity and pH Relationship

In water, ammonia exists in equilibrium between the toxic species, ammonia (NH$_3$) and also the non-toxic species, ammonium (NH$_4^+$) depending upon factors such as the temperature, salinity, and pH of the water (Bower and Bidwell, 1978).

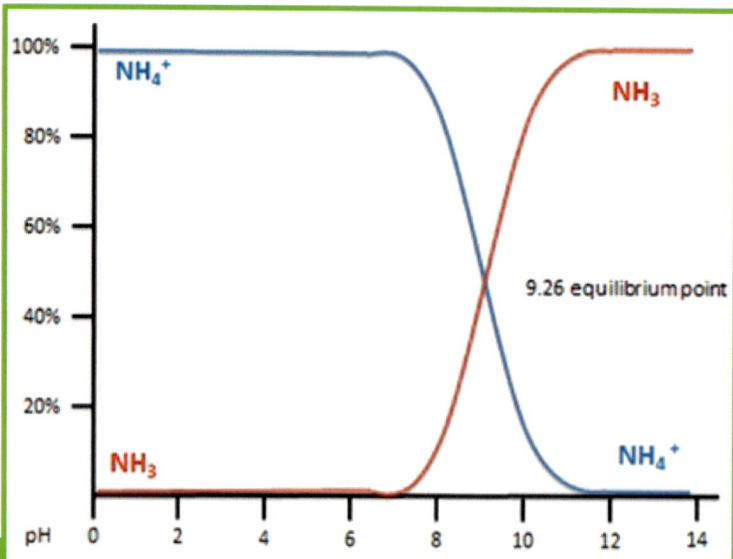

Figure 5.6 – Percentage of NH$_3$ and NH$_4^+$ over pH Scale

System pH has the geatest influence on the predominant form of ammonia in the water. It is for this reason, that during animal transports, the pH is often artificially lowered in hopes of lowering the toxic form of ammonia. As the pH increases, more hydroxide ions (OH$^-$) are present, pulling more hydrogen ions from the NH$_4^+$ molecule, converting the NH$_4^+$ molecule to the NH$_3$ form, and thus increasing the toxic component of the TAN. In most circumstances, NH$_3$ constitutes less than 10% of TAN. Ammonia testing methods measure TAN, so it is important to understand that results obtained by the water quality test does not distinguish between the toxic and non-toxic forms. To determine the toxic component of a TAN result at a given pH, salinity, and temperature, use the chart shown in Figure 5.7.

Temperature Degrees C	pH 7.5	pH 7.6	pH 7.7	pH 7.8	pH 7.9	pH 8.0	pH 8.1	pH 8.2	pH 8.3	pH 8.4	pH 8.5
10	0.459	0.577	0.726	0.912	1.15	1.44	1.80	2.26	2.83	3.54	4.41
11	0.495	0.622	0.782	0.982	1.23	1.55	1.94	2.43	3.04	3.80	4.74
12	0.533	0.670	0.842	1.06	1.33	1.67	2.09	2.61	3.27	4.08	5.08
13	0.574	0.721	0.906	1.14	1.43	1.79	2.25	2.81	3.51	4.38	5.46
14	0.618	0.777	0.976	1.23	1.54	1.93	2.42	3.02	3.78	4.71	5.85
15	0.665	0.836	1.05	1.32	1.66	2.07	2.60	3.25	4.06	5.05	6.28
16	0.717	0.900	1.13	1.42	1.78	2.23	2.79	3.49	4.36	5.42	6.73
17	0.772	0.970	1.22	1.53	1.92	2.40	3.00	3.75	4.68	5.82	7.22
18	0.831	1.04	1.31	1.64	2.06	2.58	3.23	4.03	5.02	6.24	7.73
19	0.895	1.12	1.41	1.77	2.22	2.78	3.47	4.33	5.39	6.69	8.28
20	0.963	1.21	1.52	1.90	2.39	2.98	3.73	4.65	5.78	7.17	8.87
21	1.04	1.30	1.63	2.05	2.57	3.21	4.01	4.99	6.20	7.69	9.49
22	1.12	1.40	1.76	2.20	2.76	3.45	4.30	5.36	6.65	8.23	10.1
23	1.20	1.51	1.89	2.37	2.97	3.71	4.62	5.75	7.13	8.81	10.8
24	1.29	1.62	2.04	2.55	3.19	3.98	4.96	6.17	7.64	9.43	11.6
25	1.39	1.75	2.19	2.74	3.43	4.28	5.32	6.61	8.18	10.1	12.4

Figure 5.7 - Percentage of Toxic Ammonia (NH_3-N) of Total Ammonia in Seawater for Samples with Salinity Between 32 ppt and 40 ppt (Spotte, 1992) (Bower and Bidwell, 1978)

5.1.5 Nitrifying Bacteria

Nitrifying bacteria are a quintessential part of any closed or semi-closed aquatic system. These bacteria are responsible for the oxidation of ammonia to nitrite and nitrite to nitrate; a process that allows toxic chemicals such as ammonia, to be converted to the much less toxic nitrate ion. The exact species of bacteria that are responsible for this reaction have been debated; however, the bacteria that primarily facilitate ammonia oxidation are referred to as ammonia oxidizing bacteria (AOB), including but not limited to *Nitrosomonas* and *Nitrosospira* genera; whereas, those that promote nitrite oxidation are referred to as nitrite oxidizing bacteria (NOB), including but not limited to *Nitrobacter* and *Nitrospira*. Nitrifying bacteria tend to colonize in 'dark' places in a life support system or exhibit that has plenty of oxygenated water flow; this includes system plumbing, biotowers, sand filters, and substrate. These bacteria will colonize on their own with appropriate conditions; however, it is common practice to expedite or facilitate their colonization. This can be conducted in a few different ways. For more information on exhibit seeding, see Section 9.2.3.

5.1.6 Denitrification

When nitrifying bacteria are working efficiently, the level of nitrate in the system begins to rise. There is some evidence that nitrate at too high a level interferes with thyroid function in some species of elasmobranchs (Morris et al., 2011). Since nitrate is the fully oxidized state of nitrogen, its removal must occur using a reduction mechanism, called denitrification.

Methanol-based denitrification is generally done in batches; some of the water from the aquarium is moved to a separate holding sump or basin for the duration of the process. This water is sent through designated filters where bio-filtration occurs. Methanol (CH_3OH) is injected into the system to provide a carbon source for the denitrifying bacteria. To remove 1 mg of nitrate, 1.90 mg of methanol must be added. The addition of methanol will also reduce the amount of oxygen in the water, achieving the anaerobic conditions necessary for this process to occur. The following reaction will take place (Wiesmann et al., 2007):

$$5\ CH_3OH + 6\ NO_3^- \rightarrow 3\ N_2 + 5\ CO_2 + 6\ OH^- + 7\ H_2O$$

Another method is a sulfur-based denitrification system. Instead of being a batch process, this may be accomplished as a side-stream, constant process. This side stream's flow should be kept low to create the low oxygen levels needed. This process utilizes autotrophic bacteria that are sulfur oxidizers. The formula for this reaction is as follows (Lampe and Zhang, n.d.):

$$55\ S + 20\ CO_2 + 50\ NO_3^- + 38\ H_2O + 4\ NH_4^+ \rightarrow 4\ C_5H_7O_2N + 25\ N_2 + 55\ SO_4^{2-} + 64\ H^+$$

Over time, a sulfur denitrification system will increase the acidity of a closed loop system, therefore, it may be necessary to add a base, such as sodium hydroxide (NaOH) to the aquarium to raise the pH. In a saltwater system, sodium hydroxide is a particularly good choice because the sodium is a component of sodium chloride and other salts, and the hydroxide is a component of water. A buffer solution may also need to be added to an aquarium to help prevent large changes in pH that may occur due to a denitrification system.

When operating a sulfur denitrification system, the sulfate levels in the aquarium system may become elevated. Regular testing of sulfide levels should be performed to verify safe levels. Additional steps may be needed to remove the added sulfur.

5.2 Chlorine and Bromine

There are many types of microorganisms in seawater. Some may prove beneficial, but many are pathogenic and if left unchecked in an exhibit can cause serious health concerns. Chlorine and bromine are considered sterilizing agents; they non-selectively kill all microorganisms, not just the harmful pathogens (Spotte, 1991). An exhibit pool can never be rendered truly sterile because there is a constant input from the animals, their keepers and the environment.

When chlorine in the form of bleach (active ingredient is sodium hypochlorite), is added to water for disinfection, the following reaction occurs:

$$NaOCl(aq) + H_2O(l) \leftrightarrow HOCl(aq) + Na^+(aq) + OH^-(aq)$$

When sodium hypochlorite is added to water it reacts with hydrogen ions to form hypochlorous acid (HOCl), which is the primary disinfection agent. The hypochlorous acid has a net neutral charge, which allows it to diffuse across the bacterium's cell wall causing lysis (breakdown of the cell membrane) or inhibition of the cell's primary functions such as metabolism. This process causes disruption to the bacteria cells and disinfects the water.

The use of sodium hypochlorite also maintains a residual oxidant in water, which in turn continually disinfects the water and keeps it free from harmful bacteria such as *Escherichia coli*. Although this process may seem like a great method, it also comes with its challenges. Two of the biggest problems with the use of sodium hypochlorite as an oxidant is over-chlorination and combined chlorines. Combined chlorines primarily refer to free chlorine that has reacted with the contaminants in the water and have produced a disinfection byproduct. When the free chlorine or hypochlorous acid combines with organic waste it produces an organic, chlorinated compound or a nitrogen containing chlorinated compound known as a chloramine. These compounds have a longer lifetime than free chlorine (meaning they don't react as quickly), which allows them to be found in the water column longer, and they are also responsible for the chlorinated "swimming pool" smell and eye irritation. There are some other byproducts that also occur in the process of chlorine disinfection in water. These by products include trihalomethane compounds, haloacetic acids, chloroform, and bromoform. These byproducts levels are mostly managed by performing water changes on the system. In the case of over-chlorination, it may be necessary to add sodium thiosulfate, which is a reducer that can neutralize chlorine in the system. It is important to measure free and total chlorine in the water system prior to neutralization with sodium thiosulfate. The best practice is to dose 1:1 molar (M) ratios of chlorine to thiosulfate ion to reduce only to the target level. If the technician overdoses sodium thiosulfate, it could negatively affect the ability to disinfect the water over a long period of time until all of the thiosulfate ion is neutralized.

The pH of the water system is also a very important factor when it comes to chlorine disinfection. The pH of the water essentially determines how effective chlorine is at disinfection. When sodium hypochlorite is added to water, it immediately forms an equilibrium with hypochlorous acid. Both hypochlorous acid (HOCl) and the hypochlorite (OCl⁻) ion are forms of free chlorine; however the hypochlorous acid is the active form of free chlorine and as it is consumed, the equilibrium creates more hypochlorous acid from the sodium hypochlorite that is added to the water. The pH is a contributing factor because at a lower pH, the equilibrium favors hypochlorous acid and at a higher pH the equilibrium favors the hypochlorite ion.

The best known method for testing for chlorine and bromine in water is by the DPD (N, N-diethyl-p-phenylenediamine) method, which was developed by Dr. Thomas Palin in 1957. This is the very common clear to pink test for most basic pool test strips, test kits, and the spectrophotometric method. When the DPD is added to water containing chlorine, the chlorine oxidizes the DPD to form two oxidation products: Würster dye (magenta/pink color) and imine (colorless). When running a DPD test, it is actually measuring the intensity of the pink color that is generated by the Würster dye, which can be then correlated to the amount of chlorine or bromine in the sample.

5.3 Phosphate

All living organisms contain phosphorus. Phosphorus is an important element of life as a component for cell membranes, as an energy source, and for other biochemical processes. Phosphorus is a very reactive component making it readily absorbed and generally available in aquatic environments as either an organic or inorganic phosphate.

Phosphates (PO_4^{3-}) can be created within the closed aquatic system or imported from the outside. Phosphate occurs as a by-product of mineralization of dead matter such as plants, bacteria, feces, uneaten food, fish slime etc., which are all internal contributors. Dead plant material or rotting food particles settle either on the substrate or within the filter. Rinsing or backwashing filter materials and/or hydro vacuuming the gravel can significantly reduce potential phosphate accumulation from these internal sources. It is important to note that replacement water can also contain phosphate, sometimes surprisingly high concentrations, even if reverse osmosis (RO) units are in use. Depending on the RO membrane condition and system setup, it may be necessary to use a deionization (DI) component to effectively remove phosphate from source water. Additives such as pH stabilizers, carbon, and frozen fish food are potential external phosphate sources. Avoiding phosphate containing products as well as testing of the replacement water for phosphates can further help prevent accumulation. Additives, carbon, pH buffers, and the water should be monitored and replaced if necessary.

Inorganic phosphate (as orthophosphate) is the soluble form. It is readily available and quickly absorbed by plants. Organic phosphate refers to phosphate that is part of a cell structure or organically bound in other ways. Organic phosphate must be broken down by bacteria in order to become soluble orthophosphate. One source of organic phosphate in aquarium systems is the food that is fed. The filters and substrate have to be cleaned regularly before the organic phosphate is mineralized to inorganic orthophosphate. Some marine and especially reef aquarium set-ups must rely on less frequent water changes. These often employ a delicately balanced filtration based on live rock and/or the need for nutrient supplementation for coral growth, among others. To compensate for less frequent water changes, a protein skimmer can be attached, which will remove many waste particles that would otherwise be broken down to soluble orthophosphates.

Unfortunately, protein skimmers usually do not work in freshwater aquariums and cannot be substituted for less frequent water changes. More than 90% of the phosphate contained in the aquarium is organic phosphate. The common test kit measures the inorganic soluble orthophosphate, not the organic form, the total phosphate, or total phosphorus content. Phosphate tests may give results in units of orthophosphate (PO_4^{3-})

or orthophosphate as P (PO_4-P). It is important to consider that a conversion factor is needed when data is reported differently. The PO_4-P form only accounts for the mass of phosphorus, not the four oxygen atoms; therefore, 1 mg/L PO_4-P = 3.06 mg/L PO_4^{3-}. There is a wide range of phosphate tolerance levels for aquatic animals. Corals are a sensitive species and cannot tolerate high levels of phosphate because of the interference with calcification (Simkiss, 1964). It is a best practice to determine a limit on a species by species basis.

Planted tanks have an advantage in that plants are capable of storing and consuming phosphates. Plants can only take up orthophosphate, thus reducing the levels. Saltwater tanks can imitate this by using macro algae into a refugium or sump. In reef aquariums Kalkwasser (calcium hydroxide) can remove phosphate. At a pH above 8.9 phosphate precipitates in the water as insoluble phosphate and flocculates out. Marine aquariums kept above a pH of 8.4 allow some phosphate to be bound to rocks and substrate in an insoluble form; it will become soluble if the pH drops below 8.

Phosphate cannot be entirely removed from the aquarium since organic phosphate is constantly converted into inorganic soluble, orthophosphate; however, phosphates can be controlled with a good maintenance schedule aimed at keeping organic phosphates at a minimum.

5.4 Copper

Copper (Cu) is a transition metal that is found in human consumable drinking water from <0.005 mg/L to >30 mg/L (World Health Organization, 2004). Copper can be toxic to aquatic organisms depending on the concentration and the species. Many aquatic invertebrates and some elasmobranchs species have exhibited sensitivity to this element at levels considered safe for most marine teleosts. It is important to check copper levels of source water used to house aquarium animals.

Copper has been used as a common quarantine treatment in the industry for decades. The treatment harnesses the toxic properties of copper to help aid teleosts who have invertebrate parasitic infestations (most commonly used on ciliates like *Cryptocaryon*). This practice must be closely monitored and maintained to ensure the treatment concentrations are at levels toxic enough to interrupt parasite life cycle but not so much so that it is toxic to the host. Therapeutic range should be reached within 3 - 7 days. A typical therapeutic concentration is reached at 0.150 mg/L, but should be monitored as to not exceed 0.200 mg/L copper. This target concentration may vary somewhat depending on the differing institutional protocols and several other factors. Some notable influential factors may include veterinarian decision, species sensitivity, tank life support components, such as presence of protein skimmer, use of ozone and even if the system has gravel/substrate or not, tank history with previous copper treatments, infestation loading, etc. Therapeutic levels of copper are usually maintained for at least

21 days. During this time frame the parasite has typically gone through two life cycles. It is important that water quality testing be completed daily to monitor copper levels and ensure proper treatment levels. It is also important to monitor fish behavior; with the most obvious being feeding interest, as each species seems to have a range of sensitivity.

5.5 Alkalinity

Alkalinity is a measure of water's resistance to changes in pH or its buffering capacity. What is being measured is the buffering of carbonate and bicarbonate in the water. These buffer levels can be measured through titration in which an acid (the titrant, such as sulfuric acid) is slowly added to the sample water (the titrand) until the equivalence point (the point at which all of the carbonate and bicarbonate is converted to carbonic acid at the pH level 4.5). In Figure 5.5, the inflection points (located at the intersection of the red lines) represent the transition of carbonate (CO_3^{2-}) to bicarbonate (HCO_3^-) to carbonic acid (H_2CO_3).

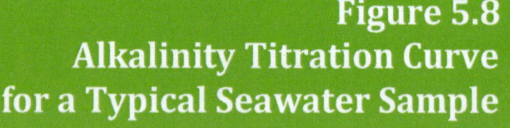

Figure 5.8
Alkalinity Titration Curve for a Typical Seawater Sample

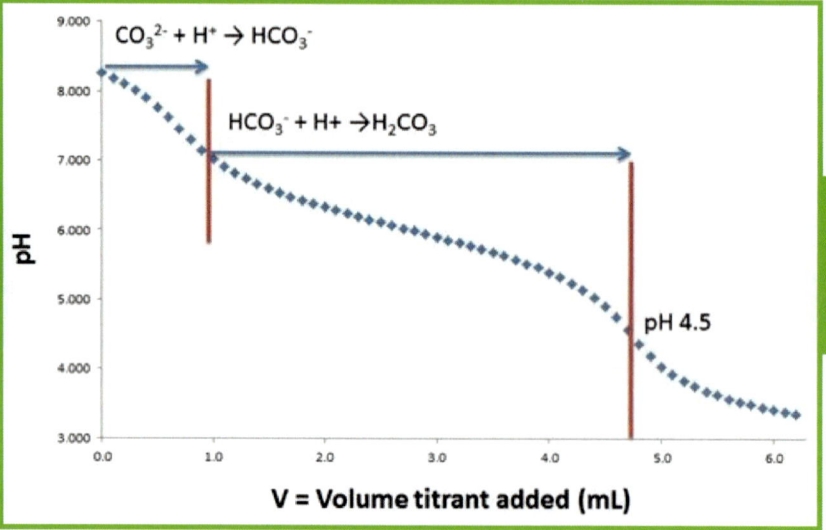

Total alkalinity is the sum of all titratable bases, including carbonate, bicarbonate, hydroxides, borates, silicates, and other bases (Rice et al., 2012), but in practical terms, alkalinity can be thought of as the sum of bicarbonate and carbonate (Spotte, 1992). Carbonate alkalinity refers only to the alkalinity that is contributed by carbonate and bicarbonate. In the zoo and aquarium industry, total alkalinity results and carbonate alkalinity results are often referred to interchangeably, due to the very small contribution from other bases. Although an increase of carbon dioxide lowers the pH of seawater, it does not alter the alkalinity measurement.

Alkalinity can be measured in parts per million expressed as calcium carbonate (mg/L as $CaCO_3$) or in milliequivalents per liter (mEq/L) or in degrees KH (derived from German: Karbonathärte). Understandably, there can be a lot of confusion between these units, even though they all can be interconverted through a simple conversion factor (Appendix 19.1.4). In fact, there is often confusion between the terms alkalinity and hardness due in part to this nomenclature. Units of alkalinity expressed as $CaCO_3$ does not describe the calcium content of the water and there may not even be carbonate present in the water. These units simply denote an alkalinity concentration equal to what $CaCO_3$ would contribute. Units of alkalinity expressed as degrees KH (Karbonathärte), is are not a measure of the total water hardness, which is based on the sum of calcium and magnesium concentrations.

Many chemical processes in the water are inhibited by the absence or abundance of alkalinity. Bacteria that are essential to the nitrogen cycle, for example, rely on alkalinity to be truly effective. Nitrification reduces alkalinity and denitrification increases alkalinity (Spotte, 1992). When adding acid to a pool to drop its pH, one must consider alkalinity levels, as a highly alkaline pool will require a higher volume of acid to achieve the desired pH.

5.6 Calcium and Magnesium Hardness

Calcium and magnesium are major cations (ions with a positive charge) that are found naturally in seawater at concentrations of around 400 mg/L and 1300 mg/L respectively (see Appendix 19.3). These ions are used in important biological processes such as coral skeleton and invertebrate exoskeleton growth and can be depleted from the water quickly as animals use these ions.

Calcium and magnesium contribute to the total hardness of water. Processes such as reverse osmosis, ion exchange, and chemical softening treatment are used to reduce calcium and magnesium and the associated hardness (Rice et al., 2012). Total hardness is expressed as the sum of the calcium and magnesium concentrations, expressed as calcium carbonate in milligrams per liter, according to the following formula (Rice et al., 2012):

Hardness, mg equivalent $CaCO_3$/L = 2.497 [Ca, mg/L] + 4.118 [Mg, mg/L]

The preferred method for measuring total hardness involves making calculations after the separate measurement of the calcium and magnesium concentrations. Calcium and magnesium can be measured using ion chromatography (IC), atomic absorption spectroscopy (AAS), inductively coupled plasma (ICP), or a titration using ethylenediaminetetraacetic acid (EDTA). Since IC, AAS, and ICP require very expensive instrumentation and highly trained analysts, the titration method is most often used in water quality laboratories in the zoos, aquariums, and by reef keeping hobbyists.

In the EDTA titration method, the EDTA combines first with the calcium in the water. When the pH is elevated sufficiently, magnesium will precipitate out as magnesium hydroxide. Analysis of calcium is carried out at a pH of roughly 12-14 and EDTA is added until the indicator solution changes color. There are many indicators that work, such as murexide (ammonium purpurate), which changes from pink to purple at the end point, and eriochrome blue black R indicator, which changes from red to blue (Rice et al., 2012).

5.7 Dissolved Organic Carbon

Organic compounds refer to molecules that contain carbon. The term "organic" originates from an early belief that these compounds were only made by living organisms (Brady et al., 2000). Compounds such as carbon dioxide and sodium carbonate, are considered inorganic carbon compounds. Carbon-containing chemicals are either dissolved in the water itself, referred to as dissolved organic carbon (DOC) or suspended in the water as small particles, referred to as particulate organic carbon (POC) which can include single cell organisms (Holmes-Farley, 2004). Together, these carbon sources are called total organic carbon (TOC). Natural waters, freshwater aquariums and saltwater aquariums contain a great variety of soluble organic compounds. These include such compounds as sugars, fatty acids, humic acids, tannins, vitamins, amino acids, proteins, and urea. DOC is a broad classification for organic molecules of varied origin and composition within aquatic systems. The "dissolved" fraction of organic carbon is an operational classification used to describe compounds below 0.45 micrometers in size. A practical definition of "dissolved" typically used in marine chemistry is all substances that pass through a glass microfiber filter.

DOC in marine and freshwater systems is one of the greatest cycled reservoirs of organic matter on Earth. The source of DOC depends on the body of water. In the wild, organic carbon compounds are a result of decomposition processes from dead organic matter such as plants or marine organisms. In an aquarium the major source of dissolved organics is the natural biological processes that accompany having a tank full of fish that are fed often. Fish feed, fish wastes, and other particulate organic material are colonized by bacteria which break the material down into dissolved substances. The basic step is for particulate carbon to become dissolved carbon. Simply put, more fish and more fish feed means a higher concentration of organic substances.

There are many ways to control the amount of organic carbon in an aquarium, and there are ways to remove both of the two general types of organic material (particulate and dissolved). First, limit the amount of particulate carbon. This does not necessarily mean reducing the number of fish in the tank or reducing the feeding amount; it means cleaning the mechanical filter component of filtration systems often because the filter is where a majority of the particulate material will get trapped. If the system is heavily stocked, one might have to clean this often. Organic material trapped in a filter is detrimental to the aquarium environment. Sometimes, on smaller systems, activated carbon in filters can help remove some of this material. Aquarium systems with a substrate should be cleaned regularly with a siphon vacuum or gravel washer to help limit DOC. The gravel at the bottom of an aquarium is a likely place for particulate organic material to collect, so removal will help reduce system DOC. Getting rid of the organic material on a regular basis will go a long way towards keeping an aquarium healthy and keeping disease away. A protein skimmer/foam fractionator can also aid in removal of DOC, see Section 9.3.4.

5.8 UV-254

Most organic carbon compounds that accumulate in aquatic exhibits absorb light in the UV range. UV absorption measurements can therefore be used as an indication of the concentration of organic compounds present in a body of water (Rice et al., 2012). UV absorption can often be used to monitor effectiveness of carbon adsorption, coagulation, foam fractionation, and other methods used to reduce or remove organic carbon from exhibit water. UV absorption can also be used to determine the identity and concentration of organic disinfection byproducts; separation chemistry by high performance liquid chromatography (HPLC) is an excellent technique for this purpose. In the absence of this expensive instrumentation, a readily available substitute is to utilize UV-254.

UV-254 is a measurement of the amount of light at the 254 nm wavelength that is absorbed by aromatic organic compounds in a sample. This measurement is often interpreted as a surrogate measurement for dissolved organic carbon (DOC) or for the trihalomethane (THM) formation potential of the water. The measurement does not include all organics, which must be determined by testing total organic carbon (TOC) using specialized instrumentation, but it does provide an estimation of organics present, and can show changes in the presence of these compounds. There are several potential interferences to be aware of with this test, including nitrate, nitrite, and bromide, which can be found in most exhibits. In addition, oxidants such as ozone and reducers such as sodium thiosulfate can absorb UV light at wavelength 254 nm (Rice et al., 2012). It is important to note that UV absorption measurements do not directly measure dissolved organic carbon, may not correlate between exhibits and water sources, and the data should be reviewed with care.

5.9 Adsorption and Absorption (Carbon and Turbidity)

Absorption and adsorption are two very different processes that are easy to mix up due to their similar sounding terminology. Adsorption is the adhesion of a molecules to a surface. Absorption involves the taking up of molecules by a volume of another substance.

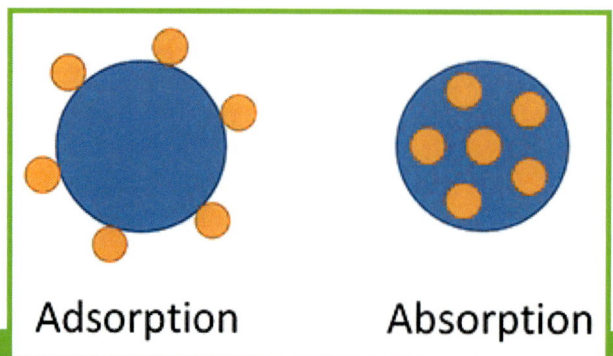

Figure 5.9 - Molecules Engaging in Adsorption Versus Absorption

Activated carbon is highly porous adsorbing material that is used in aquariums because it adsorbs a variety of undesired substances such as copper and other metals, and dissolved organic carbon, which often contributes to a yellowed coloring in aquarium water and odor. The extent to which these substances will adsorb to the activated carbon media is related to the chemical form they are in, the size of the substance relative to the pores of the carbon, contact time, and age of the media. The use of activated carbon improves water clarity through the adsorption of these undesirable molecules.

Turbidity can be thought of as a measure of water clarity, since it is a measurement of the light scattering caused by suspended and colloidal matter. These particles cause the light to be scattered and absorbed instead of transmitted. It is important to understand that turbidity does not measure particle size or suspended particles in the water and should be used more as a qualitative value for gauging changes within an exhibit. Turbidity measurements involving the scattering of light at 90° incident to the light beam is known as nephelometry and is measured in nephelometric turbidity units (NTU). Light absorbing compounds, such as activated carbon, may cause negative interference as well as colored substances (Rice et al., 2012).

A turbidimeter is usually calibrated using formazin standards, which are available pre-made and sealed because they are difficult to prepare. In aquarium water, clear looking water has turbidity below the lowest standard of the calibration, so turbidity levels are an approximation that can be used to gauge trends, instead of being relied upon for reproducible quantitative results. In addition to the problems with measurements outside of the calibration range, slight variations in sample cuvettes, air bubbles, fingerprints and cleaning methods may cause variability in measurements, particularly on the low range.

Turbidity can also be measured outside of the laboratory using a continuous turbidity monitor that is plumbed into the life support system of an exhibit. It is important to follow manufacturer's specifications and place them in locations where air entrainment is minimal. With all inline electrode monitoring systems, it is important to compare and verify results against laboratory-generated values to ensure the equipment is working properly since inline equipment can foul and fall outside of calibration.

5.10 Testing for Bacteria: Coliforms and Enterococci

In the case of the nitrogen cycle, many species of bacteria are beneficial, but some species found in water may be harmful, most often originating from animal feces. Since it would be impossible to test for all of the potential harmful microorganisms, indicator bacteria are used to detect and quantify the efficacy of the disinfection of the exhibit water using the same assays developed for monitoring recreational water for humans. The indicator bacteria are not considered pathogens, but rather serve as a proxy of other microorganisms which may cause gastrointestinal illness, such as viruses and protozoans.

There are two types of indicator bacteria recommended by the US EPA used for recreational water monitoring: *E. coli* (freshwater only) and *Enterococcus* (marine and freshwater). Total coliforms and fecal coliforms are not recommended for recreation water monitoring, due to a stronger correlation between *E. coli* and *Enterococcus* and gastroenteritis incident rate (US EPA, 1986).

Total coliforms are still used by the United States Department of Agriculture (USDA), and Animal and Plant Health Inspection Service (APHIS), to determine the suitability of exhibit water for housing marine mammals, with the upper limit set as 1,000 MPN/100 mL (Coakley & Crawford, 1998). If levels rise above 1,000 per 100 ml of water, the USDA mandates two additional retests in 48-hour intervals (Coakley & Crawford, 1998). If the average of the three tests is above 1,000, actions must be taken to eradicate the bacteria. Partial or full water changes and chemical treatment/sterilization are just two examples of such actions. The US Fish and Wildlife Service sets the same limits for sea turtle rescue programs. It is also a good husbandry practice to monitor indicator bacterial levels in exhibits housing marine birds and sea turtles. *Enterococcus* is actually the indicator species suggested by the United States Environmental Protection Agency for marine waters (US EPA, 1986), but changes to the USDA regulations have not been made.

Coliform bacteria and enterococci can be measured by two culture based methods: membrane filtration reported as CFU (Colony Forming Units) or multiple tube fermentation reported as MPN (Most Probable Number). The IDEXX Quanti-tray method is an adaptation of the multiple tube fermentation.

Sodium thiosulfate is added to collection bottles to dechlorinate the water, which would otherwise affect the bacteria results and is useful to reduce oxidants that are present in ozonated systems. Sampling containers may come with a sodium thiosulfate tablet already inside; be careful not to lose it while collecting samples. Do not skim the surface of the water, collect samples at a consistent depth and location for trending. Leave air space in the bottle after collecting and use aseptic techniques to avoid sample contamination (Rice et al., 2012), meaning taking care not to touch the mouth or interior of the sample bottle during collection. In the laboratory, aseptic techniques refer to a set of procedures designed to minimize the possibility of contamination by using a clean work area, sterile reagents and media, sterile handling procedures, and good personal hygiene (Thermo Fisher Scientific, n.d.). Work areas and gloved hands should be cleaned and wiped down with 70% alcohol before and after work. Ensure reagents and equipment are sterilized by either purchasing pre-sterilized supplies, or by proper use of an autoclave. Do not unwrap sterile supplies or uncover containers until they are ready to be used. If one has to remove a cap and place it on the work surface, place the cap with the opening facing down (ThermoFisher Scientific, n.d.). If samples cannot be processed within one hour after collection, refrigerate the samples for a maximum holding time of eight hours, between transport, storage, and processing (Rice et al., 2012).

6 Laboratory Chemistry and Specialized Chemical Additions

The majority of work performed in a water quality laboratory is procedure-based and only requires a well-trained technician; however, proper water quality management requires a firm understanding of the chemistry that drives these testing methods and the chemistry that drives the balance and management of a healthy aquarium system.

6.1 Molarity

There are many ways to express the concentration of a solution, or in other terms, how solute is dissolved in a volume or mass. Units such as parts per million (ppm) and milligrams per liter (mg/L) seem more straightforward, but certain mathematical calculations (such as preparing stock solutions and determining the appropriate amounts of a chemical to complete a reaction) necessitate expressing concentration in units of molarity. Molarity is defined as the number of moles of a substance per liter of solution (M or mol/L). A mole is Avogadro's number of atoms or molecules or ions (6.022×10^{23} mol^{-1}). The atomic mass of an element is the number of grams containing Avogadro's number of that element's atoms and the molecular mass of a compound is the sum of the atomic masses of the atoms in the molecule (Harris, 2001). The atomic mass of an element is found on the *Periodic Table of the Elements* (see Appendix 19.10).

For example, the molar mass of carbon is approximately 12.011, meaning that 6.022×10^{23} atoms of carbon have a mass of 12.011 grams. To determine the molecular mass of carbon monoxide (CO), add the atomic mass of carbon with that of oxygen (12.011 g/mol + 15.999 g/mol) for a total molecular mass of 28.010 g/mol. If there are multiple atoms of one element in a formula (indicated by a numerical subscript) as in carbon dioxide (CO_2), then multiply the atomic mass of that element by the total number of atoms in the molecule and add that to the other atomic masses found in the molecule (12.011 g/mol + 2(15.999 g/mol)) = (12.011 g/mol + 31.998 g/mol) = 44.009 g/mol. Molar ratios play an important role in *stoichiometry,* which refers to the relationships that govern the relative quantities of substances taking part in a chemical reaction. Additional information about stoichiometric calculations can be found in Section 17.4.

6.2 Chemical Reactions

Chemical reactions follow strict stoichiometric relationships which can be used to predict reactions and their byproducts, and allow understanding of aquatic life support systems at the molecular level. In a chemical reaction, substances interact to form completely different substances with different properties. For example, both sodium and chlorine on their own are hazardous materials, but upon a violent reaction, metallic sodium and chlorine gas form solid sodium chloride (NaCl), better known as table salt.

$$2Na\ (s) + Cl_2\ (g) \rightarrow 2NaCl\ (s)$$

In a chemical reaction, the law of conservation of energy and the law of conservation of matter are obeyed, meaning that energy and matter cannot be created or destroyed; it can only change form. The law of conservation of matter is demonstrated by balancing chemical reactions, so that the mass of the reactants match the mass of the products. In the reaction above, the mass of the products is equal to the mass of the reactants: 2 sodium atoms and 2 chlorine atoms, even though the number of molecules is different. For every 2 moles of Na, 2 moles of NaCl are formed; a 1:1 molar ratio. For every 1 mole of Cl_2, 2 moles of NaCl are formed; a 1:2 molar ratio.

Molar ratios can be used to calculate how much of a chemical is needed to create a product in a chemical reaction, which reactant is the limiting reagent, or how much product will be formed based upon the quantity of the reactants. An example is determining how much lanthanum chloride ($LaCl_3$) is needed to react with phosphate to form a precipitate that can be mechanically filtered out of an exhibit, as seen in the following reaction:

$$La^{3+}\ (aq) + PO_4{}^{3-}\ (aq) \rightarrow LaPO_4\ (s)$$

For a single mole of phosphate, one mole of lanthanum chloride is needed. The mass or volume of lanthanum chloride needed to remove a given amount of phosphate can be calculated based on this molar relationship and converted into grams using the molecular weight.

Understanding how to interpret and balance chemical reactions is extremely useful for calculating chemical dosage and ensuring that the proper amount of reactant(s) are added to the system.

6.3 Buffering Aquatic Systems

It is often necessary to adjust the pH of an aquatic system, by adding buffer. The process of buffering, in the scientific community, means adding a substance that strives to maintain pH at a set point. In the professional animal care industry, buffering can be used to maintain, raise or lower pH. When buffering a system, operators are not directly manipulating the pH; they are manipulating the buffer capacity of a system (more often represented by the measurement of alkalinity). Higher alkalinity means higher buffering capacity, lower alkalinity means lower buffering capacity. There are several ways to buffer up and down with each method having its own pros and cons.

6.3.1 Buffer Up

Sodium Bicarbonate

One of the most common ways to buffer up a system is to use sodium bicarbonate (bicarb). The bicarb method is traditionally used to increase the alkalinity of a tank. Occasionally, triple buffer may be necessary to incur a higher pH value.

Triple Buffer

In some instances the addition of a triple buffer may be desirable instead of the addition of sodium bicarbonate alone. Triple buffer includes sodium carbonate (Na_2CO_3) and borax ($Na_2B_4O_7$) as well as sodium bicarbonate ($NaHCO_3$). This combination increases the potency of the buffer for situations where bicarbonate alone cannot raise the pH to desired levels. It is also effective for more drastic and long lasting results.

6.3.2 Buffer Down

Phosphate Buffers

Phosphate buffers may be added to control pH at a lower set point. A 1:1 dry mixture of potassium phosphate (KH_2PO_4) and sodium phosphate (NaH_2PO_4) can be used to lower pH. This can be used when systems are empty in preparation for animals. However, if animals are already present in the system, this may be too great of change for them to endure. There are a number of commercially available buffers used to maintain a lower pH when makeup water is highly alkaline or hard. For freshwater species, the desired pH range can be widely different and buffers should be chosen for maintaining pH at the endemic range for the animals.

Acid Drip

Muriatic acid is commonly used to lower the pH in established systems. One reason for choosing muriatic acid over another pH lowering chemical is due to its effectiveness in low doses. Muriatic acid drips accomplish this due to its approximate pH of 0.1. With this low of a pH, it is considered a dangerous chemical and can cause serious chemical burns and respiratory damage. Large quantities (50 gallon drums) can be sourced directly from most chemical companies. Small quantities (1 gallon) can be obtained through a local hardware store or the local pool supply store. The containers are sometimes labeled with dosing instructions, but are generally only applicable to freshwater exhibits. Due to having live animals versus an empty swimming pool, it is the industry norm to administer a muriatic acid as a diluted aqueous mixture and slowly dripped into the exhibit over period of time. A drip into an exhibit can be accomplished in many ways via carboy, peristaltic pumping system, liter/meter pump system or any other sealed drip mechanism. It is also good practice to follow the simple chemistry rule of thumb: always add acid to water not vice versa.

Carbon Dioxide Injection

Replacing acid drips with carbon dioxide (CO_2) in alkaline water is an effective, reliable, and economical method of controlling pH levels. Carbon dioxide is a safer alternative than acids and an effective chemical for lowering the pH of various alkaline waters. When CO_2 is dissolved in water, it goes through a series of chemical reactions as shown below.

$$CO_2 + H_2O \leftrightarrow H_2CO_3$$
$$H_2CO_3 \leftrightarrow H^+ + HCO_3^-$$
$$HCO_3^- \leftrightarrow H^+ + CO_3$$

Initially, dissolved CO_2 forms carbonic acid, which subsequently dissociates into bicarbonates, carbonates and hydrogen ions. The hydrogen ions reduce the pH. Continuous water quality analysis, via a pH controller box and injection system taken directly from exhibit, is suggested to mediate and monitor the effectiveness of CO_2.

6.4 Chemicals Used in Zoos and Aquariums

There are many different chemicals used in laboratory applications. See Appendix 19.2 for a partial list of common chemicals used in aquarium and zoo water quality laboratories and aquatic life support facilities. This list includes the chemical name, common name or synonym and the chemical formula. Just like with animals, the common name is not always the best one to use. It is important to know that the right chemical is being used when making a solution or communicating with a colleague.

6.5 Artificial Salt Mixes

Aquariums and zoos that house marine animals need a source of clean saltwater. Facilities on the coast may have the ability to pull saltwater directly from the ocean or bay. Natural seawater is not always the easy road; biofouling and recruitment of planktonic local species are two challenges that come with natural seawater. Inland facilities or coastal facilities with poor water sources need to make artificial seawater for their exhibits.

Making saltwater artificially can be done in two ways: from a packaged fully manufactured mix or from a mix that is prepared on site and is made to match the needs of the facility and local water sources. Packaged manufactured mixes are convenient, easy to store and make saltwater quickly. The downside is they cost more than an onsite mix and cannot easily be customized. An onsite mix costs less, can be tailored to local water sources and can be adjusted daily if needed. The downside is they require preparation time, are more difficult to store and they take more staff time.

When making saltwater from an onsite mix, the first step is to determine what the recipe should be from the freshwater available and contributions from the major salt compounds. By mixing the local waters with the 6 major salt compounds, this initial mix can be tested to determine the starting point. From there, the mix can be fine tuned with minor and trace elements as needed by the animal collection. Refer to Appendix 19.3.1 for a list of element concentrations found in natural seawater that are either considered to be essential to aquatic health or potentially toxic and therefore should be evaluated when making an artificial salt mix. Refer to Appendix 19.3.2 for a partial list of common salts used to make artificial saltwater in aquarium and zoo water quality laboratories and life support facilities. Refer to Appendix 19.3.3 for an example of an artificial salt recipe used at the Steinhart Aquarium with local San Francisco drinking water.

6.6 Lanthanum Chloride

Algae growth is common in most water features at any zoo or aquarium. The use of lanthanum chloride to reduce the amount of phosphorus in water features is a common practice to limit the amount of algae growth, since phosphorus is considered the limiting nutrient for algae growth. Lanthanum (La) is a silvery-white metallic rare-earth element and is the first element in the Lanthanide Series in the *Periodic Table of the Elements*. Lanthanum chloride is a salt and is non-toxic when added to water systems. Although it has no known role in biological systems, it is extremely reactive with phosphorus. When lanthanum chloride is injected into a water filtration stream, it quickly reacts with any available phosphates to form the fine, white precipitate, lanthanum phosphate. This white precipitate is easily filtered out of the filtration stream by sand filtration. The reaction of lanthanum with phosphorus is relatively quick and works best if the injection point is just prior to the sand filtration. The amount of lanthanum chloride dose should be based on the estimated amount of phosphorus desired to remove based on a 1:1 molar ratio of lanthanum to phosphorus as indicated in the reaction:

$$La^{3+} (aq) + HPO_4^{2-} (aq) \rightarrow LaPO_4 (s) + H^+$$

Lanthanum chloride is managed differently when it is first initiated than when it is held at a maintenance level. When starting the initial lanthanum chloride dosing, phosphate levels should be tested before addition and then daily to monitor the progress. If the supplier of the lanthanum chloride does not provide a calculator for dosing, the authors recommend a very conservative dose to start. That amount can then be increased if a drop in phosphate levels is not realized. Once the ratio of lanthanum to phosphate results in a steady reduction in phosphate, continue that amount until the desired levels of phosphate are reached. Transition the initial dosing level to maintenance levels, using enough lanthanum chloride to prevent an increase in phosphate. Confirm this with weekly testing. Ensure that the phosphate test being used has a range of accuracy low enough to accurately test the desired levels of phosphate to be achieved. The addition of lanthanum chloride must occur slowly via a metering pump to avoid precipitation in the exhibit and damage of the acrylic.

For more information on how to effectively dose lanthanum chloride into a life support system see Section 9.3.5.

7 Pumps and Motors

Every aspect of a life support system plays a specific role in the treatment of the water. These components, whether they serve the mechanical or chemical requirements of the water, are the heart of a functional life support system. These range from the pumps that move water through the system to the valves that control the direction of the water.

7.1 Centrifugal Pumps

Centrifugal pumps are common across the life support industry and operate under basic physical principles. Centrifugal pumps are suited to moving large amounts of water quickly and efficiently.

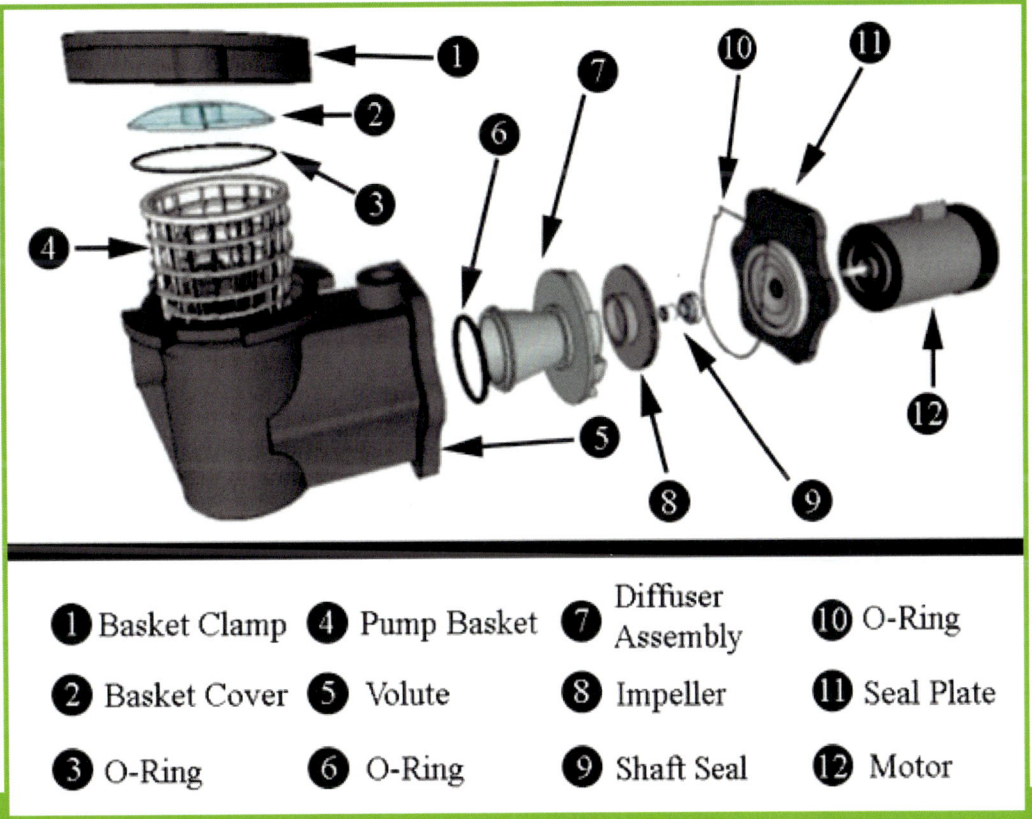

Figure 7.1 - Centrifugal Pump Exploded View

1 Basket Clamp   4 Pump Basket   7 Diffuser Assembly   10 O-Ring

2 Basket Cover   5 Volute   8 Impeller   11 Seal Plate

3 O-Ring   6 O-Ring   9 Shaft Seal   12 Motor

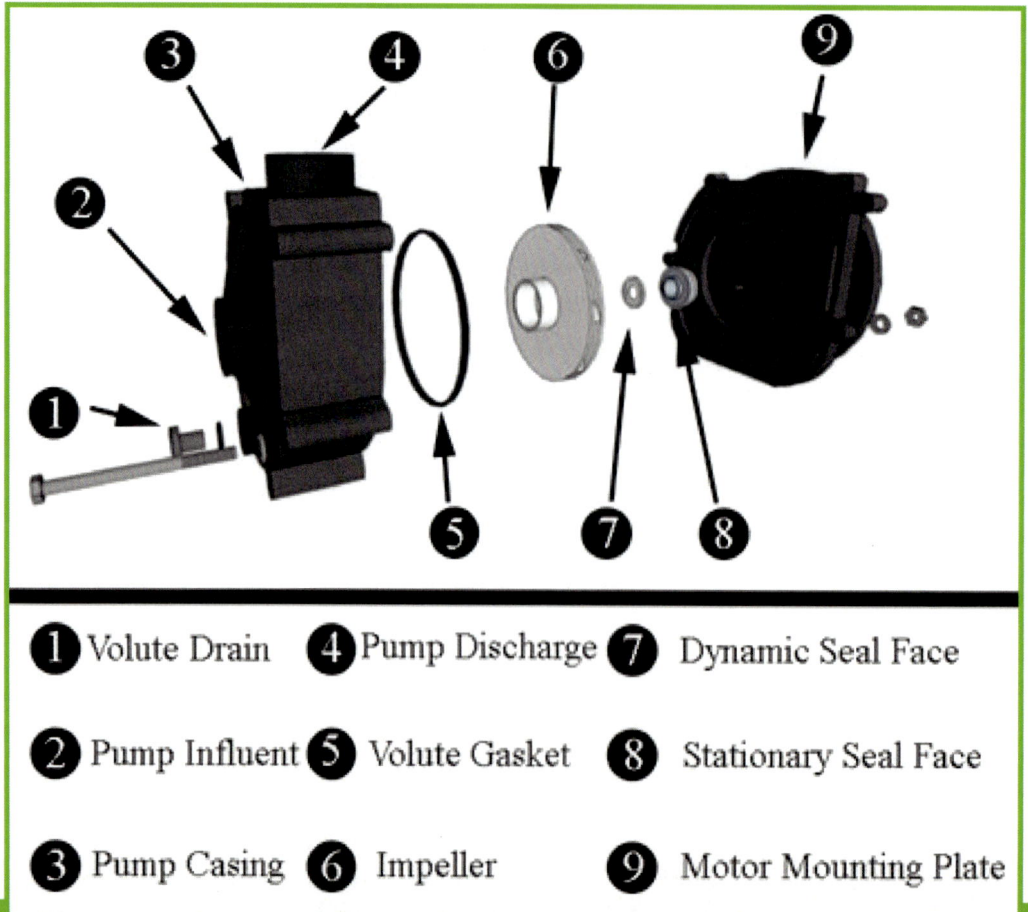

1 Volute Drain   **4** Pump Discharge   **7** Dynamic Seal Face

2 Pump Influent   **5** Volute Gasket   **8** Stationary Seal Face

3 Pump Casing   **6** Impeller   **9** Motor Mounting Plate

Figure 7.2 - Centrifugal Pump Wet End Exploded View

Water enters the suction inlet of the pump and encounters the impeller. The impeller is the rotating pump component which transfers energy from the pump motor into the water. The rotational force is transferred to the water by the backward swept fins at its face. This rotational force causes the water to travel towards the outside edge of the pump casing, where it is directed out of the discharge of the pump. This process is constant and imparts pressure as the water exits the pump. Centrifugal pumps are not typically self-priming and require water at the level of the impeller in order to be primed (the point at which the pump begins moving water). Centrifugal pumps are the most common pump found in life support systems. These pumps are extremely varied in design and purpose and can be constructed from cast iron, stainless steel, plastics, and fiberglass.

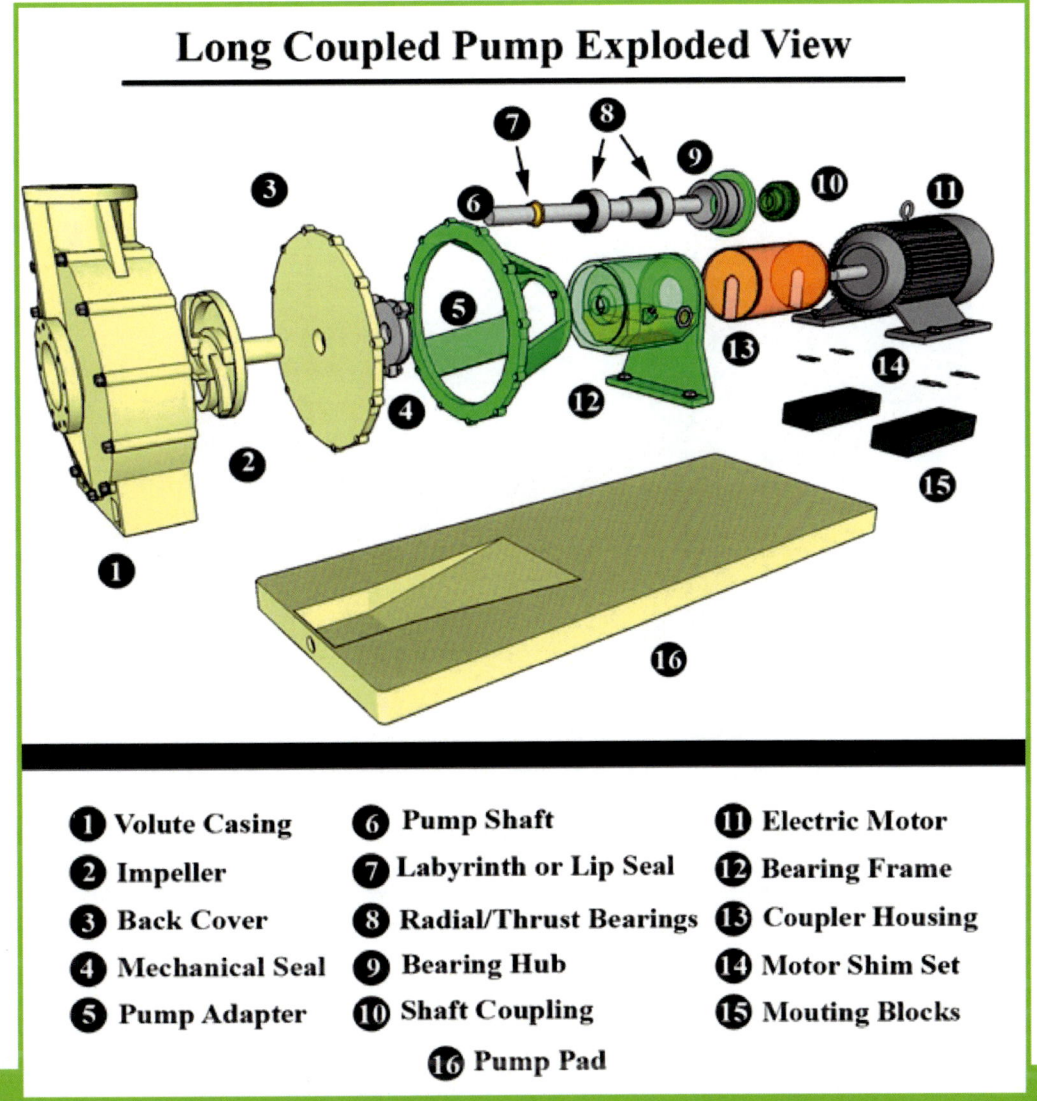

Long Coupled Pump Exploded View

① Volute Casing ⑥ Pump Shaft ⑪ Electric Motor
② Impeller ⑦ Labyrinth or Lip Seal ⑫ Bearing Frame
③ Back Cover ⑧ Radial/Thrust Bearings ⑬ Coupler Housing
④ Mechanical Seal ⑨ Bearing Hub ⑭ Motor Shim Set
⑤ Pump Adapter ⑩ Shaft Coupling ⑮ Mouting Blocks
⑯ Pump Pad

Figure 7.3 - Long Coupled Pump Exploded View

7.2 Positive Displacement Pumps

A positive displacement pump makes fluid move by trapping a fixed amount and forcing (displacing) that trapped volume into the discharge pipe. As a result, these types of pump will produce flow regardless of the pressure on the discharge end. In the LSS field, these types of pumps are typically found in low flow applications such as chemical dosing.

7.2.1 Diaphragm Pumps

A diaphragm pump uses a membrane to pull water into the suction side of the pump and then push it out of the discharge side. A diaphragm pump incorporates two check valves (valves that only allow fluid to move in one direction) in order to accomplish this. Figure 7.4 shows this action:

Figure 7.4 Diaphragm Pump

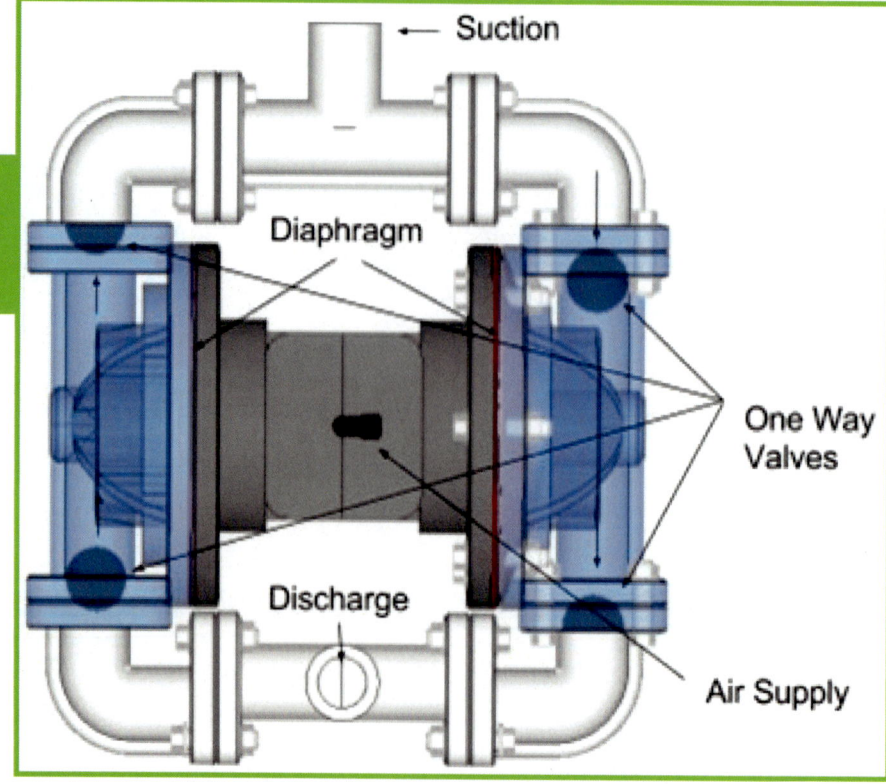

As the membrane expands, a vacuum is created, which draws fluid into the chamber. When the membrane collapses, the fluid is forced out of the discharge side. Plunger and piston pumps operate under a similar principle. Diaphragm pumps can be used moving liquids that have a high degree of sludge and particulate matter. These pumps can also run dry without damaging the pump.

7.2.2 Peristaltic Pumps

A peristaltic pump employs a set of rotating rollers pinching a continuous section of flexible tubing against the pump casing in order to force fluid out of the pump discharge. The peristaltic pump is ideally suited to pumping corrosive fluids as there is no contact between the corrosive fluid and the pump's mechanical components. Peristaltic pumps can be used for metering in chemical additions, as seen in Figure 7.5.

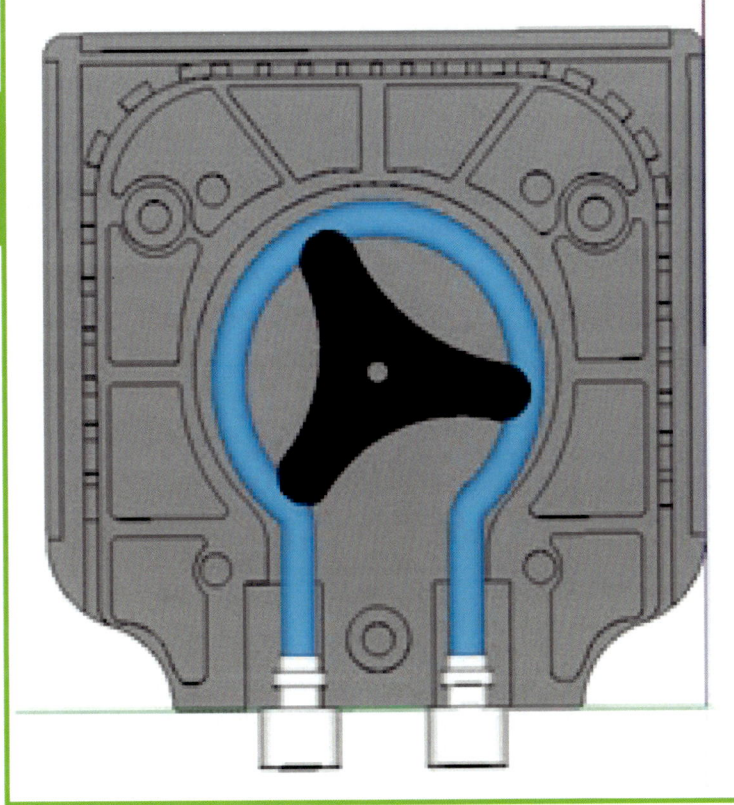

**Figure 7.5
Peristaltic Pump**

The roller in the middle of the casing is forced against the tubing which contains the fluid. As this roller rotates, the tubing is pinched against the casing of the pump. As the pinched section of tubing moves around the casing, a vacuum is created behind it, which draws fluid forward. As that roller releases the tubing on the other end of the casing, that fluid is discharged out the other end of the pump.

7.2.3 Flexible Impeller Pump

A flexible impeller pump is a positive-displacement pump that, by deforming impeller vanes, draws the liquid into the pump housing and moves it to the discharge port at a constant flow rate. The flexibility of the vanes enables a tight seal with the internal housing, making the pump self-priming while also permitting bidirectional operation.

7.3 Motors

Motors, within the context of life support systems, supply the power to move water from point A to point B. There are many different types of motors as well as sizes. This introduction will cover frequently used terms and standardized codes used throughout the industry. Within the scope of this manual, only alternating current (AC) motors are discussed.

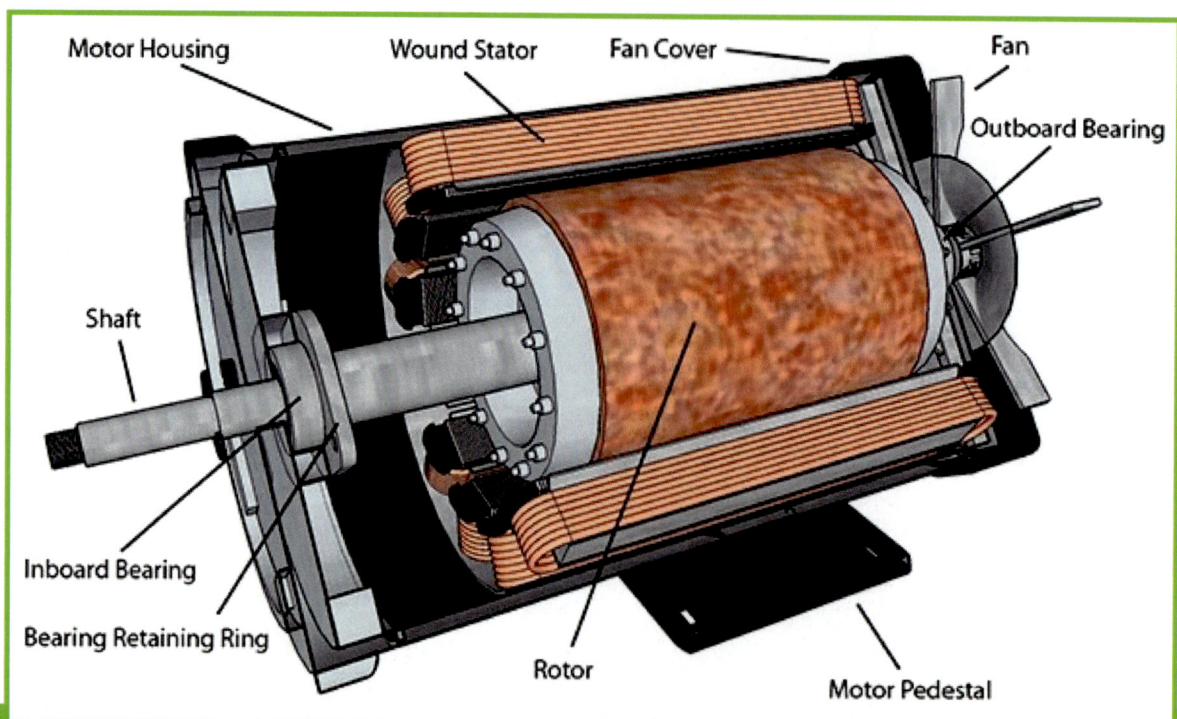

Figure 7.6 - Motor Cut Away View

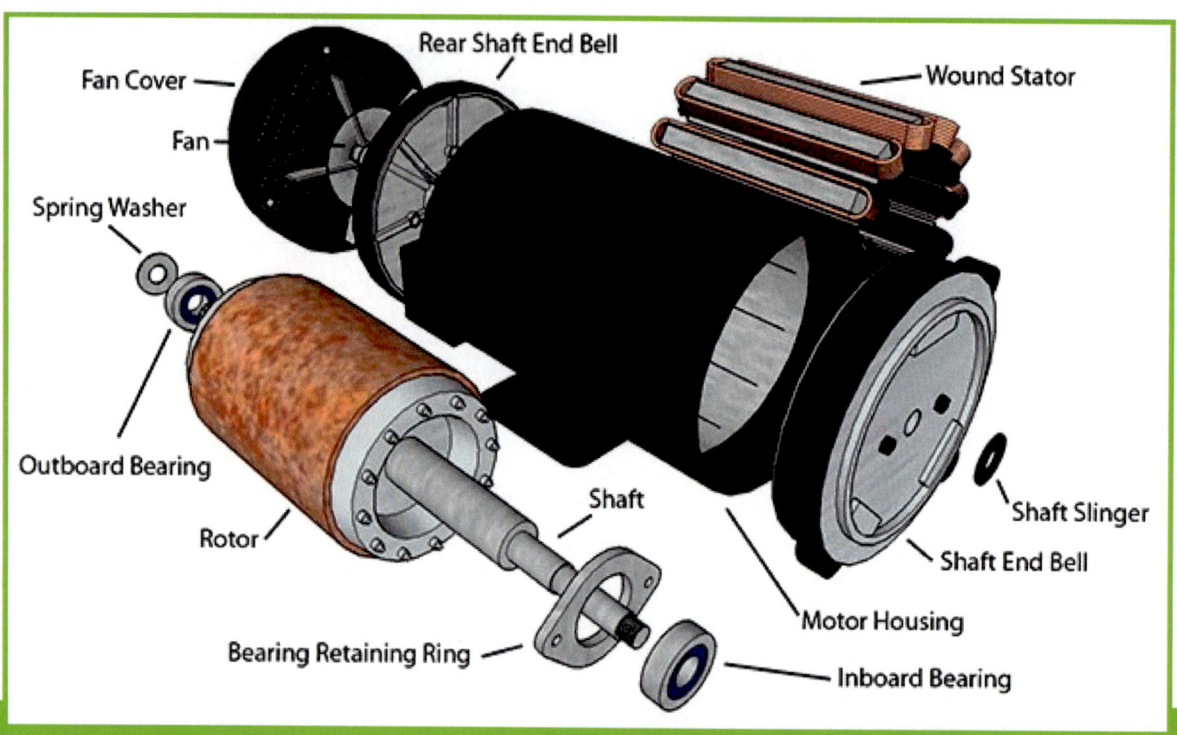

Figure 7.7 - Motor Exploded View

7.3.1 Types of Motors

There are many ways to classify AC induction (creation of electromotive force by magnetic field) motors but two of the more common methods are based on the electrical phase and type of motor. Different types of motors are useful because manufacturers have designed motors for different environments and purposes, some of which can be found in life support systems.

Open Drip-Proof (ODP): These motors can handle some water dripped from above and are not rated for outdoor use.

Totally Enclosed Fan Cooled (TEFC): These motors are enclosed, making them suitable for outdoor and wet locations. The motor is cooled by an external fan, which is mounted on the shaft, blowing air across the external surface of the motor.

Totally Enclosed Non-Ventilated (TENV): These motors are smaller, usually 5 horsepower and lower, where the surface area ratio to volume is large enough that heat will discharge into the ambient environment without an external or internal fan.

Hazardous Location Motors: These motors are a specialty totally enclosed type and will have sub-categories depending on location and application. Class I motors are rated as explosion proof and are used with potentially explosive liquids, vapors, and gases. Class II motors are rated as dust ignition proof are used in locations that may contain combustible dusts (for example, around coal, grain, and flour).

Single Phase Motor: When using a single conductor to supply power to the motor, a supplementary means to start the motor is required. Single phase motors are categorized by the differing methods used to start the motor. Many single phase motors can only rotate in one direction (clockwise) but some motors have the capability to rotate clockwise or counterclockwise. The methods of starting single phase motors are shaded pole, split phase, and capacitor use.

Shaded Pole Motors: With a size of 1/100 - ⅙ HP, these use a shaded pole mechanism of starting the rotation and have copper shorting rings delaying the magnetic field build-up, thus making the rotation appear to be from the main pole to the shaded pole.

Split Phase Motors: With a size of 1/25 - ½ HP, two separate windings of differing resistance create a delay in the current flow which causes the rotor to move. The starting winding will be disconnected when the motor reaches 75% of its speed and will then continue running as an induction motor.

Capacitors: The use of capacitors in motors from 1/25 to 15 HP is common. There are three different ways that capacitors are used to start motors. The first being the capacitor start induction run. In this version, the capacitor creates a time delay similar to the split phase method. In this case, after the rotating field has started the rotor, the starting switch will open as the motor approaches full speed and will then run as an induction motor. A single value capacitor style has a capacitor that is built in series on one of the two windings. The starting torque for these small motors usually has values that are 100% or less than full load torque ratings. In a two value capacitor motor, a capacitor is used on each winding, starting and running. After the motor has started, that capacitor will drop out and the motor will run as a two phase motor.

Three Phase Motors: These motors use three conductors (A, B, C legs) to power the motors. These motors will start and run in the direction of the phase rotation of the incoming power. Less electricity is used to power three phase motors than similar single phase versions, making them preferable in terms of energy conservation. Swapping out two of the three conductors will change the direction that the motor is rotating, while swapping all three conductors will keep the rotational direction the same (Cowern, n.d.).

7.3.2 Motor Terminology

There are many terms that are needed to completely define a motor and the work that is accomplished. Below are some of the more common terms needed to complete the picture:

Full Load Amps (FLA): The amount of current drawn when a motor is running under a full load.

Run Load Amps (RLA): The amount of current drawn when a motor is running under a normal load.

Locked Rotor Amps (LRA): This is also known as starting inrush amps, which is the amount of current a motor draws under starting condition when full voltage is applied. Motors will often pull 300% or more current than FLA when started at full voltage.

Service Factor Amps (SFA): The amount of current a motor will draw under the service factor load (overload) situation. For example, a SF of 1.10 can handle a 10% overload.

Efficiency: The percentage of input power converted to work output.

Frequency: The Hertz (cycles) for which a motor is designed to be operated. In the U.S.A., normally it is 60 Hz while internationally, 50 Hz is commonplace.

Full Load Speed: The speed (RPM) that a motor will run at full-rated output torque or horsepower.

Variable Torque: When the amount of torque required is low at low speeds and increases as speed increases (centrifugal pumps).

Poles: The number of magnetic poles that appear within a motor when power is applied which will always be in pairs. The number of poles work with the frequency to determine the synchronous speed of the motor, as seen in Figure 7.8.

Poles	Synchronous Speed	
	60 Hz	50 Hz
2	3600	3000
4	1800	1500
6	1200	1000
8	900	750
10	720	600

Figure 7.8 - Number of Poles and Synchronous Speed

Power Factor: The ratio of actual power used to apparent power flowing through the circuit.

Service Factor: A multiplier that indicates the amount of overload a motor can be expected to handle.

Slip RPM: The difference between synchronous speed and full load speed.

Synchronous Speed: The speed at which the magnetic field is rotating. It can be used to approximate the motor's speed under a no load condition.

Ambient Temperature: Maximum safe room temperature when operating a motor continuously under a full load condition. Standard is 104°F (40°C).

Temperature Rise: Amount of temperature gain expected within the winding from non-operating to full load continuously operating.

Time Rating: Motors are either rated for continuous duty or intermittent duty (actuators).

Torque: Twisting force exerted by shaft of a motor. Measured in pound inches, pound feet, ounce inches (for small motors), or newton meters.

Horsepower: A unit describing the amount of work a motor can do in a given timeframe. For example, a 1 HP motor produces 33,000 ft lbs in one minute. A 1 Metric HP motor produces 735.5 N-m in one second.

Full Load Torque: The rated continuous torque that a motor can support without overheating.

Peak Torque: The maximum amount of torque required of a motor at any point during operation.

Pull Out Torque (Breakdown Torque): The maximum amount of torque available from motor shaft when a motor is operating at full voltage and running at full speed.

Pull Up Torque: The lowest point of the torque speed curve for a motor that is ramping up a load to full speed.

Starting Torque (Locked Rotor Torque): The amount of torque a motor produces when it is started at full voltage and the shaft is locked in place.

7.3.3 Motor Frame Size

Motor frame sizes have been standardized by the National Electrical Manufacturers Association (NEMA). There are three generations of standards with the original grouping from 1952 and earlier, the U frames from 1952 – 1964, and the T frames from 1964 to the present. Base plate mounting hole spacing (E and F dimensions) and the shaft height (D) will be the same if the 3-digit code is the same for all three generations. Please refer to the charts in the Appendix (19.7.1 and 19.7.2) for frame sizes for Open Drip-Proof Motors and Totally Enclosed Fan Cooled Motors. Additionally, in the Appendix, Sections 19.7.3 and 19.7.4, there is a chart for NEMA standardized frame dimensions and NEMA standardized shaft keyseat dimensions.

Fractional Horsepower Motors: These motors, typically only go up to 3 HP, cover frame sizes that are a 2-digit code. 42, 48, and 56 are quite common. Each frame size refers to a specific shaft height, shaft diameter, and base mounting hole pattern. Shaft height for these frames can be calculated by taking the 2-digit code and dividing it by 16. So for example, a 42 frame size will have a shaft height of 2 5/8" (42/16 = 2 5/8"). Since the frame size code does not pertain to a particular horsepower or speed, that information must be on hand when ordering a replacement (Cowern, n.d.).

Integral Horsepower Motors: These motors are the 3-digit code variety. The shaft height can be calculated by taking the first two digits and dividing by 4. For example, a 143T frame has a shaft height of 14/4 = 3.5". The third digit does not directly refer to a dimension, but comparatively larger numbers will reference that the rear bolt holes have been moved further back, such as 143 and 145.

Frame Size Categories

C – Flange Mounted Motor: The most common type of face mount motors which have female threaded mounting holes on the motor face and a specific bolt pattern on the shaft end which allows mounting.

D – Flange Mounted Motor: A special type of mounting flange that has a flange diameter larger than the motor body with holes that are designed to allow a pass-through bolt from the back of the motor to the mating part.

H: Is used on some fractional HP 56 frame size motors which are designed to be used for mounting in either 56, 143T, or 145T situations.

J: Is used with 56 frame motors that are designed for jet pump service.

JM: The shaft is designed to be used with a mechanical seal. This frame has a C face.

JP: The shaft is designed to be used with a packing type of seal. This frame has a C face.

S: The shaft for this frame designation is shorter than normal dimensions and is designed to be coupled to the pump with a flexible coupling.

T: Indicates the motor is from 1964 and later.

U: Indicates the motor is from 1952 to 1964.

Y: The mounting configuration deviates from the standard dimensions.

Z: The shaft deviates from the standard dimension.

8 Valves

There are a variety of different valves used in life support systems. All of them control the flow of water, but in different ways. Butterfly valves, ball valves, check valves, gate valves, and globe valves are the most common.

8.1 Butterfly Valves

A butterfly valve can be constructed out of plastic or metal and utilizes a disk between its housing to control the flow of water. In the closed position, the broad side of the disk is perpendicular to the water's flow direction. In the open position, the disk is rotated so that its broad side is parallel to the direction of the water flow. The casing of the valve is most often lined with rubber, so that the disk's edges seat against it in the closed position, as the rubber creates a seal and prevents water from leaking past. Butterfly valves have a relatively small footprint compared to other types of valves, which makes them ideal for large-scale operations. Figure 8.1 is an example of a butterfly valve.

Figure 8.1 - Butterfly Valve

8.2 Ball Valves

Ball valves can be constructed out of a variety of metals, plastics, and even ceramic. A ball valve controls the flow of water in much the same way as a butterfly valve. The key difference being that the "disk" is a sphere in a ball valve. The sphere has a hole from one side to the other, like a "tunnel" through the sphere, allowing fluid to pass through. In the closed position, this hole is perpendicular to the water flow, thus the fluid contacts the solid side of the sphere and ceases to move. In the open position, the hole is in line with the inlet and outlet of the valve. Ball valves are unique for this in that, when fully open, the sphere acts as a section of pipe. This makes ball valves the least restrictive to flow, resulting in less friction or head loss when fully open than other valves. Figure 8.2 shows a ball valve in both positions.

Figure 8.2 - True Union Ball Valve

8.3 Gate and Knife Valves

Gate and knife valves are not used as frequently as butterfly or ball valves in LSS systems. These valves utilize a gate or wedge in the path of the water to restrict or allow flow, as is illustrated in Figure 8.3. Gate and knife valves can be made out of metals and/or plastics. Gate valves are not the best choice for throttling flow because they tend to produce erratic results; however, they are often used in these situations (such as on the discharge of protein skimmers) since the cost of globe valves tends to be prohibitive.

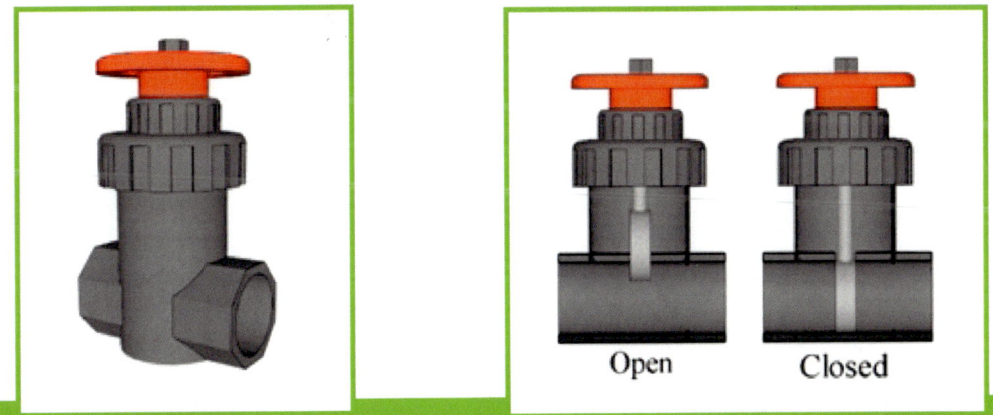

Figure 8.3 - Gate Valve

8.4 Globe Valves

Figure 8.4 depicts the basic anatomy of a globe valve. Fluid is free to flow from left to right as long as the plug is not contacting the baffle in the center. Globe valves are used for throttling purposes, as minor changes in the position of the plug create predictable changes in flow. A globe-type valve is not ideal for operations where maximum velocity needs to be maintained because of the baffle and plug in the center. Water flow through a valve of this type experiences substantial friction due to the changes in water direction through the valve. These types of valves are often used for municipal water applications where water pressure requires frequent adjustment.

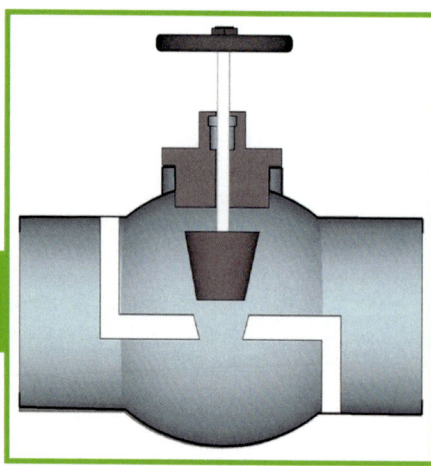

Figure 8.4 - Globe Valve

8.5 Check Valves

Check Valves are valves which allow a fluid to move in one direction, but not the other. These types of valves are beneficial in cases where fluid is being pumped upward to great heights. If the pump should fail or lose power, the fluid in the pipe would remain at a point beyond the check valve until the pump issue is resolved. Check valves are often placed in-line, after a centrifugal pump to prevent backwards flow across the impeller when the pump is de-energized. As discussed previously, check valves also allow a diaphragm pump to operate. There are several types of check valves, including ball type and swing type. Examples of these check valves (in the order listed) can be seen in Figures 8.5, 8.6 and 8.7.

Figure 8.5 - Swing Type Check Valve

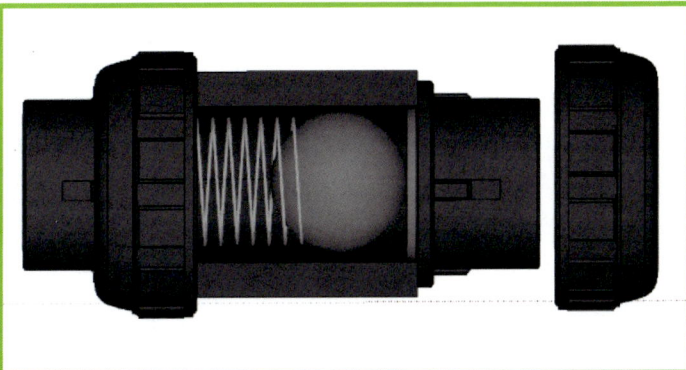

Figure 8.6 - True Union Ball Type Check Valve

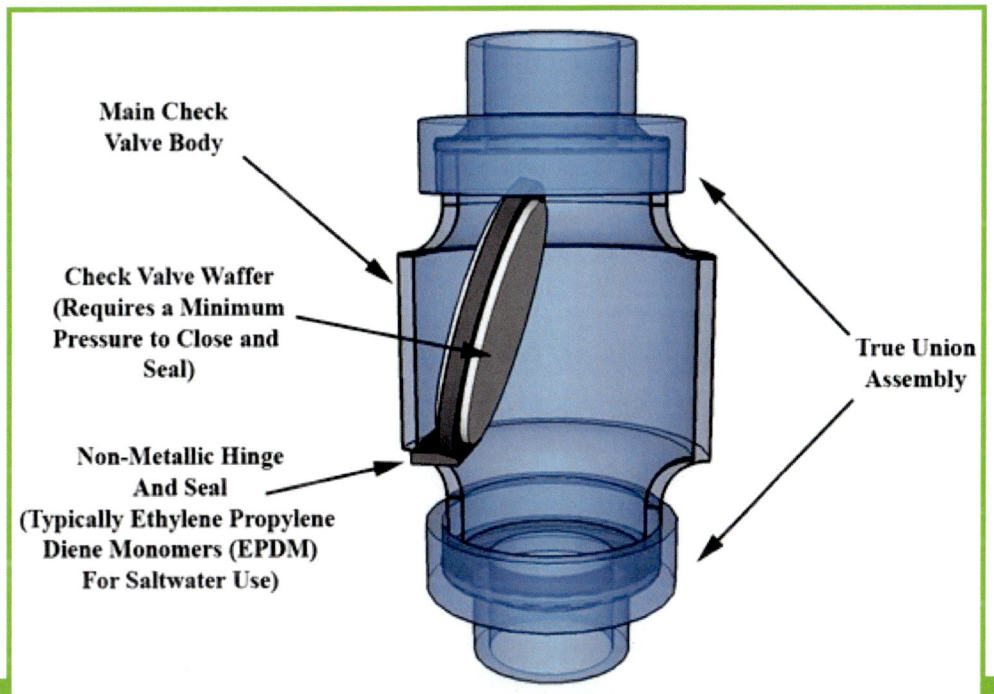

Main Check Valve Body

Check Valve Waffer (Requires a Minimum Pressure to Close and Seal)

Non-Metallic Hinge And Seal (Typically Ethylene Propylene Diene Monomers (EPDM) For Saltwater Use)

True Union Assembly

Figure 8.7 - Non-Metallic True Union Flapper Type Check Valve

8.6 Diaphragm Valves

A diaphragm is a thin, pliable sheet of material that forms a divider. In diaphragm valves, the diaphragm will usually divide the moving components of the valve from the flow of fluid through the valve.

A diaphragm valve works by moving the diaphragm; either stopping or directing the flow of water. Diaphragm valves may be 2-way or 3-way valves. There are diaphragm valves with more ports, but these are generally made by having multiple diaphragms.

In a 2-way diaphragm valve, the diaphragm is pushed across the flow of water to touch the valve body on the other side of the valve, stopping the flow of water. The inside of the valve will often have a rubber lining that creates a seal with the diaphragm. Releasing the pressure on the diaphragm opens the valve. If pressure on the diaphragm is lost, the valve may be pushed open by the water moving through it, as seen when there is a loss of air pressure on a pneumatic diaphragm valve.

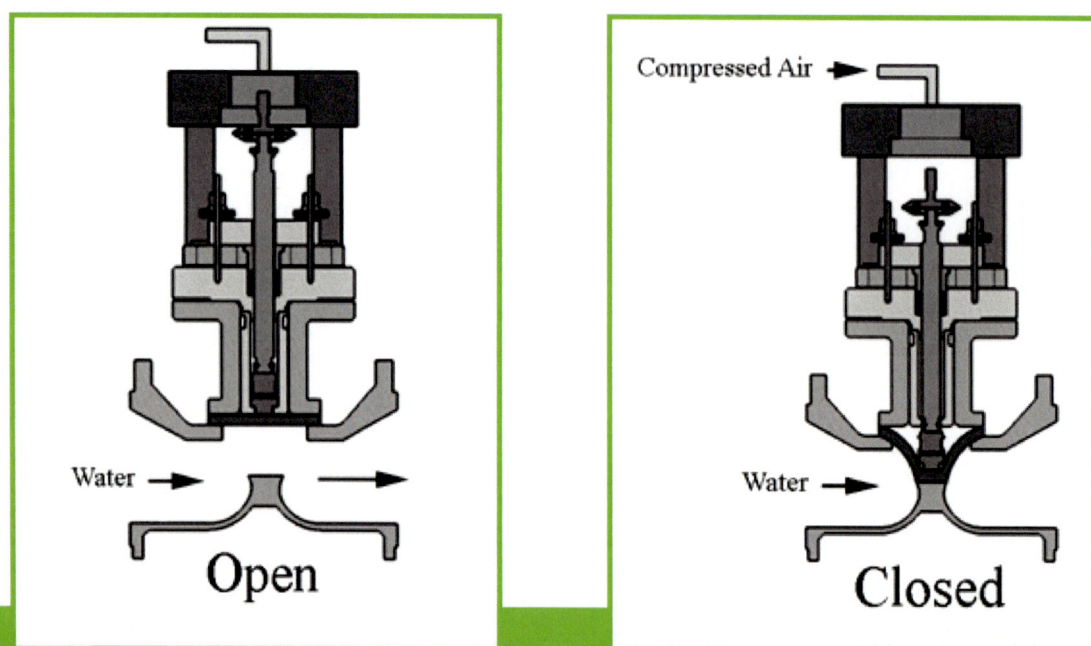

Figure 8.8 - Pneumatic Diaphragm Valve

3-way diaphragm valves operate the nearly the same as 2-way diaphragm valves. The diaphragm is not limited to only closing and opening the valve. A 3-way diaphragm valve will close one of the three ports, leaving two ports open, selecting which direction the water will flow. At any given time two ports will be open and one will be closed; therefore, these valves are not for stopping water flow, but directing water flow. The most common design has a plunger or plug attached to the diaphragm. When the diaphragm is not under pressure, the plunger or plug will close the port opposite the diaphragm. When the diaphragm is placed under pressure, it will press into a saddle or weir in the valve, closing one of the other two ports, while also pressing the plunger or plug out of the way, allowing water to flow through its port. In this configuration, one of the three ports will always be open, no matter the position of the diaphragm. When installing these valves, be aware of the position of the diaphragm in the event of a loss of pressure; the fluid moving through the valve may push on the diaphragm and close the port with the plunger or plug.

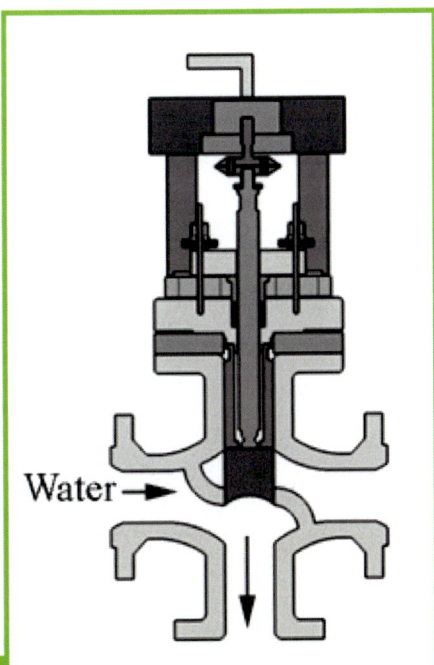 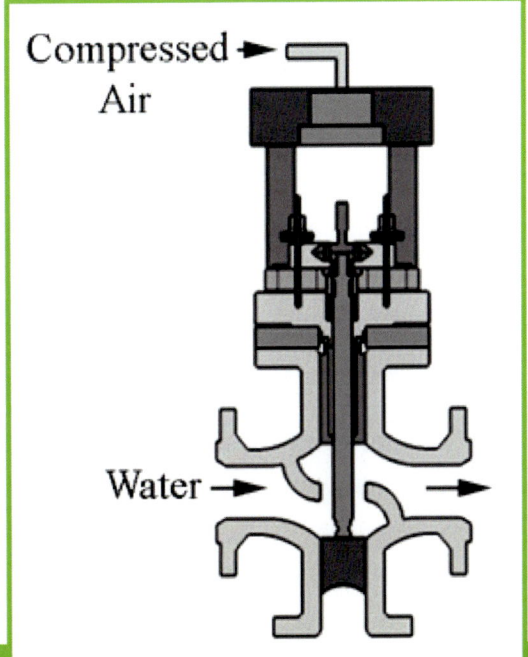

Figure 8.9 - 3-Way Pneumatic Diaphragm Valve

Diaphragm valves are designed either as saddle diaphragm valves or as straight-through diaphragm valves. In a saddle diaphragm valve, a saddle or weir is across from the diaphragm, allowing the diaphragm to move less distance to close the valve. This design causes more turbulence in the water, due to an obstacle in its path of flow. Straight-through style diaphragm valves do not have this obstacle, much like a ball valve; however, the diaphragm will have to travel further and be placed under more pressure to close the valve.

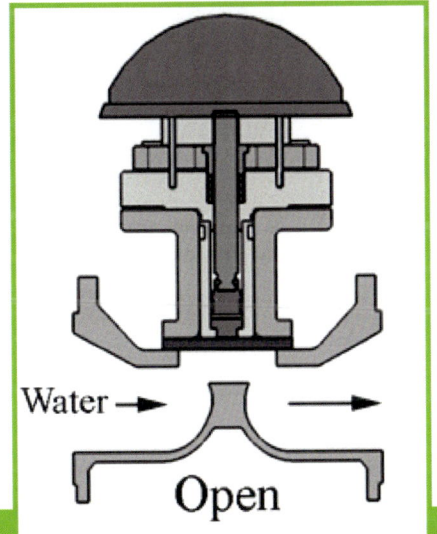 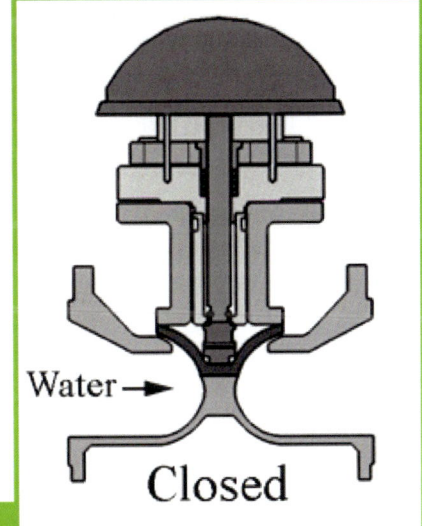

Figure 8.10 - Saddle Diaphragm Valve

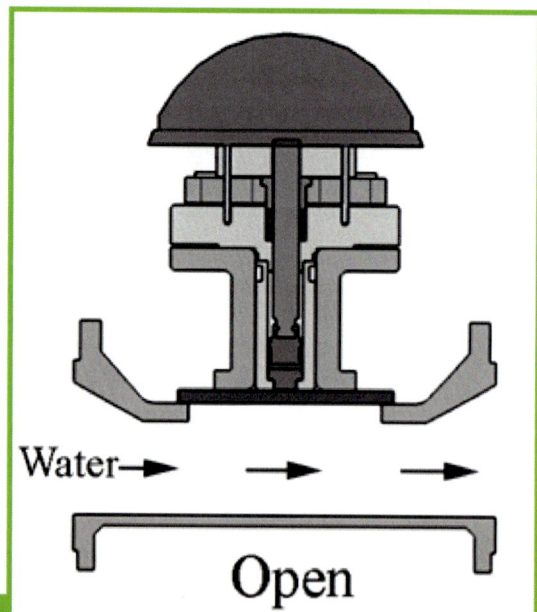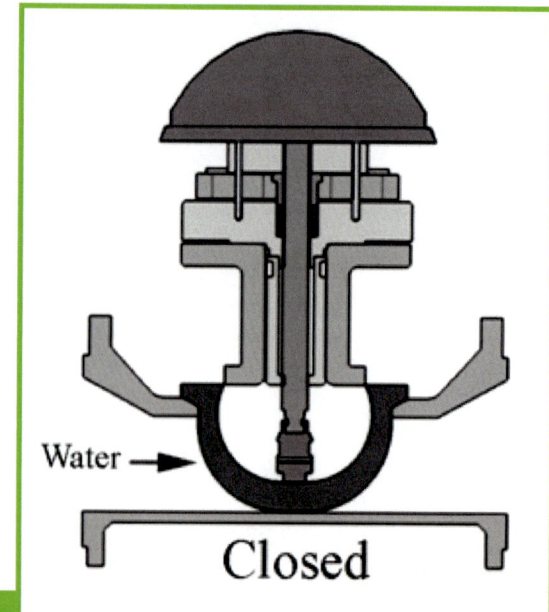

Figure 8.11 - Straight - Through Diaphragm Valve

Diaphragm valves may be controlled pneumatically, hydraulically, or manually. If pneumatically operated, corresponding equipment, such as an air compressor or air lines, will be needed and maintained to operate the diaphragm valves. In the event that water intrusion is found in the air lines, the valve should be tested for diaphragm integrity.

8.7 Valve Actuators

An actuator is any device used to open or close a valve. This manual will concentrate on the three types typically found in an LSS application: manual, pneumatic, and electric. Actuators of all types typically include a manual override mechanism such as a hand wheel and may include feedback mechanisms for signaling to a programmable logic controller (PLC) or supervisory control and data acquisition (SCADA) system.

A manual actuator employs levers, wheels, or gears in order to move the valve stem and is operated directly by a person. For example, the handle or gear operator on a typical butterfly valve.

An electric actuator is powered by an electric motor acting through a gearing assembly in order to effect a change in the position of the valve stem. Of the various designs found in this category, the most common in the LSS field is the cam-on-shaft type. This design is commonly found on both ball and butterfly valves as both are quarter-turn applications. Additionally, electric actuators are found in multi-turn applications such as on large gate and globe valves.

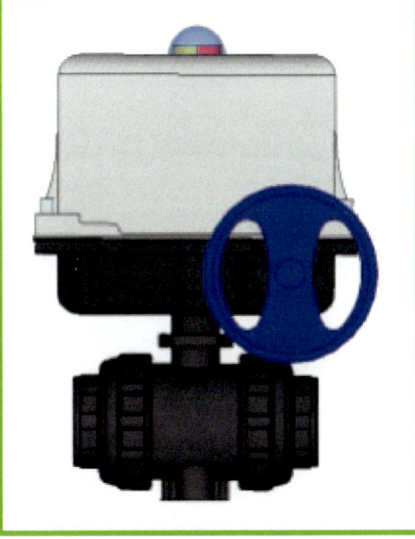

Figure 8.12 - Electric Actuator on a Ball Valve

A pneumatic actuator is one designed to allow the valve to be moved by air (or another gas) pressure, typically by means of a piston assembly. These actuators can be ideal in fail-safe applications when equipped with a spring return mechanism. This design provides the power to move the valve position by means of a loaded spring. An example of a fail-safe application is one where the valve must close immediately upon the loss of utility power in order to prevent water loss from a system or in order to prevent the flooding of a mechanical space.

8.8 Valve Issues: Water Hammer

A phenomenon known as "water hammer", or "hydraulic shock", is caused by a pressure surge that occurs when flowing liquid significantly decreases velocity, stops, or changes direction. This can be caused by a pump suddenly decreasing in speed, a check valve closing due to a pump being shut off suddenly, by quickly opening or closing a valve, or by air trapped in a length of plumbing. The severity of the water hammer relates to the inertia of the water. Damage can occur if the hammer is severe enough. Plumbing can shake violently, causing pipes, fittings, or supports to break, and pumps may become damaged. In extreme cases, the buildup of pressure can cause plumbing or pressure vessels, such as sand filters, to explode. Water hammer caused by changing valve positions can be avoided by opening and closing valves slowly. Water hammer caused by check valve slamming can be avoided by reducing flow significantly before turning off pumps, and only opening valves slightly before turning pumps on, then proceeding to open the rest of it slowly. For pumps using a variable frequency drive, the ramp up and ramp down time can be increased. For swing type check valves, a weight can be attached to the shaft that the flapper is attached to (see Figure 8.8). The added weight slows down the flapper, lessening the hammer. When starting a system, make sure to vent air properly from sand filters.

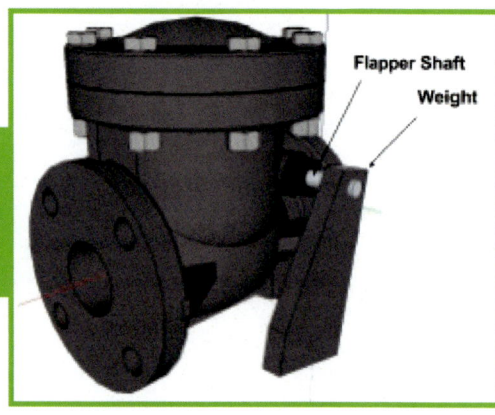

Figure 8.13 - Swing Type Check Valve with Weight

8.9 Valve Materials

Control valves can come in a variety of materials. These include but are not limited to metals such as copper or stainless steel but in aquarium/zoo settings most are plastic. It is important to choose the right material for the application. Metal valves are typically used in higher pressure or chemical applications such as drinking water or coolant loops. Plastic valves are typically found in most life support applications because of their reliability, ease of installation, strong corrosion resistance, and overall cost effectiveness.

Butterfly valves are found in both metal and plastic components. Wafers come in different forms of metal, some with protective coatings, and plastic. Most bodies are composed of PVC or cast iron. Some internal stem components are metal despite the wafer/disk being plastic. Be sure to monitor functionality and replace when parts become increasingly difficult to move. For more information please refer to Section 8.1 on butterfly valves.

Ball valves are typically composed of plastics or metals. Materials typically used include but are not limited to PVC, CPVC, polypropylene, copper, and stainless steel. Most small life support systems contain ball valves. Please refer to Section 8.2 on ball valves for further information on usage and how they function.

Check valves can be found in stainless steel as well as plastic. These are typically composed of all plastic, including the moving components. Some incorporate springs for reliability. These are typically composed of stainless steel in aquarium and zoo settings. It is possible for these to break down over time and lose functionality. For more information please refer to Section 8.5 on check valves.

8.10 Valve Placement

Valve placement is very critical when designing or building a life support system. In an ideal setting valves would be placed on the suction and discharge lines of all system pumps, bypasses of filtration systems, as well as inlets and outlets to exhibits. Placement is key to maintain the following goals: redundancy, exhibit isolation, equipment isolation, and redirection of water. Check valves should be placed on any line with the potential to back siphon. Most are located above main pumps to protect the impeller from spinning backwards. In some cases, check valves will be placed on the suction lines of pumps to prevent loss of prime.

9 Filtration

Filtration is an important component of maintaining water quality in exhibits. In this chapter, mechanical, chemical, and biological filtration are discussed.

9.1 Mechanical Filtration

Mechanical filtration is the process by which particulate matter is removed from the water. There are numerous ways this can be accomplished. Mechanical filters commonly used in LSS are sand filters, drum filters, bead filters, screens and sieves.

9.1.1 Sand Filters: Rapid Rate, High Pressure, Gravity Fed

For most operators, sand filters are the primary means of mechanical filtration for large scale exhibits. Sand filter manufacturers provide a wide range of sizing options, from homeowner (backyard swimming pool) models, to large commercial sized filters. Sand filters come in two configurations: vertical or horizontal. Each style has benefits and some drawbacks, depending on the application. Horizontal styles allow for a greater surface area (read filtering area) per vessel and in some cases can even be stacked to double the surface area per square foot of floor space needed. In the case of horizontal style, the filtering bed is very shallow compared to verticals which can be a drawback. Vertical style sand filters take up less floor space per filter but that corresponds to a smaller surface area of filtering capacity. These filters provide a deeper sand bed, which makes it harder for particulate matter to travel through the filter without being trapped by the sand.

**Figure 9.1
Vertical Sand Filter**

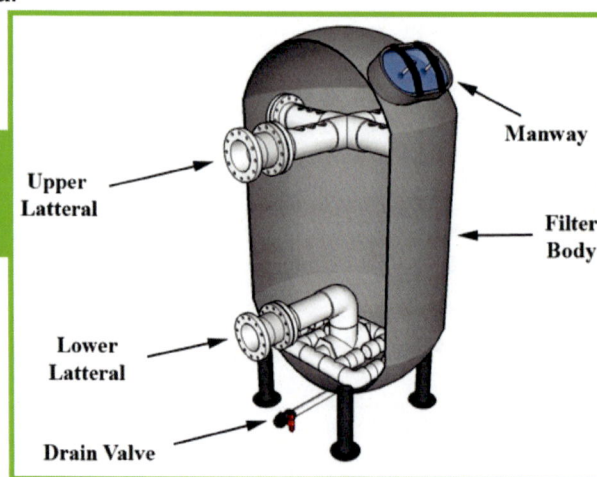

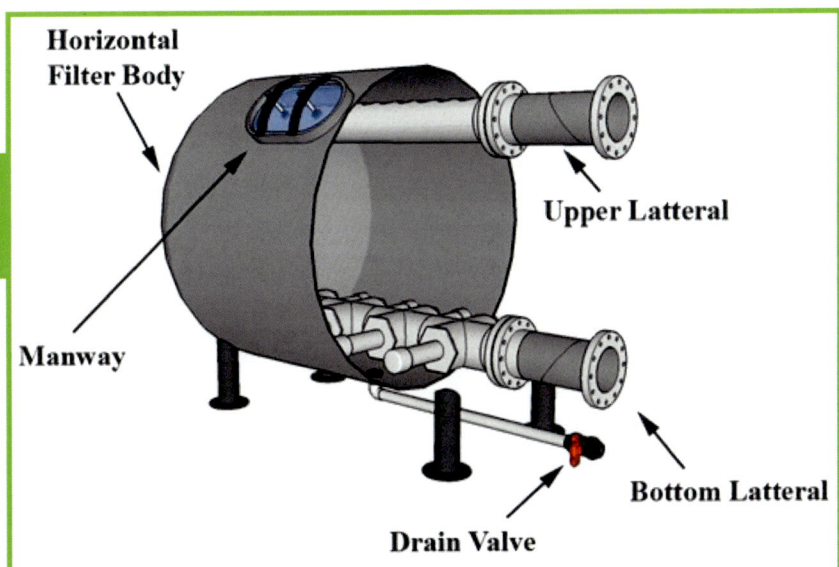

Horizontal
Filter Body

Upper Latteral

Manway

Bottom Latteral

Drain Valve

**Figure 9.2
Horizontal Sand Filter**

Sand Filter Operations

All sand filters operate in the same manner, despite small differences in piping layout and valve placement. During normal operation in filtering mode, dirty exhibit water is pumped into the top of the filter, and is distributed evenly throughout the filter through a series of diffusers or laterals. It is then filtered through the sand bed where the angularity of the jagged individual grains of sand trap particulates, and then exits the filter vessel through a series of laterals (underdrain) at the bottom of the filter. When the filter is cleaned, a process called backwashing, the flow of water is reversed through the filter. This can be accomplished by either switching a series of valves or changing the position of a multi-port valve. The water then enters the filter through the lower laterals, fluidizing the sand bed, effectively freeing the particulate debris to flow out of the filter through the upper laterals where it can be directed towards a sanitary system or a recovery system, depending on the facility setup. Backwash source water can be different depending on the system and facility needs. Many large systems will use filtered water from a shared header to provide the necessary water for the backwash. Some smaller systems will use untreated exhibit water pumped in with a valve alignment change to perform the backwash. This can cause problems over time, because particles can clog the lower laterals or allow dirty water to be captured in the lower portion of the sand bed. Some systems use non-potable cold water or municipal water, while other systems may use a combination of all of these, depending on seasonal availability (when heated or cooled exhibit water is at a premium), changes in bio-load conditions, or for when a large water change needs to be conducted.

Standard Operation of High Pressure Sand Filters

It is important to understand the nomenclature used in the operation of high pressure sand filters. The following lists important terms and concepts.

Filtering flow rate: The filtering flow rate is generally a function of the surface area of the filter and type of media installed. All manufacturers will provide a loading rate for their sand filters based upon the application. This will typically run anywhere from 9 gpm/ft² - 15 gpm/ft² (360 lpm/m² - 600 lpm/m²).

Backwash flow rate: Manufacturers will provide a recommended backwash flow rate for their sand filters based upon the application. This will typically run anywhere from 15 gpm/ft² - 20 gpm/ft² (600 lpm/m² - 800 lpm/m²) depending upon the density of the media installed, temperature, and salinity.

Backwash trigger points: There are a few metrics that can be used to determine when a filter needs to be backwashed. These can be set for when flow rate is less than 75% of nominal flow rate, influent pressure is more than 10 psi - 12 psi higher than effluent pressures or running time is greater than 168 hours (one week).

Pressure: All sand filter vessels will have a maximum pressure rating from the manufacturer; care must be taken not to exceed that rating (50 psi is fairly common) to avoid damaging the vessel.

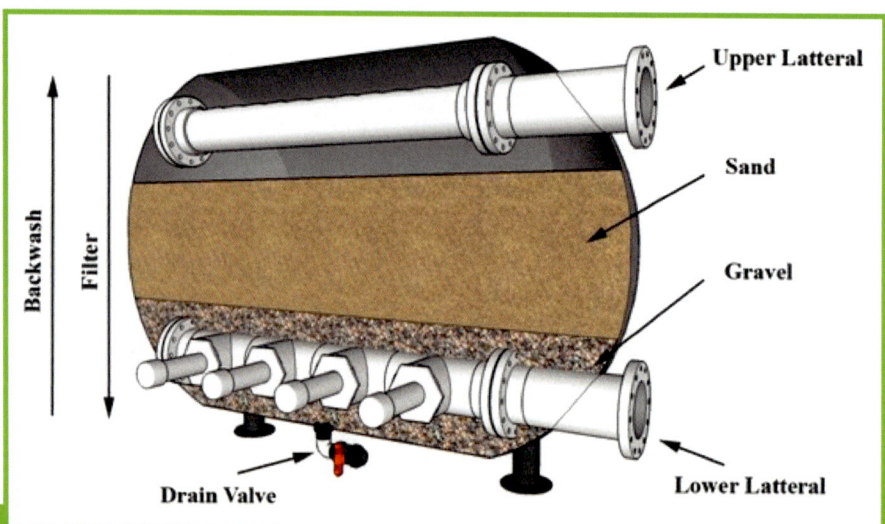

Figure 9.3 – Horizontal Sand Filter with Media

Sand grain sizes: Filter grade sand is pre-washed sand that is available specifically for filter applications. It can be composed of 0.35 - 0.45 mm, 0.45 - 0.55 mm, 0.55 - 0.65 mm, 0.65 - 0.75 mm, or 0.75 - 0.85 mm, depending on application and design specifications. The larger the grade of sand, the less particles it can filter out and debris can make its way deeper into the sand bed.

Gravel: It is standard practice to place a bed of gravel on the bottom of a sand filter to cover the lower laterals, providing a good foundation to place sand. This allows for separation between the sand and laterals and prevents the sand from completely caking over the laterals. The gravel also supports the laterals and prevents them from cracking under the weight of the sand. In some cases, seen most often with vertical filters, a decreasing gradient of gravel sizes will be used with just a small layer of sand on top. The most common gravel sizes used in filter media applications are ⅛ in × ¼ in and ¼ in× ½ in gravel (3 mm × 6 mm and 6 mm × 12 mm).

Glass filter media: Recycled crushed glass filter media is an alternative to silica sand in some applications such as gravity fed sand filters and marine mammal pools. The media is made out of recycled glass from the window and door manufacturing industry. Compared to silica sand media, glass media provides filtration ability with the same or less restrictive pressure and generally more consistent flow rates per square foot of filter surface area. Glass media also requires less backwash flow and pressure because it is 20% lighter per cubic foot than silica sand. A distinct advantage of glass media is that it has much less surface porosity than silica sand and, therefore, does not hold unwanted particles such as bacteria or other organics. This reduces clumping and channeling, making glass particularly suited for mammal systems. The downside to glass media in mixed taxa systems is that glass media does not provide much, if any, surface area for nitrifying bacteria to take residence.

Standard Operation of Gravity Fed Sand Filters

Gravity fed sand filters operate very similarly to high pressure sand filters. Untreated water is pumped on top of the sand filter media and is then allowed to slowly trickle through the sand and out the laterals on the bottom. The main difference between these is that gravity fed sand filters are open on top and simply allow gravity to pull the water through the media instead of using pumps to push water through the sand bed.

Potential Problems Associated with Sand Filters

Channeling: Channeling occurs when a broken lateral or sand clumping creates a hole through the filter media bed to the laterals, effectively allowing water to bypass the sand and return to the exhibit unfiltered. Jetting the sand bed can occasionally fix the problem if the sand is clumping. In the case of a broken lateral, the sand and gravel will need to be removed and the lateral replaced.

Sand clumping: Sand clumping can be a major problem with sand filters, because it will cause higher pressures, lower flow rates, and will lessen the effectiveness of the filtration process. Clumping can be caused by improper backwash flow rates (too low), improper backwash durations (not allowing all of the particulate matter to leave the sand bed), improper backwash frequencies (too long between backwashes) or as a result from dosing with flocculants. Clumping can also be a symptom of undersized filtration.

Broken laterals: Broken laterals will create a channel in the sand bed that will allow gravel and sand to be blown into the piping and back into the exhibit. The sand may clog venturis and heat exchangers, resulting in the need for them to be serviced and cleaned. Broken laterals require removal of the sand and gravel and replacement of the broken lateral.

Clogged laterals: Clogged laterals can cause higher than normal pressures, lower flow rates and problematic backwashes. Occasionally, an increase in flow can free the debris from the laterals, but it is often necessary to remove the sand/gravel and physically clean the laterals and reinstall.

Excessive backwash flow rates: Excessive backwash flow rates will fluidize the sand bed too high and flush out the sand with the effluent of the backwash, reducing the sand bed.

Flocculant use: When flocculants such as lanthanum chloride, aluminum sulfate (alum), ferrous sulfate, or ferric chloride-sulfate are frequently used in a system, proper filter maintenance must be performed or it will cause problems in the sand filter. The flocculants will start binding the sand together and clumping up the sand.

Annual inspections: Sand filters should be opened up yearly and the sand bed inspected for problems. Ensure that the sand bed depth is correct, that there is no channeling, that the sand isn't clumping, and that the sand is generally in good condition. If these conditions are observed, inspection frequencies should be adjusted, especially if it is a problematic system, such as, a high bio-load system. The sand is properly inspected by digging down several inches and taking a sample. The sample can then be placed under a dissecting microscope and inspected. The edges of the sand round out over time, decreasing particle entrapment. When this happens the media will need to be replaced.

Safety: When inspecting sand filters, follow the facility's lockout/tagout policy to isolate the sand filter from the system. If there is a need to go inside the vessel, it should be considered a confined space and the operator must follow the facility's policies for entering confined spaces.

Remediating sand filters: Sand filter media will not last forever and eventually needs to be replaced. In normal operations, this should be every 7 to 10 years. Ensure that the sand filter is isolated from the system and all lockout/tagout policies have been followed. Care must be taken not to damage the laterals when removing the sand and gravel. Remove and clean the laterals while the filter is empty. If the sand filter is small or a horizontal style filter, fill the vessel below the laterals with gravel or sand, depending on the application, and reinstall the laterals. If the sand filter is a vertical type, water can be added to help distribute the weight of the gravel and sand. Finish covering the laterals with the gravel or sand. Follow all safety guidelines in regards to entering the vessel and inhalation of the sand dust.

9.1.2 Rotating Drum Filter

The use of rotating drum filters (RDFs) is becoming increasingly prevalent in life support systems due to the desirability of more efficient alternatives to sand filters. RDFs are mechanical, self-cleaning filters that use gravity for water flow across the filtration screen. Unlike pressurized filters, such as high rate sand filters, water does not need to be pushed through the media. Significant reduction of pumping head requirements is the result of this design, reducing energy costs. Particulates and solids are caught on the inside of the screen and removed. The untreated water flows by gravity into the filter panels from the center drum. Solids are separated from the water by a microscreen cloth fitted on the two sides of the filter panels while the clean water passes through the cloth to the outside of the drum.

RDFs are self-cleaning, which can save cartridge replacement costs and backwashing labor costs associated with manually operated systems. RDFs require a relatively insignificant amount of water for self-cleaning. This water can be from an outside source (domestic freshwater), or from the process stream. In aquarium applications, valuable salt water is not needed for filter cleaning which can result in large cost savings.

Rotating drum filters have a higher initial investment cost compared to other mechanical filtration options, such as sand filters. RDFs may be difficult to replace sand filters retroactively, due to their requirement for gravity draining. RDFs are best suited where original design allows for placement of the RDF at an elevation higher than the desired effluent.

Figure 9.4 - Rotating Drum Filter

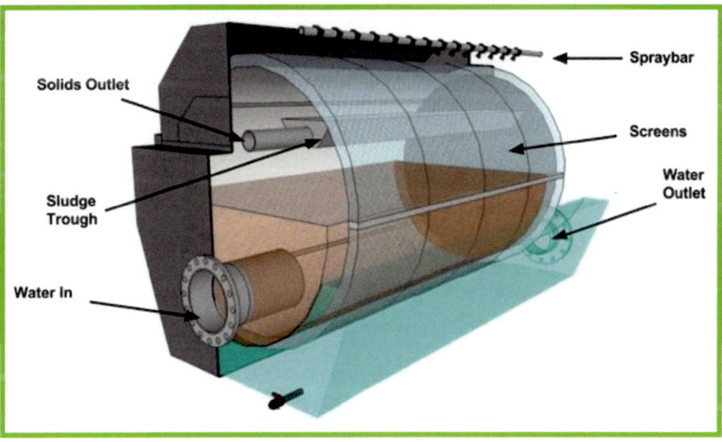

9.1.3 Bead Filters

Bead filters are a relatively new type of mechanical filtration for zoo and aquarium life support systems. The vessels are similar to sand filters but use small polyethylene beads instead of sand. These filters operate differently than sand filters: water flows from the bottom up inside the vessel where the floating beads catch the particulate matter. When backwashing, a propeller or air injected into the filter disturbs the beads and cause debris to fall off and settle on the bottom of the filter, where it is either passively or actively drained out. The beads provide a good surface for nitrifying bacteria to colonize. Bead filters use a smaller amount of water to backwash than sand filters.

9.1.4 Sieve and Screen Filters

Sieve and screen filters do not operate on the same principle as other mechanical filters. For a sieve or screen filter, water is pushed through small pores in the filter while other matter is left behind. Screen filters can be made from paper, threads of cotton/nylon/polyester, or even stainless steel mesh. Screen filters are more commonly used where the volume of water to be filtered is relatively low. Too much pressure through a sieve or screen can force algae and other particles too far into the screen, making it difficult to clean. Screens can be made to filter out particles even smaller than 1 micron, which makes them more effective than most media filters, but a nuisance to maintain or replace in large scale operations.

9.2 Biological Filtration

Providing bio-filters for nitrification and denitrification is a major part of any life support system design and plays a critical role in supporting the nitrogen cycle.

9.2.1 Nitrification and Bio-filters

Bio-filters are designed to operate at low pressure and contain large amounts of surface area to allow nitrifying bacteria to colonize and thrive. These types of filters promote the nitrogen cycle (see Section 5.1 for more information). Trickle towers, submerged media, fluidized bed, bio-reactors, pressure sand filters, and static bed filters are typically used as bio-filters. Examples of the types of media used in these filters can be seen in Figure 9.4. The media provides a suitable surface for the bacteria to be exposed to the nutrients and oxygen within the flow stream. Bio-filters are best placed after the primary mechanical filtration stage to minimize fouling of the media. The level of nutrients, dissolved oxygen, and suspended solids will determine the best style of filter to be used and its location within the filter stream. Sufficient dissolved oxygen within the biofilter is required to maintain populations of nitrifying bacteria. Bio-filters that are either open top or are in clear vessels should be kept dark to allow the bacteria to grow and minimize growth of algae.

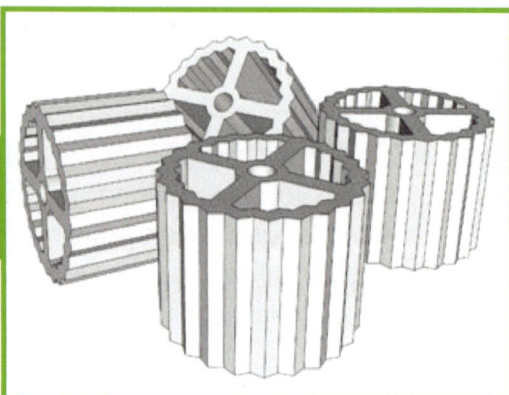

Figure 9.5 – Bio-media

9.2.2 Denitrification

Biological filtration helps to remove toxic ammonia and nitrites from the water; however, the buildup of nitrate over time in a system, may cause animal health concerns. In closed systems, nitrogen (as nitrate) will accumulate and eventually reach hazardous levels, requiring other processes to denitrify the water.

Water exchanges may be used to remove unwanted nitrogen (and other accumulated materials) from a system. In systems that send filter backwash water to sanitary sewer and then refill with new makeup water, this process will often be enough to keep the nitrogen levels within acceptable ranges. Closed loop systems with infrequent water exchanges will need an additional process to remove the unwanted nitrogen from the water.

A practical solution is a side-stream denitrification system on the LSS system. Generally, the flow through these side streams needs to only be less than 1% of the total flow of the system. There are many different kinds of denitrification systems in use within the aquarium industry.

One method of denitrification is a methanol-based heterotrophic bacteria denitrification system (see Section 5.1.5). Methanol is an organic electron donor. In this method, dissolved oxygen levels must be kept very low (preferably less than 1 mg/L) to create the necessary hypoxic conditions.

In the denitrification process, nitrogen is removed from the water as nitrogen gas (N_2). Once the nitrogen level in the side-stream batch of water reaches less than 1 mg/L, it is returned back into the system. The water is then filtered or sent through foam fractionators until the turbidity is lowered and finally disinfected before being sent back into the main system, because the organic byproduct of this process increases the turbidity of the water.

This batch treatment method of denitrification requires a large basin or sump that can be dedicated to the process, and also requires a steady dose of methanol. When the system is shut down, biological activity is reduced and may take a long time to recover upon startup. When using a methanol-based denitrification system, be careful to avoid the introduction of methanol into the main exhibit.

In a sulfur-based denitrification system, a reactor filled with sulfur flakes allows bacteria such as *Thiobacillus denitrificans* and *Thiomicrospira denitrificans* (Lampe and Zhang, n.d.) to reduce ammonia to nitrogen gas (N_2) (see Section 5.1.5). A second reactor is used as a carbon source, often filled with crushed scallop shells. The scallop, oyster, and clam shells also help buffer the water after the process, which lowers pH levels and consumes alkalinity. The buffering material can also be mixed in the sulfur bed rather than in a separate vessel. The sulfur reactor is rebedded every three to six months, or as needed.

A sulfur denitrification system also tends to suppress the ORP of an aquarium. If ozone is used in the system, ozone generators will increase their output to maintain the same oxidation reduction potential when a sulfur-based denitrification system is brought online.

9.2.3 Exhibit Seeding

The development of well-established biological filtration is essential to maintain appropriate water quality parameters in recirculating aquatic exhibits. The process in which ammonia is converted to nitrite and nitrite is converted to nitrate is known as nitrification. Nitrification is carried out by a multitude of bacterial species commonly referred to as ammonia oxidizing bacteria (AOB) and nitrite oxidizing bacteria (NOB). These bacteria are ubiquitous in nature and will establish a sustainable population provided the appropriate water quality parameters and food source (nitrogen). Seeding is the addition of a nitrogen source to enhance propagation of AOB and NOB bacteria for biological filtration purposes. Three methods typically employed to add the nitrogen source used to start a new aquarium include live fish, tolerant to low levels of ammonia and nitrite; addition of substrate from cycled aquaria, either from another fish tank or from a biofarm; and chemical sources of nitrogen. This section will describe these methods and offer guidance for establishing a new aquarium.

Cycling by Live Animals

A new aquarium can be started by the introduction of a small number of aquatic species which are known to tolerate the temporary increases in ammonia and then nitrite. This method requires careful monitoring of water quality parameters to confirm the expected rise and fall in ammonia, followed by the rise and fall of nitrite, and subsequent rise in nitrate. Should the ammonia or nitrite increase above the tolerance level of the animals, or the alkalinity drops, quick corrective actions are needed to restore the water quality parameters to ensure the safety of the species involved. Animal feeding rates should be closely controlled and monitored as not to overfeed, because uneaten food will contribute to nitrogenous wastes in the system and overload an underdeveloped biological filter quickly.

Cycling by Bacteria in Substrate/Live Cultures

Another method involves the addition of pre-seeded biological media taken from another aquarium which has well-established biological activity. While this method may be effective, it is important to stress that cross-contamination precautions should be taken if the pre-seeded media is collected from an already established system housing healthy livestock. Alternatively, developing a biofarm for this specific purpose will eliminate the risk associated with collecting and using media from already established systems. Setting up and maintaining a biofarm can be achieved by placing biomedia in a container with an aeration source and routinely adding urea or ammonium chloride to feed the bacteria. Some facilities set up small recirculating systems that allow for the temporary installation of sand filters, fluidized beds, bioreactors and other life support system components that are allowed to colonize with bacteria before being removed and permanently installed on an exhibit. Additionally, additive bacterial starter cultures for marine and freshwater systems can be purchased specifically for this purpose (Jones, 2014); however, LSS disinfection systems (UV, ozone, and fractionation) should be taken offline prior to their addition to allow efficient colonization in the LSS.

Cycling by Chemical Additions

The addition of ammonium chloride or urea in carefully calculated doses is another method commonly used to develop strong populations of AOB species. The frequency and amount of chemical addition can be calculated by taking into account the system's daily input of protein originating from the animal's diets. Uneaten food or waste excreted by the animals contributes to nitrogenous waste, which is broken down or decays into ammonia. The conditioning of water within ranges of the desired livestock and nitrifying bacteria can significantly reduce cycling time to support overall health of the systems and inhabitants. Proliferation of AOB and NOB may be improved by several methods: adding small continuous dosing of ammonium chloride or urea over a twenty-four-hour period in lieu of one-time daily doses of these additives, reduction of salinity in marine systems to ranges between 22-26 ppt, and increasing temperatures of systems up to 30°C temporarily (Hovanec, 2015).

Nitrification occurs at various locations within a life support system and exhibit, such as biofilms in plumbing, biotowers, undergravel etc.; however, the majority occurs within mechanical filters, such as high rate sand filters. These filters provide excellent water flow and surface area for the bacteria to colonize on. If mechanical filters need to be reloaded with new media, it is usually good practice to save some of the top layer of media to reload into the filter containing the new media to speed up biofilter establishment.

Like most living organisms, AOB and NOB species can survive in many conditions; however, parameters such as pH, temperature, salinity, and alkalinity can be manipulated to provide conditions in which these species will thrive (DeLong & Losordo, 2012). AOB species are also salinity specific; therefore, when using already established media it must be adapted to the desired salinity. For example, do not seed a new marine exhibit with media from a freshwater exhibit. Figure 9.5 compares some important differences between Marine AOB and NOB species (Hovanec, 2015).

Marine AOB Species	Marine NOB Species
Growth inhibited at NH_3-N > 5 mg/L	Growth inhibited at NO_2-N > 5mg/L
Intolerant of nitrite (above 5 mg/L NO_2-N)	Tolerant of low Oxygen environments
Doubling time ~30+ hours	Doubling time ~40+ hours

Figure 9.6 – Comparison of Marine Ammonia Oxidizing Bacteria (AOB) and Nitrite Oxidizing Bacteria (NOB)

Troubleshooting

Occasionally issues may arise in the development of appropriate AOB and NOB colonies for biological filtration. In addition to the previously mentioned parameters, water flow, total surface area, biological load, dissolved oxygen levels, and LSS design can all contribute to less than ideal results (Hovanec & Jones, 2015). Nitrifying bacteria are a living component of the life support system; therefore, when trying to establish a biofilter, water quality testing should begin immediately. Dissolved oxygen and alkalinity are consumed in the nitrification steps and need to be maintained. Nitrification is also an acidic process, due to carbon dioxide production, which can lower the pH drastically if system alkalinity is not maintained at appropriate levels. The wellbeing of the biofilter should always be considered before making any changes to the operation of the life support system. The addition of pharmaceuticals or other additives could potentially compromise the integrity of the biofilter.

9.3 Chemical Filtration

Chemical filtration plays an integral role in aquarium systems and is carried out by means of absorption, adsorption, and ion exchange. These processes are used to treat make-up water before it goes into an aquarium system, and as part of an aquarium system's filtration scheme.

9.3.1 Ion Exchange

Ion exchange systems can be used for efficient removal of unwanted dissolved ions from water by exchanging one ion for another. An understanding of how different ions affect aquarium water quality is vital to ensure that ionic imbalances do not occur. All water has dissociated salts that form charged ions, unless these ions are removed. Positively charged ions are called cations and negatively charged ions are called anions. The most common cations in aquariums are sodium, calcium, and magnesium, and the most common anions include carbonate, bicarbonate, borate, sulfate, chlorate, potassium, chloride, and silica (DeSilva, 1999).

An ion exchange system replaces undesirable ions in the water supply with more acceptable ions. A sodium zeolite water softener is the most widely applied use of ion exchange. It reduces the hardness of the water by replacing calcium, magnesium, and even iron, with sodium ions.

$$\begin{bmatrix} Ca \\ Mg \end{bmatrix} \cdot \begin{bmatrix} SO_4 \\ 2Cl \\ 2HCO_3 \end{bmatrix} + Na_2 \cdot Z \rightarrow Z \cdot \begin{bmatrix} Ca \\ Mg \end{bmatrix} + \begin{bmatrix} Na_2SO_4 \\ 2NaCl \\ 2NaHCO_3 \end{bmatrix}$$

Figure 9.7 - Calcium and Magnesium Ion Exchange with Sodium

Potassium ions can be substituted for sodium ions. It may be beneficial to use potassium chloride salt instead of sodium chloride salt in scenarios where excess sodium ions could be harmful to aquarium inhabitants.

An ion exchange filter can treat the hardness of the water, and when combined with an activated carbon filter, the additional removal of sediments, fluorine, chlorine, bromine, copper and other potentially harmful ions can be made possible. This combination will prepare water from most municipal water supplies for use in aquarium systems or in preparation of saltwater makeup. Alternative treatments may be required for other types of water sources.

Complete ion exchange can also be achieved by replacing all cations and anions with H^+ and OH^- ions. This process, called deionization, is useful for treating water that will be used to mix saltwater or to lower salinity of a system suffering from evaporation loss. It is often combined with a reverse osmosis filtering process to produce reverse osmosis filtered deionized water (RODI). RODI water is too pure to be used directly for freshwater aquariums.

The media used for ion exchange varies greatly and is dependent upon the ions targeted for removal. Typically, chemically active synthetic resins in the form of small (1 mm) beads are used. There are four main categories of resins used for ion exchange. Their properties can be found on the table in Figure 9.8.

Category	Uses	Make Up	Regeneration
Strong Acid Cation (SAC)	Softening and full demineralization	Sulfonic acid groups	Hydrochloric acid
Strong Base Anion (SBA)	Softening and full demineralization	Quaternary ammonium functional groups	Sodium hydroxide
Weak Acid Cation (WAC)	Dealkalization and partial demineralization.	Carboxylic groups	Hydrochloric acid
Weak Base Anion (WBA)	Dealkalization and partial demineralization	Primary, secondary, or tertiary amine groups	Sodium hydroxide

Figure 9.8 - Ion Exchange Resin Categories

The regeneration solution of ion exchange resins can give clues as to which category it fits in. Always follow the manufacturer's recommendations for resin regeneration.

Ion exchange resins are primarily used in the treatment of water before it goes into the aquarium; however, some resins are specifically designed to be used as part of the aquariums filtration. Ion exchange resins are typically employed for freshwater use, but there are some that work in both fresh and saltwater. Follow the manufacturer's recommended application.

Ion exchange uses the charge of ionized molecule to bond the molecule to an oppositely charged surface. The charged surface usually exchanges an ion, such as Na^+, in the process. Chemically active synthetic material (1 mm beads) is used as a cation (+) or anion (-) resin. These resins have a wider application in freshwater situations and are limited in saltwater applications, for example, deionization in freshwater pretreatment processes.

9.3.2 Absorbtion

Absorption is the taking up of molecules by a volume of another substance, often involving a molecular sieving or a removal of molecules on a basis of size. There are some specialized resins that use absorption to remove impurities. Refer to Section 5.9 for more information.

9.3.3 Adsorbtion

Adsorption is when molecules become physically attached to a surface. Polar molecules (with hydrophilic and hydrophobic ends) attach to either solid surfaces or at water and gas interface (bubbles). Some bonds are stronger or even permanent, while other bonds are weak and can be disrupted or reversed (via pH or temperature changes) causing desorption. Granulated activated carbons and protein skimmers are two examples.

Granulated activated carbon is the most common and cost effective chemical filter. It removes heavy metals, some medications, organic compounds, chlorine, ozone, and color. It comes in many different grades and forms for different purposes.

9.3.4 Protein Skimmers

Protein skimmers, also called foam fractionators, are common LSS components for saltwater aquaria. The design consists of a vessel of water that is injected with gas, most commonly air, with the goal of producing a large air-water interface. The air enters the vessel and produces bubbles. Surfactants such as proteins, amino acids, nitrogenous compounds, detritus, and a variety of other substances are attracted to the surface of the bubbles due to their non-polar nature. The surfactants may be hydrophobic or amphiphilic (containing both hydrophilic (polar) and hydrophobic (nonpolar) portions). The air bubbles, with the organic compounds attached, make their way to the surface of the vessel, which is fitted with a reduced cylindrical or conical lid, and are forced out the top of the lid in the form of foam. The foam moves at a higher velocity, where it overflows into a collection vessel and discharges to waste. Removing these substances is beneficial to water quality because it relieves some of the nitrogen load that would normally be handled by the biological filtration and other system components. Foam fractionation is typically used in a flow through configuration in aquaria, although batch methods may also be used in some aquaculture settings (Lekang, 2013).

There are several variables that affect the efficiency of protein skimmers. These include contact time, bubble size, air to water ratio, flow characteristics inside the reaction chamber, and reaction chamber height and diameter.

Contact Time/Dwell Time

Contact time, or dwell time, through a given reaction chamber can be calculated by dividing the volume of the reaction chamber by the flow rate through the chamber, as seen below:

$$\textbf{Contact Time (minutes)} = \left(\frac{\textbf{Chamber Volume (gallons)}}{\textbf{Flow Rate (GPM)}} \right)$$

A typical flow-through protein skimmer has a contact time of 1.5 - 2.0 minutes (Lekang, 2013). Increased contact time allows for more material to attach itself to the surface of the bubbles. Increasing the contact time will also give the surfactants in the water more opportunities to come into contact with bubble surfaces. Decreasing the contact time may not allow for bubbles to collect enough material to form a stable enough surface, and it may not allow time for material to be effectively removed from the water before it exits the reaction chamber. Longer contact times promote the increase in the amount of material removed from the water.

Air Dwell Time

The ratio of dwell time between the air and water is commonly referred to as bombardment rate. The suggested value of this ratio is 10, meaning that the water dwell time is 10 times longer than the air dwell time (Escobal, 2000). Dwell time calculations for the air in the reaction chamber involve several forces that must be considered. The gravitational and drag forces act on the bubble, pulling the bubble down in the water column. The upward force of the bubble comes from the buoyancy of the bubble. As long as the upward force is greater than the downward force, the bubble will rise in the water column. Bubble size affects each of these forces, making it another important factor in fractionator efficiency.

Bubble Size

Protein skimmers rely on surface area to collect organic material; therefore, bubble size has an impact on efficiency. Small bubbles will have a higher surface area to volume ratio than larger bubbles. The recommended bubble size for foam fractionation is 0.5 - 0.8 mm (Reclos, 2004). Larger bubbles have more buoyant force, and will rise faster in the water column, causing turbulence and reducing contact time with the surfactants in the water. Smaller bubbles have less buoyant force, and may not rise in the water column, possibly leading to bubbles being carried out of the reaction chamber by the flow of water. The density of the water affects bubble size and stability; experiments using foam fractionation in freshwater have shown poor or no removal of surfactants (Lekang, 2013).

Air to Water Ratio

In addition to bubble size, the ratio between the volumes of air to water is also important. In an ideally designed fractionator, the amount of material removed from the water is independent of water flow. Instead, the removal capabilities depend on the amount of airflow present (Weeks, 1992). The recommended ratio of air to water is 13% (Fossa and Nilson, 1996), with the highest productive ratio of 16% (Escobal, 2000). The rule of thumb of 90 cm^2 cross-sectional area per kg of feed added to the system, 20 L/min of air is recommended (Timmons, 2013). This ratio affects the superficial velocity of air inside the reaction chamber, which can be calculated by dividing the gas flow by the cross section of the reaction chamber (Lekang, 2013).
A typical superficial velocity ranges from 0.001 - 0.038 m^2 (Lekang, 2013). Low superficial velocity will not achieve optimal removal, since the surface of the bubbles may become saturated with material before reaching the top of the reaction chamber. A higher superficial velocity will produce a wet foam and turbulence in the reaction chamber (Lekang, 2013).

Flow Characteristics

Protein skimmers can be designed to use co-current flow, counter-current flow, or a hybrid of the two. Co-current flow protein skimmers inject air and water at the bottom of the reaction chamber; the water and air mixture exits at the top of the reaction chamber. Since the bubbles rise with the water, the bubbles only interact with the water immediately surrounding it as it rises. Counter-current flow protein skimmers inject air at the bottom of the reaction chamber and water at the top of the reaction chamber. The bubbles interact with new water coming into the reaction chamber as they rise through the water column. The water exits at the bottom of the reaction chamber. Hybrid skimmers inject water and air at the bottom of the reaction chamber. After the water rises in the chamber with the bubbles in a co-current fashion, it changes directions and returns to the bottom of the chamber in a counter-current fashion. In both counter-current and hybrid protein skimmers, as long as the downward rate of the water does not exceed the raise rate of the bubbles, the water will leave the reaction chamber free of bubbles. In a properly functioning protein skimmer, the upper ⅔ of the reaction chamber will contain all the air bubbles, while the bottom ⅓ will contain no bubbles (Escobal, 2000).

Reaction Chamber Size

The height and width of the reaction chamber both play important roles in determining the effectiveness of a protein skimmer. Increasing the height of the reaction chamber will have no effect on the superficial velocity of a protein skimmer, it will only increase the contact time; however, increasing the diameter of the reaction chamber will decrease the superficial velocity. This means that a reaction chamber with a larger diameter will be able to process a higher flow rate than if the height of the reaction chamber were to be increased. In general, it is recommended that a cross-sectional area of 90 cm^2 per kg of food is used as a starting point for sizing a protein skimmer (Timmons, 2013). Multiple reaction chambers can be used to meet the cross-sectional area recommendation with similar effectiveness. The height of the reaction chamber is then used to control the contact time within the chamber. A height to diameter ratio of 3:1 - 10:1 is typical (Deckwer, 1992).

Sizing

The theoretical productivity of an individual foam fractionator is nearly impossible to calculate (Timmons, 2013); however, there are some general guidelines that can be followed when sizing a fractionator. Sizing foam fractionators based on a desired turnover rate and contact time as well as including at least one turnover (99.99%) of the system per day is recommended (Escobal, 2000). Sizing an exhibit with more fractionation capacity than required will result in times during which foam production will decrease or stop, which may be desirable. This may happen when the water does not contain enough surfactants to create stable foam.

Other Design Considerations

Due to the nature of protein skimmers, there are several considerations that need to be made when adding them to a system. Protein skimmers operate at ambient pressure, meaning that they need to be placed higher than their discharge destination. Fractionators are typically discharged into a sump or degas tower to allow dissipation of microbubbles, although some facilities discharge them directly into the exhibit. Frictional losses on the effluent line should be kept as minimal as possible to allow for the greatest range of adjustment from the effluent valve.

Protein skimmers operate most efficiently with a steady water level in their reaction chamber. Care should be taken to ensure that they receive a consistent flow rate. Systems using a venturi for air injection should monitor air flow and be controlled by a rotameter. Both the venturi and rotameter benefit from regular cleaning. This can be done by removing them from the skimmer and rinsing with freshwater, or freshwater can be sucked through the rotameter where it will break up any salt deposits that form at the throat of the venturi, with the system running.

Systems using ozone injection into the protein skimmer should have the top of the collection cup vent to an ozone destruction unit. Ozone destruction units that use a vacuum pump should include a vent at the top of the collection cup to allow ambient air to be pulled in. Without this, the water level in the reaction chamber can be affected and the collection cup can collapse from the buildup of negative pressure.

A smooth and clean riser cone is required for best efficiency. Many commercial protein skimmers can be equipped with an automated washdown system. This system typically uses system water to rinse the inside of the riser cone and freshwater to rinse the outside of the riser cone and the inside of the collection cup. The collection cups are typically plumbed to a drain or a collection vessel. Small models may have an easily removable collection cup that can be separated from the body and cleaned.

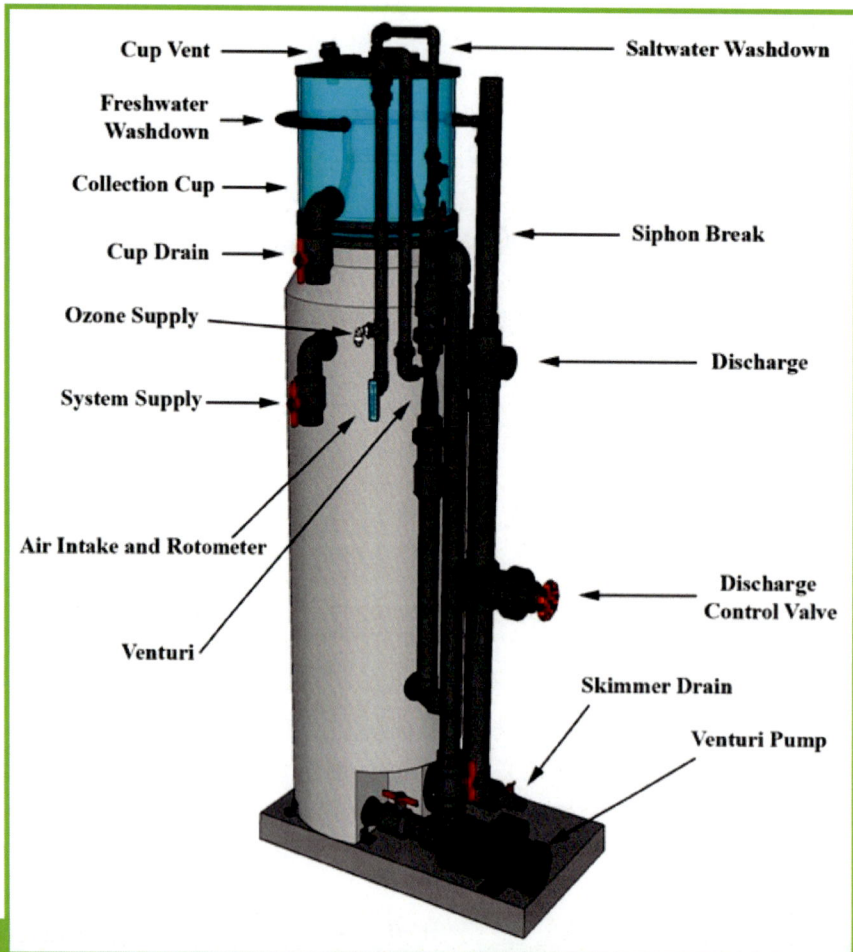

Figure 9.9 Protein Skimmer

9.3.5 Phosphate Reduction

There are a number of methods used to reduce phosphates in an exhibit; one method for phosphate reduction is dosing with lanthanum chloride ($LaCl_3$). This section will cover lanthanum chloride dosing protocols; for more information on lanthanum chloride, please see Section 6.7.

Dosing lanthanum into the discharge of a pump supplying a dedicated, sacrificial sand filter(s) is one way to control the reaction location and the by-products created during this process. Lanthanum chloride will be less likely to leach through the sand bed and into the system and exhibit if filter flow rates are reduced to 6 gpm/ft^2 – 8 gpm/ft^2 (14.4 m^3/hr/m^2 - 19.2 m^3/hr/m^2). This helps prevent a lanthanum phosphate precipitate from causing a white out of the exhibit as well as preventing it from adhering to the acrylic windows (lanthanum chloride adheres to plastics extremely well). A turnover rate of even once a week can have a positive effect on phosphate levels.

The preferred method of dosing lanthanum chloride into a system is in small amounts using a reliable metering pump. This allows specific dosing levels to be set, and the amount of lanthanum chloride dosed to be known. It is easy to overdose lanthanum chloride because small amounts can go a long way. When dosing into the effluent of a sand filter, do not overdose the lanthanum chloride. Leave a slight residual of around 0.10 mg/L phosphate so that all of the lanthanum chloride reacts in the sand filter and the excess cannot be pushed through into the exhibit and cause flocculation onto exhibit or on the gills and skin of some fishes. It is necessary to fine-tune the dose in order to achieve a downward trend of phosphate levels in the exhibit.

Location of the dosing point is critical. Do not dose or inject before a pump; this includes dosing into skimmer boxes. Lanthanum chloride can adhere to the pump impeller causing problems such as diminished flow rates, unevenness to the weight of the impeller (which will cause problems to bearings and potentially the shaft) and can clog up flushing ports on mechanical seals. Lanthanum chloride dosing should be avoided in protein skimmers because precipitates will adhere to the acrylic and plastic components, causing reduced efficiency.

Best practices for managing lanthanum chloride dosing must include safety considerations. The pH of lanthanum chloride solution is around 5, making this a caustic substance that should be treated with care. PPE such as chemical resistant gloves, chemical smock, and sealed eye protection must be worn when working with this chemical. Ensure that staff knows the location and are within an appropriate distance from an eyewash station and safety shower before working with this chemical; follow local laws and regulations. Wash any skin where lanthanum chloride has splashed with soap and water. Have spill prevention in place at the dosing site to contain accidents.

10 Disinfection and Sterilization

The disinfection (reduction of harmful pathogens) and sterilization (the elimination of all organisms) of exhibit water is an important process in any zoo and aquarium. It reduces harmful pathogens that could negatively impact animal health and also facilitates the breakdown of complex organic compounds, consequently "polishing" the water. Ozone has wide-spread use in water treatment applications, especially in the zoo and aquarium field due to its ability for use in the efficient disinfection of aquatic animal exhibits. UV sterilization is also widely used as a method to reduce pathogens and kill free-floating algae. Chlorine can be used as a method to control harmful bacteria in mammal pools as well as a way to sterilize water.

10.1 Ozone

Ozone is a molecule consisting of three oxygen atoms bonded together (O_3). It is widely used in the LSS field as a means of reducing pathogens in exhibit water. In addition, ozone is an excellent clarifying agent useful in reducing exhibit turbidity. In low doses, ozone can also be used as a micro-flocculant in protein skimmers.

Ozone is a chemical oxidizer similar to chlorine and bromine but much more unstable. This natural instability allows ozone to be effectively sequestered in treatment vessels and removed from the process flow as long as proper degas is installed prior to the water being introduced into the exhibit. This distinguishes ozone as one of the only chemical oxidizers that can safely be used on a life support system housing fish or invertebrates.

10.1.1 The Chemistry of Ozone

At standard temperature and pressure, ozone is a gas that consists of three oxygen atoms bonded together. It is a very unstable molecule, which helps contribute to its powerful oxidant properties. Ozone reacts with unsaturated carbon bonds, causing complex organic molecules to break apart into smaller molecules. These complex organic molecules are compounds which contribute to odor and discoloration of water; therefore, the application of ozone will break these compounds down resulting in a decrease in turbidity of the exhibit (increase in water clarity). Ozone also will facilitate the rupturing of microorganisms' cell walls; inactivating pathogens and viruses. Ozone could potentially disrupt nitrifying bacteria and other advantageous microorganisms in the exhibit, which is important to keep in mind when designing and operating an ozone system. After the reaction, ozone is reduced to molecular oxygen (O_2), which contributes to maintaining the dissolved oxygen concentration in the exhibit.

Ozone is a very efficient method of water disinfection; however, it needs to be controlled and operated by a properly trained and experienced technician, as there is great potential for over or under dosing situations. The production of ozone and disinfection of water is most often controlled by ORP measurements (see Section 10.1.4). While this is not a direct ozone concentration measurement, ORP measurements allow aquariums to measure the sum of oxidizing and reducing species in an exhibit. The presence of excess oxidants, called total residual oxidants (TRO) can be generally quantified with a DPD test (N,N-diethyl-p-phenylenediamine); however, it should be noted that this test cannot differentiate between the specific oxidants present (some examples are, but not limited to: ozone, hypobromous acid (HOBr), and hypochlorous acid (HOCl)). Monitoring ORP and testing TRO is very important in a marine aquarium as ozone will oxidize the bromide anion (Br^-) found in salt water to hypobromite ion (OBr^-), which is an active halogenated oxidant, and is very dangerous to marine life even in small concentrations. The bromide anion is fairly abundant in natural salt water at about 65 mg/L (Spotte, 1992); therefore, when ozonating salt water, the production of hypobromous acid is unavoidable and should be closely monitored. Over-ozonation of salt water could possibly lead to the production of the hypobromous acid (HOBr), bromite (OBr^-), and bromate (BrO_3^-) (Spotte, 1992), which is carcinogenic.

The management of an ozone system should include regular ORP monitoring and routine TRO testing. TRO should remain below 0.05 mg/L Cl (0.10 mg/L Br) or at the level that has been deemed acceptable by the operator's facility, for teleost and elasmobranch exhibits. For exhibits only housing marine mammals may be kept at a higher level to aid in continual disinfection; typically within 0.1 mg/L - 0.4 mg/L Cl (0.2 mg/L - 0.8 mg/L Br). Many fishes may show adverse reactions to TRO at concentrations below 0.05 mg/L Cl (0.10 mg/L Br). Elasmobranchs (sharks and rays) are very sensitive to even low TRO concentrations and over-ozonation; their behaviors may show precursors to such events. These behaviors could include sudden darting, irregular swimming patterns, swimming toward the surface, swimming higher in the water column, or away from exhibit influents. If these behaviors are observed, it is important to check ozone systems and TRO immediately. Long term, chronic exposure to even low levels of oxidants can cause lasting damage to aquatic animals and make them more susceptible to disease. Using animal behavior as a sole means to control disinfection systems is highly discouraged.

Care should be taken when administering pharmaceutical treatments to exhibits treated with ozone. Ozone, a powerful oxidant, may react with the pharmaceutical and either degrade it to below therapeutic concentrations or it is possible that it could react with it to produce a harmful byproduct.

When operating ozone and UV sterilizers together, there are Advanced Oxidation Processes (AOP) that may occur. Advanced Oxidation Processes lead to the generation of hydroxyl radicals (OH⁻) by first forming hydrogen peroxide (H_2O_2) before finally disassociating to H_2O and O_2. H_2O_2 is a strong oxidizer, so care should be taken if H_2O_2 production is likely. Peak hydroxyl formation occurs at a pH < 1.8, and production decreases as pH increases. At pH 5 - 10, well within a typical pH range for aquatic exhibits, oxidation by H_2O_2 is negligible (Gottschalk, 2010).

Ozone may also help oxidize nitrite to nitrate (Aiken, 1995), which is helpful if a healthy biofilter has not been established; however, it should not be relied on for the ozone to facilitate this process in case the ozone system needs to be taken offline for an extended period of time.

10.1.2 Applied Ozone Dose

Applied ozone doses (AOD) for disinfection of an aquarium should be kept between 0.10 mg/L – 1.00 mg/L (Aiken, 1995) depending on the requirement to balance the biological demand of the aquarium. An AOD should be well known and based off of ORP and TRO readings and can be calculated from the following equation (Aiken, 1995):

$$AOD = \left(\frac{dose\ of\ ozone\left(\frac{mg}{min}\right)}{flow\left(\frac{L}{min}\right)} \right)$$

The ORP of an exhibit will fluctuate based on the biological demand of the exhibit even with the AOD constant. During husbandry practices, such as cleaning or feeding, the demand will increase (decrease in ORP) due to the intentional addition of organic compounds. Exhibit cleaning will also have a similar impact on the ORP and ozone system. During these common occurrences, it may be necessary to increase the AOD to compensate and maintain appropriate disinfection levels. It is ideal and recommended to have some type of ORP controller on the exhibit, which can help regulate the AOD during such events and also protect against overdose situations by either alerting a technician to issues or shutting down the ozone feed to the exhibit in cases of a higher ORP.

10.1.3 Oxidation Reduction Potential

ORP, also known as redox, is the chief means of monitoring the dosage of ozone in a life support system and is the accumulation of reactive potential within a system of water, contributed to by many oxidizing and reducing forces. ORP measures the availability of the oxidizer (or oxidant) present in the water to react with, and thus destroy contaminants. ORP is not a direct measurement of ozone concentration in a solution, but rather a measure of the prevalence of oxidizing reactions triggered by the presence of ozone.

Oxidation is the loss of an electron and reduction is the gain of an electron, by an atom, molecule, or ion. Oxidizers are chemicals that remove an electron from another compound, thereby altering the compound's chemical structure. These electrons cannot exist in a solution alone and therefore must be accepted by another substance. In the case of a bacterium, virus, or water-borne parasite, this change in the chemical makeup of their cell structure results in the organism being severely damaged or destroyed. ORP can also measure chlorine and bromine levels as indicated in Section 10.1.1, although direct concentration testing is preferred for these compounds.

According to the World Health Organization (WHO), *"A redox potential of 650 mV (measured between platinum and calomel electrodes) will cause almost instantaneous inactivation of even high concentrations of virus. Such a potential can be obtained with even a low concentration of free chlorine but only with an extremely high concentration of combined chlorine"* (World Health Organization, 2003).

As a best practice, multiple ORP electrodes should be used on any life support system undergoing ozone treatment in order to ensure both effective sterilization and animal safety. One electrode placed in the process stream at the ozone contactor discharge ensures a proper millivolt level for effective treatment, a second electrode placed at the discharge of the de-gas/deaeration tower ensures the removal of excess oxidizer, and a third electrode placed at the exhibit return piping allows monitoring of the ORP in the exhibit itself.

10.1.4 Ozone Monitoring using ORP Probes

ORP is measured using an instrument which is essentially a millivolt (mV) meter and measures the voltage potential between two electrodes. The first of these is the reference electrode which is surrounded by an electrolyte solution and produces a consistent voltage. The reference electrode is typically a silver-silver chloride electrode, similar to pH measurements. The reference voltage is the result of the electrolyte solution oxidizing the surface of the reference electrode at a very predictable rate. The second component is the measuring electrode which directly contacts the process water resulting in a voltage which changes in relation to the concentration of oxidizer in the process stream. As the concentration of oxidizer in the water increases, the oxidation sensed by the measuring electrode increases. The resulting difference between the two voltages is the ORP and is typically expressed from -2,000 mV to +2,000 mV.

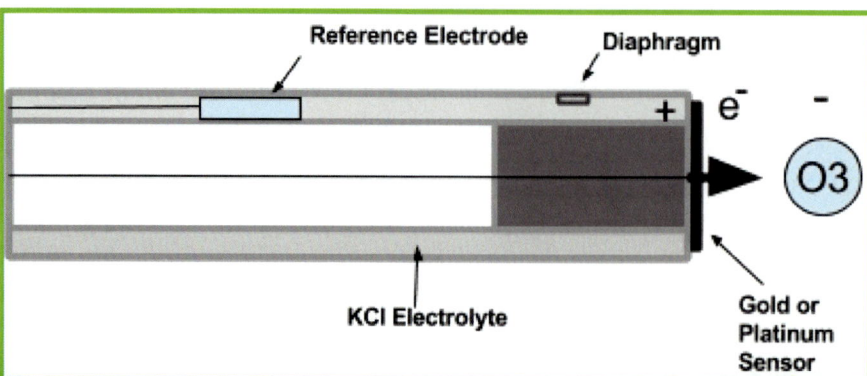

Figure 10.1 – Cross Section of an ORP Probe

An ORP electrode consists of an inert metal, such as platinum or gold, that has a low resistance to oxidizing or reducing electrons, is used for measurement. ORP electrodes differ in quality and design but most fall within a +/- 25 mV accuracy and have the ability to be calibrated to a known constant. ORP measurements may become erroneous by responding more strongly to certain chemical substances during electron exchange due to low rate of electron exchange; for example, dissolved oxygen and hydrogen peroxide treatments. With exposure to saturated dissolved oxygen levels (approximately 8 mg/L), the ORP value range may vary with pH level. Observations of ORP value fluctuations recorded during a study based on carbonate buffered water treated by the addition of different forms of oxidants, revealed that the addition of dissolved oxygen to a solution affects the ORP measurements results most noticeably at a pH of 7, with the significance decreased at a pH of 8, and lesser still at a pH of 9 (Lytle et al., 2004).

It is important to have an understanding of standard cell potentials and half-reactions to fully grasp the concept of ORP measurement. When electricity is passed through water, the substances within undergo a process called electrolysis, which involves gain or loss in electrons, also known as oxidation or reduction. Half reactions refer to either the oxidation reaction or the reduction reaction. Electrolysis is measured within what is called a chemical "cell", which is much like a battery, where chemical energy is converted to electrical energy. The standard cell potential, denoted as E^o_{cell} is the potential of the cell when all of the ion concentrations are 1.00 M, the temperature is 25°C, and any gases involved in the reaction are at a pressure of 1 atm (Brady et al., 2000). The overall reaction occurring in the cell is called a cell reaction, which is the sum of two half-reactions (oxidation and reduction), each with a characteristic potential associated with it, which is described by the following equation (Skoog et al., 2007):

$$E^o cell = \begin{pmatrix} \text{standard reduction} \\ \text{potential of the} \\ \text{substance reduced} \end{pmatrix} - \begin{pmatrix} \text{standard reduction} \\ \text{potential of the} \\ \text{substance oxidized} \end{pmatrix}$$

ORP is a measurement of the sum of half-cell reactions (oxidation and reduction) occurring within system water (which can be thought of as one big electrochemical cell). When an ORP electrode is added to system water, the electrode will act as an electron donor (in an oxidizing environment) or an electron acceptor (in a reducing environment). In reality, there are both oxidation and reduction reactions occurring simultaneously in exhibit water. The measurement of ORP can take a long time to stabilize, due to a number of redox reactions occurring.

Measuring the ORP of a solution can take 20 minutes or more, even though calibration of the electrode may only takes moments. Oxidizers, such as ozone or chlorine cause a rise in the millivolt value; therefore, higher millivolt measurements indicate an increase in disinfection capabilities, while reductants cause the millivolt value to fall and indicates a decrease in disinfection capabilities. Typical reductants found in aquatic systems are organic matter such as dust, dirt, food, bodily fluids, microorganisms, and fecal material.

ORP probes are depicted as rugged in advertisements but are quite fragile without protective guards. The probe should be stored with the electrode and reference junction submerged in the manufacturer's recommended storage solution. Before use, rinse the tip of the electrode with purified water such as RO or DI water. To begin calibration, place the probe sensory tip in the calibration solution of preference. In some cases, gently stirring or manipulating the probe in the calibration solution enhances the capability of rapid response time and stability of measurement. Too strong of a stirring may lead to unwanted saturation of air into the calibration solution, causing interference with a proper calibration. ORP electrodes should not be wiped with a dry cloth or paper towels, rinsing with deionized water is sufficient to eliminate contamination. In some extreme cases where probes may become fouled and are unable to be rinsed off, a clean and specified brush (similar to a very soft toothbrush) may be used along with DI and RO water for cleaning. Calibration solutions should remain in an opaque airtight container and should be verified regularly to maintain accurate data. In most cases it is recommended to mix calibration solutions on an as needed basis and discard after calibrations in order to eliminate erroneous data. Preserving the age of the ORP electrode sensor is reliable as long as routine operational inspections of quality are performed (external structural integrity and internal mechanics); do not allow electrode to soak in deionized water for prolonged periods of time or heat exceeding 80°C or greater to preserve longevity. It is a general recommendation that probes deemed to be in a critical application are replaced at least every year even with successful calibrations, as the loss of electrolyte within the probe or wear on the reference junction is often immeasurable.

Electrode maintenance and cleaning prompts are noted through observation of slow response time and large offset values, which could indicate fouling or coating of the probe and /or platinum (or gold) sensory tip. Always default to the manufacturer's instructions regarding the cleaning and servicing of ORP electrodes.

Scheduled maintenance and cleaning of the ORP probes are needed to obtain good results. Commonly used calibration solutions for ORP measurement are ZoBell's 600 mV solution and 200 mV Light's solution. It is also possible to use pH 4 buffers saturated with a small amount quinhydrone powder for a millivolt reading of +264 mV (+/-15%) and pH 7 buffers saturated with a small amount of quinhydrone powder for a millivolt reading of +87 mV (+/- 15%). When using any solution, it should be verified to attain accuracy. Select the appropriate single-value range for the specific needs of the testing solution (Georg Fischer, n.d). The Light's and ZoBell's calibration solutions are stable so shelf life can be months, while quinhydrone mixtures are unstable and must be discarded after every use (Water Analytics, n.d.).

10.1.5 Typical ORP Values for Exhibit, Tower, and Contactor

ORP is perhaps the most complicated and difficult to understand chemical parameter because there are so many chemical processes that affect ORP, making it too difficult to model and predict. Chemical reactions that control ORP in one aquarium may not be present or contribute to the ORP in another aquarium. An ORP level capable of maintaining the desired water quality parameters in one aquarium system might not work for a seemingly similar system. To complicate matters even more, ORP monitoring systems and measurement equipment can show wildly different results. ORP monitoring is best used as a relative parameter individualized to a particular system, as an ozone dosing control parameter. In an ozonated system, the ORP will vary at different locations in the system, such as the contact chamber, the deaeration tower, and the pool. Monitoring the ORP at these various locations verifies proper disinfection and ensures the aquarium does not get over ozonated, which could have serious results such as loss of fish life, oxidized skin and eyes in mammals, and hindered thermoregulation in aquatic birds.

The ORP in the contact chamber will have the highest ORP levels in the system. This ORP should be at least 650 mV. At ORP levels of 650 mV and higher, pathogenic bacteria will be killed within 30 seconds (Suslow, 2004).

The deaeration tower, if present, is where ozonated water from the contactor has the opportunity to mix with the rest of the system water. The ORP of the water entering the tower should still be higher than the exhibit's ORP, although not as high as in the contact chamber. Typically water entering the tower will be between 400 mV to 500 mV. By the time the water leaves the tower, the ORP needs to be down to a level safe for aquatic life. The ideal ORP of the water entering the tower will vary from exhibit to exhibit to ensure water exiting that tower is at a safe ORP for the exhibit.

The most critical ORP levels to monitor are in the exhibit pool, and acceptable levels are dependent on the type of aquatic animals that reside there. Systems housing only marine mammals typically tolerate higher levels than fish and invertebrate systems. Sharks and rays are typically more sensitive to higher ORP levels than the bony fishes. An ORP that is too high can kill the animals living in the aquarium either directly or by chronic exposure to ozone produced byproducts, such as brominated compounds; therefore, it is essential the ORP does not rise above an unsafe level. To help ensure this, it is recommended that TRO is measured along with ORP. Healthy saltwater exhibits typically have ORP values between 250 mV to 400 mV. Freshwater exhibits may have a higher ORP range of 300 mV to 450 mV. ORP levels should not be kept too low, even though lower ORP values may seem safe for animals living in the water. Systems with too low ORP values indicates that the water contains more reducing agents and is not as good of an oxidizer. Systems with low ORP values will be more difficult to disinfect due to the increased presence of reducers. Natural coral reefs typically will have ORPs between 350 mV to 400 mV (Aiken et al., 2015).

10.1.6 Ozone Production

Ozone can be generated by corona discharge or as a byproduct of UV radiation. For UV type generators, peak production of ozone occurs at 185 nm. UV type generators are typically limited to 1.0% ozone production by weight, and are significantly less efficient than corona discharge generators (Oxidation Technologies, 2017). Corona discharge generators use a high voltage electrical current that is forced to continuously jump a discharge gap between a dielectric (insulating) barrier and a grounded electrode. The resulting corona splits a percentage of the O_2 molecules in the feed gas. The resulting single oxygen atoms recombine with remaining O_2 to form ozone. The corona discharge method is the process occurring in both dielectric tube and dielectric plate ozone generators.

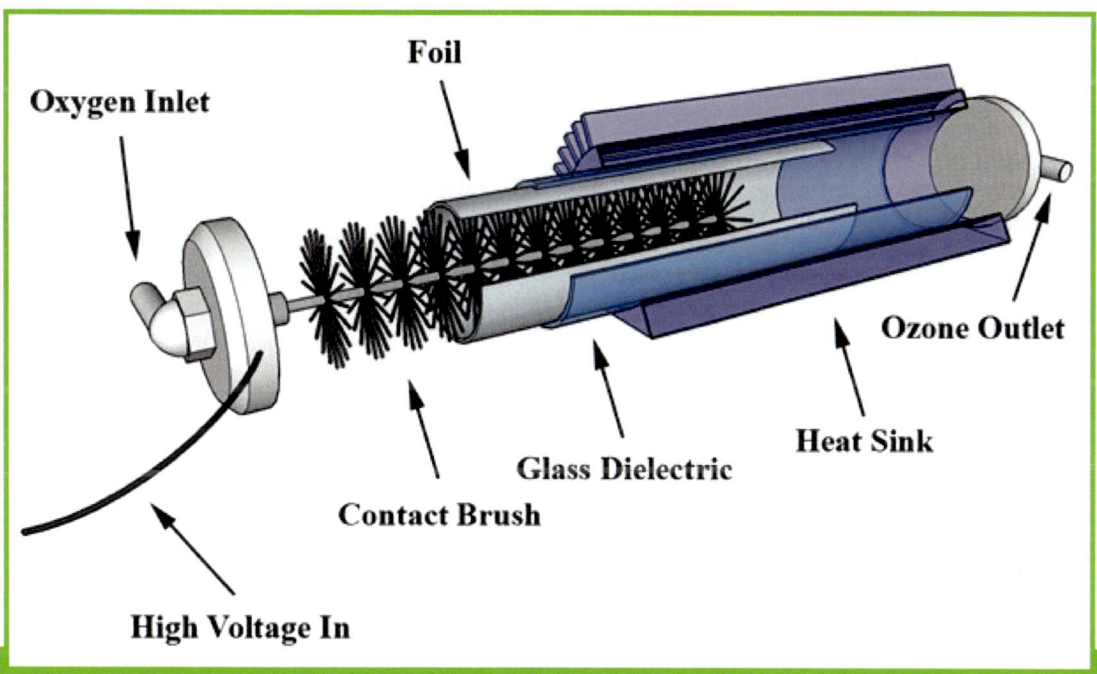

Figure 10.2 - Corona Tube Ozone Generator

Ozone generators can be fed with either dry compressed air or concentrated oxygen. Oxygen fed systems are intended to produce small volumes of highly concentrated gas and rely on compressed oxygen cylinders or oxygen concentrators. The typical output ozone concentration is 2% - 4% by weight for air fed systems. Oxygen fed systems can vary from 5% - 20% by weight with 6% - 10% being a normal operating range.

Ozone gas is both toxic and corrosive and due care must be used when selecting equipment that will make, convey, or inject ozone in a LSS setting. Atmospheric monitoring equipment should be used in any confined space when ozone equipment is present.

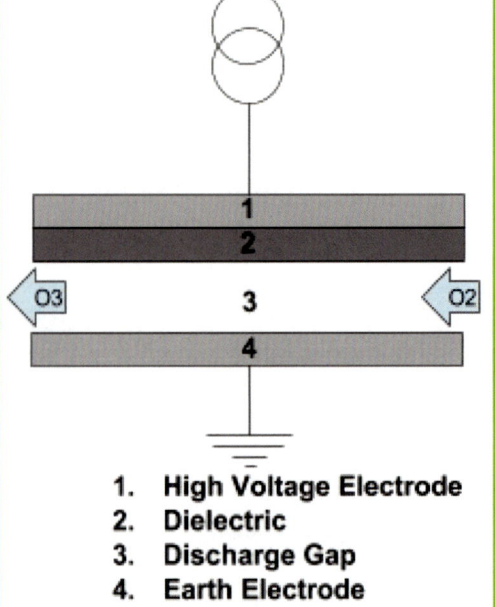

Figure 10.3 - Generating Ozone

1. **High Voltage Electrode**
2. **Dielectric**
3. **Discharge Gap**
4. **Earth Electrode**

The instability of ozone requires on-site production. The production of ozone requires specialized equipment: oxygen concentrator, ozone generator, cooling water source (if water cooled), ambient ozone sensors (for technician and public safety), and more depending on setup.

10.1.7 Ozone Generator Equipment

Ozone generators require a source for oxygen and a means for removing undissolved ozone from system water before return from the system. Oxygen may be produced from air, or pure oxygen, depending on the design.

Air-dryers

Reliable operation of an ozone generator requires that it is fed with clean, dry air. Water vapor introduced into an ozone generator will interfere with the corona discharge and will also convey contaminants into the generator chamber. The moisture content of compressed air is monitored by measuring its dew point, which is the maximum amount of water vapor a given volume of air can hold at a given temperature. Dew point is expressed in either degrees Fahrenheit or Celsius. Warm air is capable of holding much more water than cold air; a lower dew point directly corresponds to drier air. For example, a normal operating dew point for a modern air-fed ozone system should would be between -60°F and -140°F (-50°C and -100°C).

Ozone air preparation systems typically employ an air dryer in addition to cartridge filters, intended to remove oil vapor and particulates from the air feed to the generator. Air dryers are machines intended to remove water vapor from compressed air. Failure to remove sufficient water vapor from feed gas may result in the production of highly corrosive nitrogen oxides, including nitric acid, which can damage equipment (Gottschalk et al., 2010). There are two types: refrigeration and desiccant dryers.

A refrigerant dryer passes the compressed air through a heat exchanger which lowers its moisture content by cooling the air, thereby reducing its dew point. Typically, refrigeration dryers cannot reduce dew point to a useable level on their own, and are used in conjunction with a dessicant. A desiccant dryer is designed to pass air through a pressurized vessel housing material that attracts and traps water molecules. After the material becomes saturated, the water must be removed from the vessel and is typically "blown off" by opening a vent at the bottom of the vessel and using the air pressure to expel the water and "recharge" the vessel. This type of desiccant air dryer is referred to as a "Pressure Swing Adsorption Air Dryer". Another type of self-regenerative dryer is a "Thermal Swing Adsorption Dryer", where heat is applied to the regenerating chamber to help drive off moisture. Desiccant dryers of this type are generally referred to as regenerative desiccant dryers. This typically employs 2 vessels that will alternately recharge the dessicant from one vessel while air is moving through the other. The simplest air dryer uses a replaceable desiccant media, and is typically only used in relatively small systems.

Oxygen concentrators

The output of an ozone generator varies in proportion to the amount of oxygen contained in the feed gas. Simply put, more oxygen fed into the ozone generator will result in more ozone output by the generator. Many ozone production systems maximize the output of the ozone generator by incorporating an oxygen concentrator into the overall system design. These units are capable of delivering up to 95% pure oxygen to the ozone generator.

Oxygen concentrators are devices designed to separate oxygen from the compressed air feed gas and supply oxygen at levels exceeding the normal atmosphere to the ozone generator. These are specialty devices that employ adsorbent materials which trap oxygen molecules and exclude other molecules, mainly nitrogen, normally present in the atmosphere. Activated carbon, silica gel, alumina, and zeolite are examples of adsorbent materials used for this purpose. Feed gas from oxygen concentrators is typically very dry, with a dew point of about -100°F.

Destruct units

Ozone at sea level is a toxic and a corrosive atmospheric contaminant, and its release is subject to air quality management regulations as well as workplace safety standards. Ozone injected into a treatment vessel of a life support system will be consumed by the resulting chemical reactions; however, it is often the case that a certain percentage of the ozone gas injected into a treatment vessel will pass through the water column and not dissolve into solution to react with another compound. This residual ozone must be dealt with in a safe manner and not be allowed to harm the resident animals or LSS operators.

An ozone destruct unit is a device designed to remove and safely convert undissolved ozone back into oxygen. Ozone destruct units will remove ozone contaminated air from the top of a treatment vessel or directly from ozone supply piping/tubing under vacuum and pass it through a destruct chamber where it is heated and reacted with a catalyst that reverts the ozone back into oxygen. Commonly, a granular manganese dioxide/copper oxide mix is used in this application. Gas exiting the destruct unit should be vented outside the workspace to a safe location.

Fail-safes

A primary concern when designing an ozone injection system is water intrusion into ozone generators, which will destroy the cells. To avoid this, various fail-safes are typically used. Backflow preventers use an actuated valve that closes the generator effluent line when the unit loses power. This valve or an additional one may be used in conjunction with a water trap that can detect water intrusion into the gas line. When water is detected, the valve will close to protect the generator. A manual isolation valve should also be installed on the ozone generator effluent gas line. When the ozone generator is placed offline this valve should be closed, and then opened before placing the generator online again. In vacuum fed injection systems, water traps can also be used to ensure water does not backflow into equipment.

Gas flow and pressure fail-safes are also used to ensure that appropriate amounts of feed gas are provided to the generators. Mechanical or digital pressure switches are tied to generator controls in order to switch power off and close a valve on the effluent line should feed gas pressure fall outside of manufacturer's recommendations. They are an important addition to insure that the generator is not exposed to the negative pressure produced by venturi injectors, which can cause damage to certain types of generators. Gas flow sensors are used to insure that feed gas is flowing through the generator. Lack of feed gas flow shuts off power to the generator to prevent overheating and unintended variations in ozone concentration. For water cooled ozone generators, flow sensors are typically used to shut down the generator if the chilled water supply flow falls below a set point to prevent overheating.

10.1.8 Ozone Injection

There are many methods for bringing ozone into contact with the water to be treated. There are various methods for mixing the two, as well as various vessels that they can be mixed in. The needs and constraints of the system help to determine which methods may work best.

Diffuser

One method for distributing ozone is the use of a diffuser. This low tech method uses porous ceramic or stainless steel to break up the incoming ozone to produce fine bubbles. This method is only used in low pressure applications.

Venturi Injection

Another method of mixing ozone and water is with a venturi injector. A venturi injector is a device that creates a vacuum by using the *Venturi Effect*. The diameter of the venturi injector at its influent and effluent are the same, but is tapered to a smaller diameter in the center (see Figure 10.4). Immediately after the restriction, a low pressure area is formed which can be used to pull ozone gas into the water.

Many injectors are engineered with internal mixing vanes after the injection point to help mix the motive flow of gas into the water, and dissolve ozone (or other gases) into solution, and work most effectively with some downstream pressure (typically 15-25 PSI). Venturis are typically installed on a piping bypass with bypass valves (see Figure 10.5). This allows for flow adjustments which affect the pressure drop across the venturi and the air/ozone inlet. This bypass loop also allows for the venturi to be serviced or removed without stopping water flow.

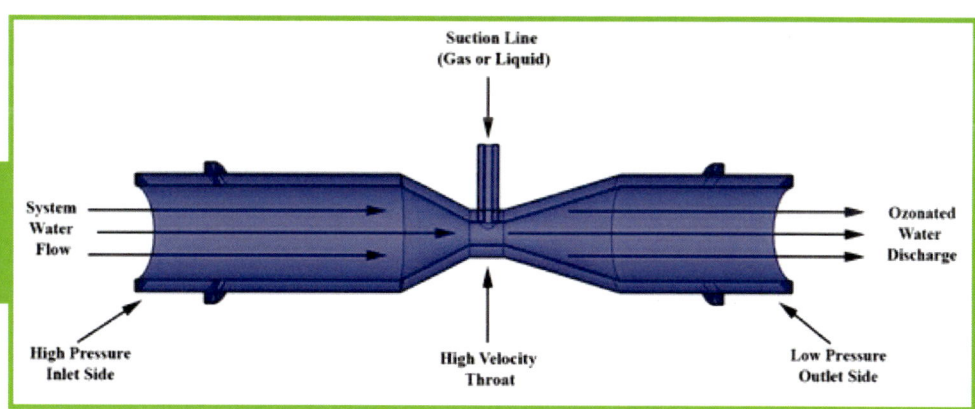

Figure 10.4 Venturi Injector

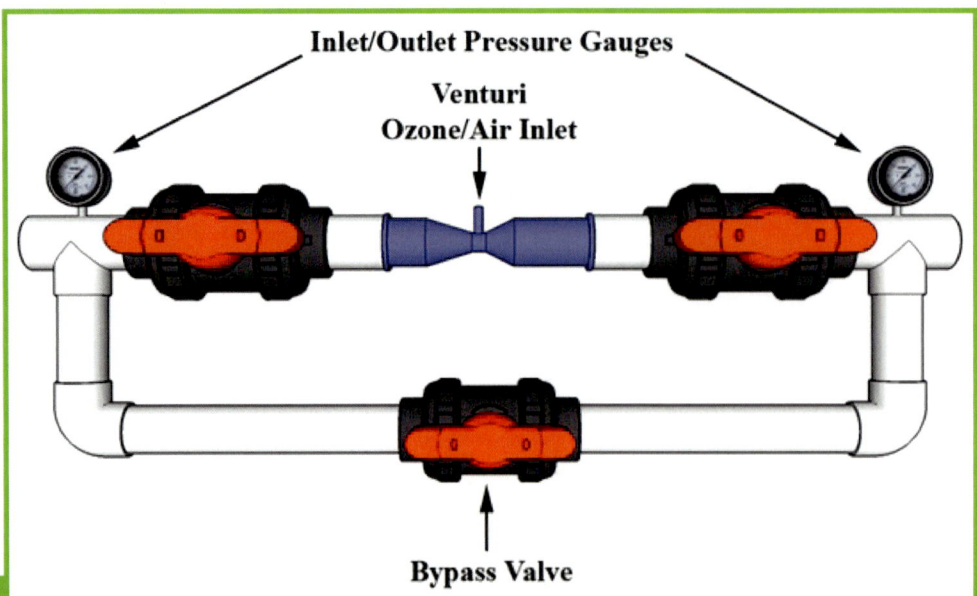

Figure 10.5 - Inline Venturi with Bypass

Low Pressure Ozone Contact Basins

In this method, a large basin is dedicated to ozone injection. Either diffusers or venturis can be used for ozone delivery. For the diffuser method, diffusers sit on the bottom of the basin. As they release ozone gas, water flows through the basin where it mixes with the ozone. Using a venturi for ozone delivery requires a secondary pump that either draws water from the main supply to the basin or recirculates on the basin. Both of these methods can allow for all of the water flowing through a filtration system to have contact time with the ozone injection point, but it requires a large footprint. Some low pressure contact basins are designed as a "tube in a tube" where the inner tube is used for ozone contacting in a co-current flow, and the outer tube is filled with degassing media. These types of basins are typically used on a side stream as opposed to the entire system flow. This method also allows for some ozone removal before water is delivered back to the system.

High Pressurize Ozone Contact Chamber

A high pressure ozone contact chamber is a vessel where mixing of the ozone and water is forced due to chamber design and the pressure allows for more ozone to dissolve into the water. Some contact chambers are designed with barriers inside that create turbulence, thereby forcing the liquid within them to mix. As the liquid moves through the contact chamber, the ozone bubbles will rise to the top and degas. Pressurized ozone contact chambers should have ozone destruct units installed to a port at the top of the chamber where undissolved gas collects (see Figure 10.6).

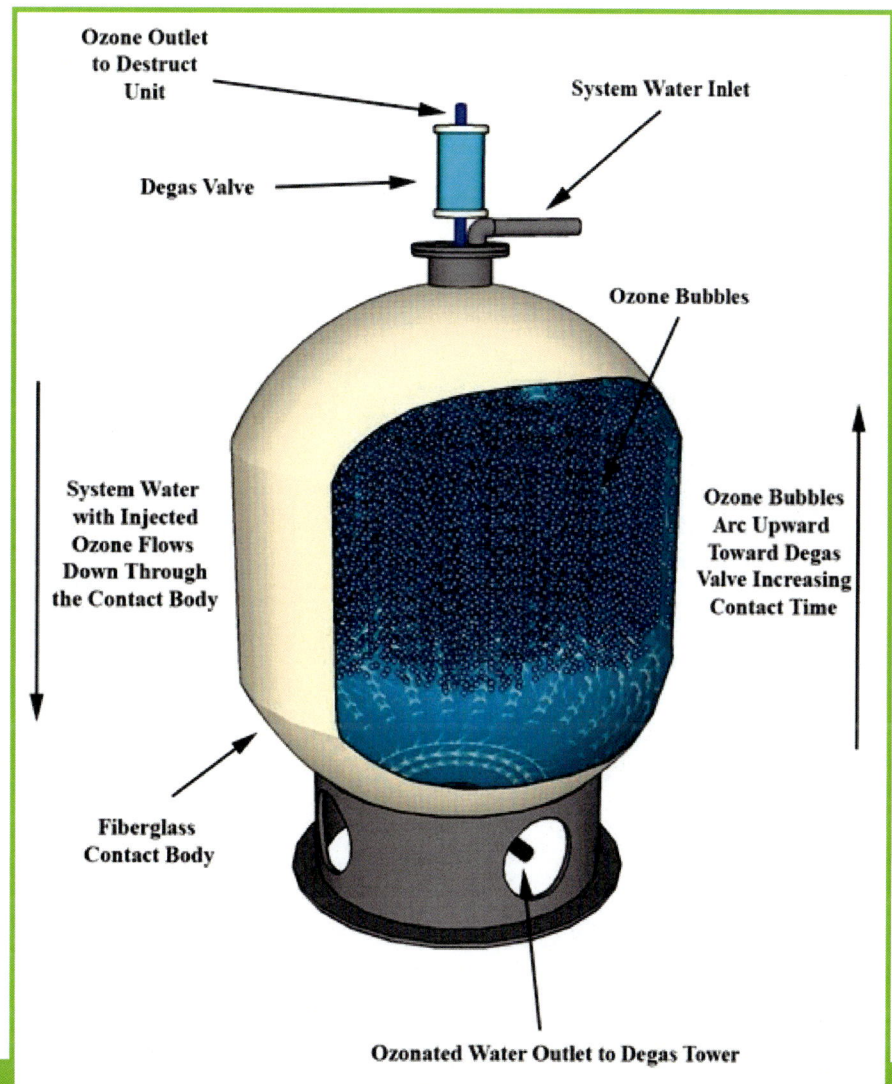

Ozone Outlet
to Destruct
Unit

System Water Inlet

Degas Valve

Ozone Bubbles

System Water
with Injected
Ozone Flows
Down Through
the Contact Body

Ozone Bubbles
Arc Upward
Toward Degas
Valve Increasing
Contact Time

Fiberglass
Contact Body

Ozonated Water Outlet to Degas Tower

Figure 10.6 - Pressurized Ozone Contact Chamber

Ozone Contact Cone

Ozone contact cones, sometimes called "Speece Cones", do not have internal barriers to create turbulence. Ozone is forced to dissolve into the water due to the shape of the cone and pressure. The water and the ozone enter through the top of the cone, where the downward velocity of the water is greater than the upward velocity of the ozone bubbles. As the mixture moves further down the cone, the diameter of the cone increases, slowing the velocity of the water. There is a point in the cone where the downward velocity of the water is no longer faster than the upward velocity of the bubbles. At this point, the bubbles move up and down between zones of varying water velocity. Stuck at this point, the gas is forced to dissolve with the water before finally leaving via the effluent near the bottom of the cone. Ozone cones can have up to 100% of the ozone gas dissolve into the water (Timmons, 2013). Once the water has left the contact chamber or ozone cone, the sidestream may recombine with the main flow of the water.

Figure 10.7 - Speece Cone

Protein Skimmers

Protein skimmers are also a common vessel used for ozone contacting in salt water systems. Instead of using air as the gas used in the fractionator, an ozone air mixture is used. Variations in the applied ozone dose (AOD) allow for either a microflocculation dose or sterilization dose. Using a low ozone dose in protein skimmer for microflocculation has been shown to decrease effluent turbidity (Phillips *et al.*, 2006). An AOD of 0.01 - 0.05 ppm is recommended for protein skimmers (Aiken, 2015). Turbidity may increase above an AOD of 0.1 ppm (Phillips *et al.*, 2006). For more information about protein skimmers, refer to Section 9.3.4 of this Field Guide.

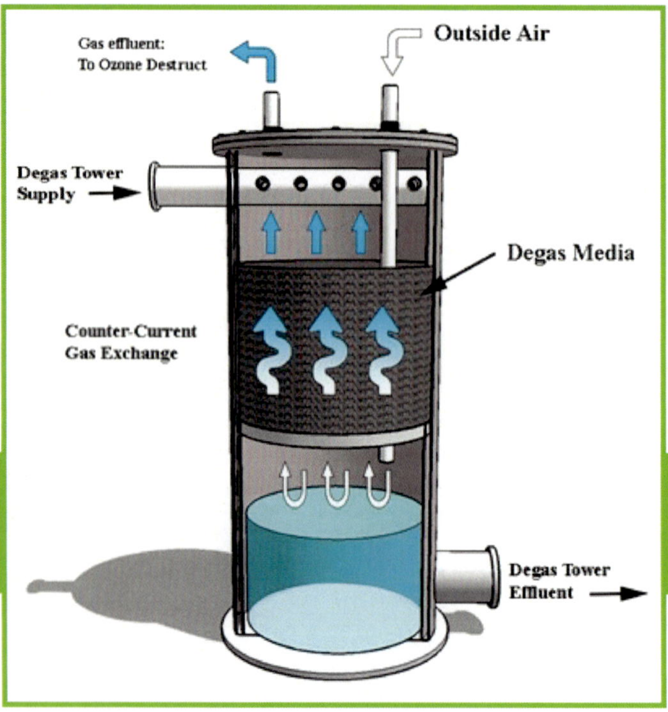

Gas effluent:
To Ozone Destruct

Outside Air

Degas Tower
Supply

Degas Media

Counter-Current
Gas Exchange

Degas Tower
Effluent

Figure 10.8
Deaeration Tower

Degas

On fish systems, ozonated water should be sent to an aeration/de-gas tower to verify the total dissolved gases, especially ozone, in the water is not too high before it comes in contact with aquatic life. Even relatively low concentrations (0.0093 ppm) of dissolved ozone can have adverse effects on the health of fishes (Gottschalk *et al*, 2010).

10.2 Chlorination

Chlorine and bromine can be used in non-fish systems as a disinfectant. In chlorinated pools there are two types of chlorine, free and combined chlorine. Free chlorine acts as a broad spectrum sterilant while non-free or combined chlorine are chlorine molecules that have combined with nitrogenous compounds such as ammonia (Partain, 2014). Combined chlorine usually is the product of ammonia and chlorine, forming chloramines. Breakpoint chlorination is the continuous dosing of free chlorine until the total chlorine matches the free chlorine in the system and chlorine demand is met.

There are several forms of chlorine that can be used for this treatment; all of them turn the same active disinfection agent (a mixture of hypochlorite ion (most active killing form) and hypochlorous acid in the exhibit, depending on system pH). Liquid chlorine solutions contain a concentration of around 10% sodium hypochlorite. A chemical metering pump monitored and controlled by a ppm or ORP probe should be used to dose this chemical accurately. Chlorine tablets contain calcium hypochlorite and can be purchased from a swimming pool supplier. The tablets must be used in specific chemical erosion feeders that need regular adjustments or an actuated valve that will open/close depending on demand. Trichlor and dichlor tablets should be used with caution as these forms of chlorine are stabilized and therefore contain cyanuric acid. Although cyanuric acid will better protect the chlorine from UV degredation, it may decrease it's effectiveness against algae, and increase the amount of contact time needed to kill pathogens in the water. A chlorine generator can be used on saltwater systems by generating chlorine from the chloride ion in the salt. The benefit of using chlorine over other oxidizers (namely ozone) is that the chlorine is residual in the pool water and actively kills coliforms and other bacteria just as they are imputed into the system. The benefit of continuous disinfection can have negative consequences if improperly or excessively administered because excess chlorine leads to health problems for the animal inhabitants. Follow all safety precautions when using any chlorine product. For most applications, 0.30 mg/L to 0.60 mg/L free chlorine is an acceptable range depending on the needs and desires of the facility. The operator must pay attention to the total chlorine result to ensure it is still within acceptable ranges set by the operator's facility and that combined chlorine is kept sufficiently low. Refer to Section 5.2 for more information regarding chlorine and bromine.

Systems often have a chlorine demand. Nitrogenous compounds and other organic matter often consumes chlorine during oxidation. Figure 10.4 represents the breakpoint chlorination curve.

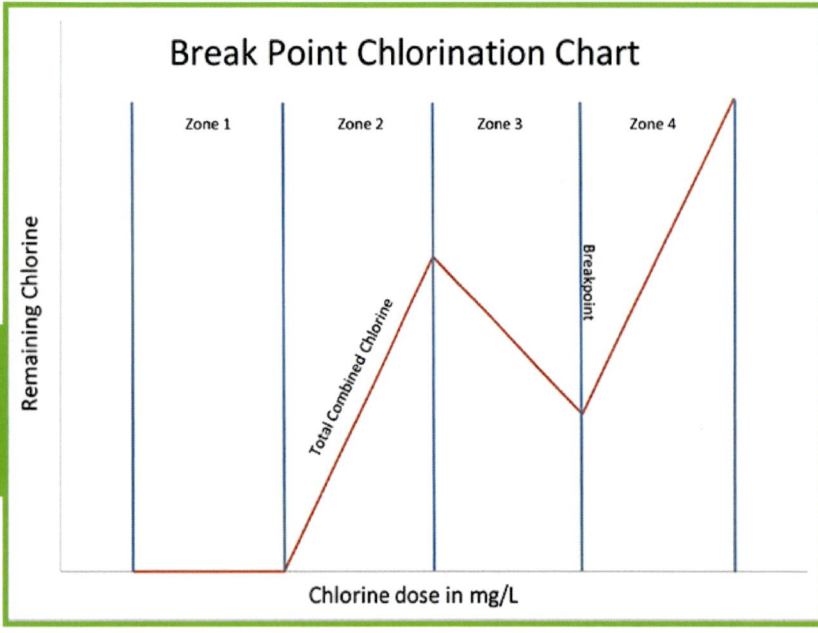

**Figure 10.9
Break Point
Chlorination Chart**

Figure 10.9 is broken down in 4 zones. Zone 1 represents the area of complete usage of chlorine. In Zone 2, the dosage increases and the chlorine begins to react with the ammonia and other nitrogenous compounds to form non free or combined chlorine. In Zone, 3 combined chlorine begins to drop and chloramines begin to breakdown. At this point, free chlorine begins to rise and correlates with dosing (break point of combined chlorines) and is represented in Zone 4.

Break point chlorination can be used to sanitize a body of water as well as remove nitrogen species from solution. In order to do this, first make sure that no animals have access to the body of water. Second, add chlorine until the demand for chlorine is satisfied by achieving breakpoint chlorination. This can be calculated as total chlorine minus free chlorine multiplied by ten; refer to a shocking agent for additional dosing calculations. For further information, please refer to a certified pool operator program.

10.3 UV Sterilization

**Figure 10.10
UV Sterilizer**

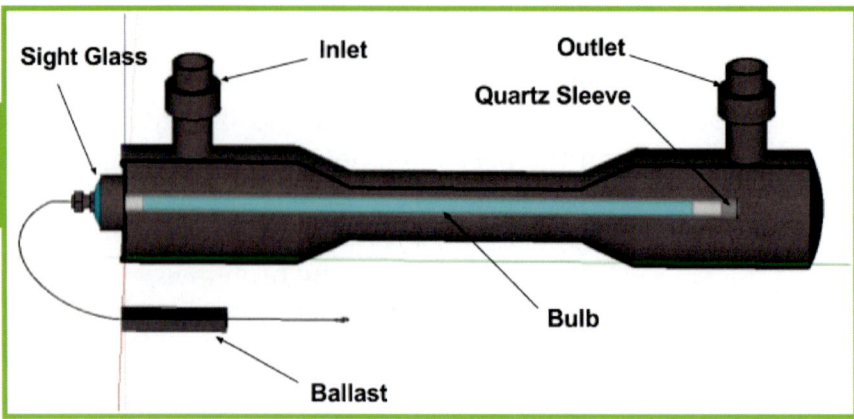

Ultraviolet (UV) sterilization is a process in which UV-C (UV rays between 200 and 280 nm, (Yanong, 2003) is used in a reaction chamber that inactivates bacteria, viruses, and algae ending their life cycle. UV sterilizers can be a very effective disinfectant if the strength of the bulb and flow rate allow for sufficient exposure. UV design ensures the water depth around the bulb allows for effective penetration of the UV light through the entire column of water. Specified flow rates ensure the appropriate doses of UV radiation is applied. This dose is typically expressed in units of microwatt seconds per centimeter squared (μW-sec/cm^2) or milllijoules per centimeter squared (mJ/cm^2). Typical doses range from 30,000 to 180,000 μW/cm^2 (30 to 180 mJ/cm^2) for pathogens found in aquaria. It is important to use the suggested dose rate indicated for a new bulb or for a bulb near end of life. UV bulbs, for best practice, should be changed at 9,000 hours of use (1 year) or sooner if the rated output has diminished below effective levels (Yanong, 2003). UV bulb output is reduced to approximately 60% at 9,000 hours (varies by manufacturer). UV bulbs operate at peak efficiency at approximately 100 ^{o}F (38 ^{o}C).

UV sterilizers usually incorporate a quartz tube, or "sleeve," to house the bulb, allowing it to operate at design temperature regardless of the process water temperature. Quartz is the chosen material because the interference to the UV wavelength is minimal and allows the transmission of almost all of the UV-C light. Quartz tubes should be inspected and cleaned periodically as they are prone to calcium deposit buildup. This can be accomplished by removing the tubes and cleaning with a dilute acid solution or denatured alcohol. Some installations and manufacturers include ports at the inlet and outlet that can be used to circulate an acid solution through the device to clean the tubes in place. This design should be considered for all installations when practical, including appropriate drains and bypasses.

UV sterilizers should receive water with the lowest turbidity possible. Suspended solids in the process water can absorb or deflect UV light, decreasing the effectiveness of the unit. UV sterilizers should be plumbed in a manner that holds water in the chamber if the flow stops. Water in the unit dissipates heat and reduces the risk of thermal shock and breakage of the quartz tube and bulb when flow is restored. Some units are equipped with temperature safeties and/or flow switches to protect the unit. These temperature and flow safeties will allow the unit to de-energize in order to prevent potential fire or shock hazards.

11 Life Support Maintenance Equipment

There are numerous varieties of common and specialized tools that an LSS Operator may require on a daily basis. Tool selection may depend on the environment the tool is being used in, and the operator's skill using those tools, in addition to task requirements. It is impractical to describe every type of tool an operator may encounter, but several specialized tools are discussed. Training on the safe use of tools is important for operator safety. It is recommended that an operator only use tools that they have been trained to use. Always follow institutional and manufacturer's guidelines for tool use.

11.1 Pump Alignment Tools

Pump alignment tools are used to precisely align the center line of a motor drive shaft to the centerline of the pump shaft. Misalignment occurs in both horizontal and vertical planes as angle (angular misalignment) and offset (parallel misalignment). Angular misalignment is the change in the gap space between coupling faces, while parallel misalignment is the difference between the shafts' centerlines (Volk, 2014). There are 3 methods that can be used to accomplish this: straight edge alignment, dial indicator alignment, and laser alignment.

**Figure 11.1
Straight Edge
Shaft Alignment**

Straight edge alignment uses a straight edge, typically a ruler or similar, to visually align the shafts (see Figure 11.1). Gaps indicate that the shafts are out of alignment. The operator can see where gaps may present by setting the straight edge across the two shafts at different points with the same diameter, typically the shaft coupling. Straight edge alignment is typically much quicker than dial indicator or laser alignment, but it lacks their precision and accuracy. A straight edge alignment is typically used to roughly align the shafts before using dial indicators or a laser alignment tool.

Figure 11.2 - Cross Shaft Dial Indicator Shaft Alignment

Using dial indicators to align shafts involves setting up the dial indicators on clamps that can be used to precisely measure the angular and parallel misalignment in either the vertical or horizontal position. There are many methods for using dial indicators for shaft alignment, but two common methods used are the rim and face method and the cross shaft dial indicator method. The rim and face method uses a dial indicator on the rim and face of the shaft coupling while attached to the stationary shaft. The cross shaft dial indicator method uses dial indicators on the rim of shaft couplings that are attached to the stationary and moveable shafts (see Figure 11.2). The shafts are then rotated together in order to measure the angular and parallel misalignment. These measurements are then used in mathematical formulas to calculate the precise adjustments needed to bring the shafts into alignment. Convenient worksheets are available for these calculations (see Section 19.10). For vertical alignment, the calculations tell the operator what size of shims should be placed under the front and rear foot bolts. For horizontal alignment, dial indicators can be used on the feet of the moveable machine to precisely measure the adjustments being made. Vertical and horizontal adjustments need to be made separately in order to accurately measure them with the dial indicators. Using dial indicators to align shafts is typically slow and requires a lot of skill.

Figure 11.3 - Laser Shaft Alignment

Laser alignment uses sensors attached to the shafts to precisely and accurately measure their alignment (see Figure 11.3). A computer system attached to the sensors keep track of both shafts positions as they relate to each other, which allows the operator to make both vertical and horizontal adjustments at the same time. Laser alignment tools also compute and relay the exact adjustments needed to the operator. Laser alignment is generally the fastest and most precise method for shaft alignment.

11.2 Motor Lifts

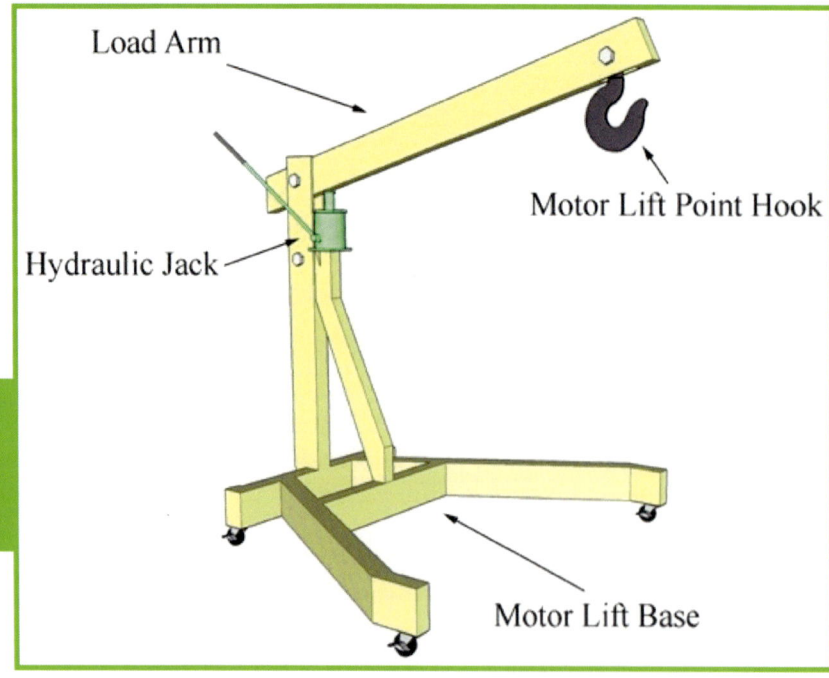

Load Arm

Motor Lift Point Hook

Hydraulic Jack

Motor Lift Base

Figure 11.4 Hydraulic Engine Hoist

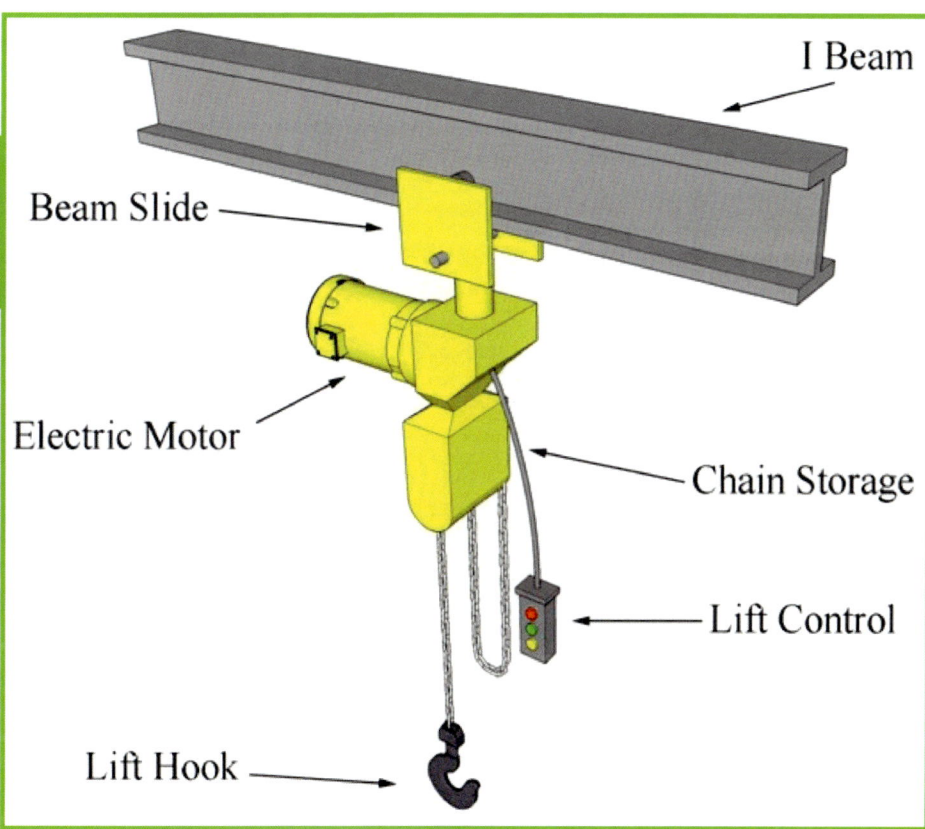

Figure 11.5 Electric Chain Hoist

I Beam

Beam Slide

Electric Motor

Chain Storage

Lift Control

Lift Hook

When working on heavy equipment, such as large pumps and motors, manpower alone may not be sufficient to maneuver them safely. Assistive devices that help lift this equipment are crucial for limiting risk of operator injury and equipment damage. Hydraulic engine hoists, ratcheting pullers, and chain hoists are commonly used in this application. Hydraulic engine hoists, sometimes called engine cranes, use a hydraulic piston mounted to a frame to lift an arm. Hydraulic engine hoists come in various weight ratings. For LSS applications, a 1 ton maximum weight limit is sufficient in most cases. Chain hoists, also referred to as chain falls, and ratcheting pullers use mechanical advantage from gear reduction to translate a small force over a long distance to a large force over a short distance. Both come in a variety of weight ratings, and chain hoists may be mechanically powered or powered by a motor. These devices are typically mounted to an anchor point mounted to the ceiling, on a trolley connected to an I-beam, or on a frame set up over the object that needs to be lifted. Multiple chain hoists and ratcheting pullers mounted in different locations may be used in tandem in order to move the objects horizontally as well.

11.3 Chain Vise

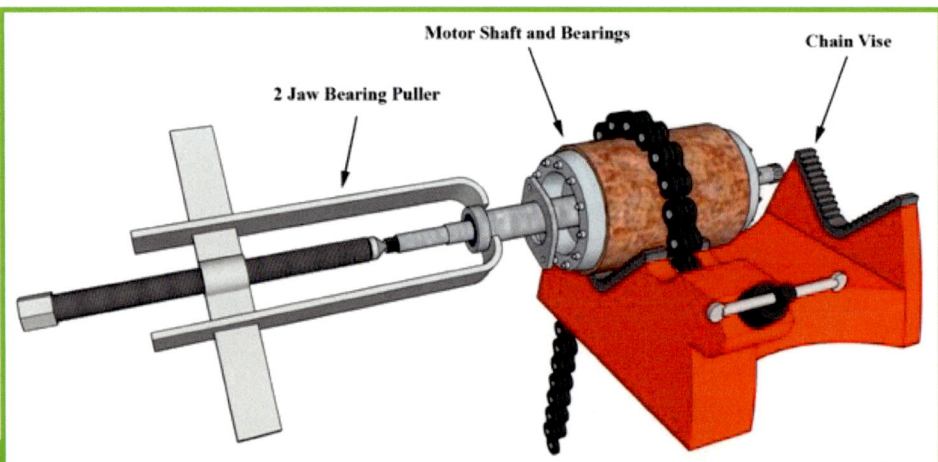

Figure 11.6 - Chain Vise with Motor Stator and 2 Arm Bearing Puller

Chain vises put tension on a chain wrapped around an object in order to hold it in place (see Figure 11.6). They are useful for holding irregularly shaped items that may not be held well by other types of vises. Chain vises come in bench top and portable stand varieties. They are particularly useful for holding large pipes, motors, and other rounded objects. Damage can occur if the vise is in direct contact with the object it is holding. A barrier, such as a cloth, can be put around the object to prevent this.

11.4 Bearing Puller

A bearing puller is a device that can be used to remove bearings from the shaft of a rotating machine or from a blind bearing hole. There are three main varieties of bearing pullers: splitter plate bearing pullers, 2 or 3 arm bearing pullers, and internal bearing pullers. Splitter plate bearing pullers use a plate that is installed behind the bearing to pull the bearing off of the shaft by applying force to the shaft in the opposite direction.

Figure 11.7 - 3 Arm Bearing Puller

A 2 or 3 armed bearing puller uses either 2 or 3 arms to grab the inner or outer race of the bearing, and then apply force to the shaft in the opposite direction (see Figure 11.7). An internal bearing puller uses an expandable collet to secure itself to the inside ring of bearing, then a slide hammer on a rail attached to the collet is used to shock the bearing out of the hole (see Figure 11.8).

**Figure 11.8
Slide Hammer
3 Arm Bearing Puller**

11.5 Bearing Fitting Tool

Figure 11.9 - Bearing Fitting Tool

A bearing fitting tool uses a shaft and impact ring in conjunction with mallet to tap a bearing onto the shaft of a rotating machine or into a blind bearing hole (see Figure 11.9). The shaft and impact ring of a bearing fitting tool fits over the shaft of the machine and is rested against the bearing being fitted. The impact ring is sized identical to the bearing being fitted to effectively transmit the force to the bearing in the correct distribution. Bearing fitting tools can be acquired in a kit that can be used on a variety of bearing and shaft sizes.

11.6 Bearing Heaters

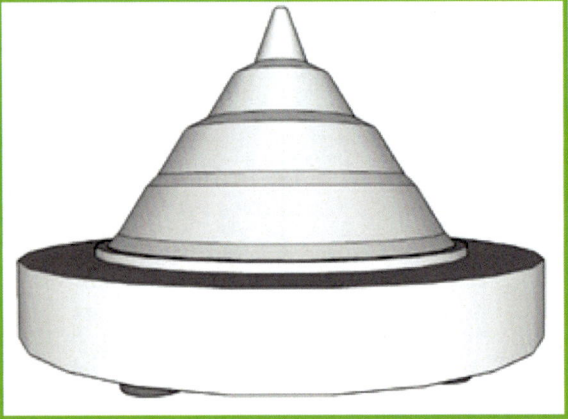

Figure 11.10 – Cone Bearing Heater

Bearing heaters are used to uniformly heat the bearing in order to expand the inner race, making installation easier. Heating a bearing can be accomplished in a number of ways including induction heating, heating plates, oil baths, and heating cabinets. Induction bearing heaters use electromagnetic induction to flow current through the bearing, which heats up due to the resistive properties of the material (see Figure 11.10). Induction heating causes ferromagnetic material to become magnetized. Most induction heaters include a demagnetization process after heating has been accomplished to rectify this. For those that do not, the bearing can be flipped 180 degrees and heated for a few more seconds. Most induction heaters have built in thermostats and thermometers to control and monitor the temperature of the bearing. Hot plate bearing heaters come in flat and conical shapes, and use conductive heating (see Figure 11.11). The bearings are placed on the hot plate, which may or may not have an integrated thermometer, until the bearing has come to the desired temperature. Oil bath bearing heating uses a heated vat of oil to bring the bearing to the desired temperature. Oil baths can be extremely hazardous and messy; they are not typically recommended unless no other option is available. Heating cabinets use convection and radiation to heat the bearings in the same way as a home oven works. Using a heating cabinet to heat bearings is a very slow process. Both oil bath and heating cabinets are very inefficient compared to hot plates and induction heaters.

Figure 11.11- Induction Bearing heater

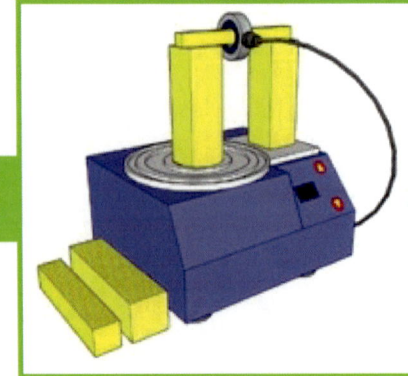

11.7 PVC Pipe Joiner

A PVC Pipe Joiner uses a ratcheting or levered mechanism to push together a pipe and fitting, while they are being held by a moveable vice or clamp. They are most often used for gasketed pvc pipe and fittings, but their application in solvent welding should not be overlooked. Pipe joiners are typically used for large diameter pipe, where human force alone may be insufficient to push and hold the pipe fitting together. With solvent welding, they can help to insure the pipe is inserted to the glue stop and hold the pipe there to prevent it from backing out. They can also be used to pull a freshly glued joint apart if the glue has not set.

11.8 Pipe Chamfer

A chamfer tool typically uses a blade to remove burrs and to create a smooth, symmetrical, sloped surface on the outer cut edge of pipe. A typical manufacturer's requirement is to have a 10° to 15° chamfer. Having a chamfered edge typically makes inserting pipe into a fitting much easier, and allows the solvent cement to be distributed throughout the joint more completely. On larger diameter pipe, it is common to use a grinder or sand paper wheel to chamfer, although a specialized large diameter chamfer is usually less messy, and produces a more precise chamfer. Chamfering the pipe is a manufacturer required step for solvent welding PVC.

11.9 Pipe Deburring Tool

A deburring tool typically uses a blade to remove burrs and create a smooth, sloped surface on the inside edge of a cut pipe. Many deburring tools can be used to chamfer the outer edge of the pipe as well. Deburring is a manufacturer required step for solvent welding PVC. Having a deburred inner edge can help decrease frictional losses in the piping system.

11.10 PVC Pipe Cutters

PVC pipe cutters use a knife-like action to cut PVC pipe (see Figure 11.12). Although many PVC pipe cutters use a ratcheting lever action to increase mechanical force, there are also electrically powered devices that use the same knife like action. A variety of saws are also widely used to cut PVC pipe, but PVC pipe cutters have the benefit of cleanliness because they do not remove any material from the pipe as they cut through it. PVC pipe cutters may not be safe or effective to use on brittle pipe caused by cold, UV, ozone, or other chemical exposure due to the potential for the pipe to shatter.

Figure 11.12 – PVC Pipe Cutters

11.11 Centering Head

Figure 11.13- Centering Head

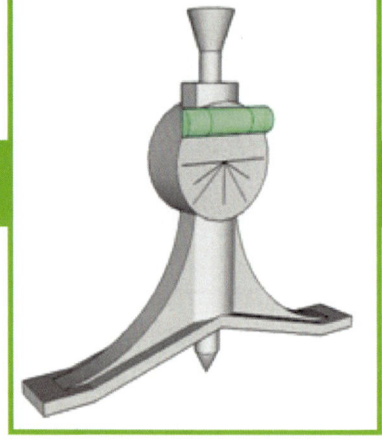

A centering head is a device that is used to mark a point that is perpendicular to a curved surface (see Figure 11.13). Some centering heads are equipped with an adjustable tubular spirit level that allows for precise angular measurements on a horizontally run pipe. Centering heads are particularly useful for installing pipe tapping saddles that may be used for mounting sensor equipment such as flow meters and in-line probes.

11.12 Torque Wrench

A torque wrench is a device that applies a set amount of torque to a nut or bolt. They come in either indicating or setting types (see Figure 11.14). Indicating type torque wrenches use a flexing indicator or dial to show the torque being applied. Setting type torque wrenches us a special mechanism that can be set to let the operator know when the set torque value has been achieved. Torque wrenches come is a variety of sizes and ranges. Typically, their measurements are inch-pounds (in·lbs), foot-pounds (ft·lbs), and/or Newton meters (N·m). Always follow manufacturer's recommendations for use, calibration and storage since all of these things can reduce the accuracy of the torque wrench if done improperly. Torque wrenches are useful in many life support applications, including plumbing, pump repair, plate heat exchanger repair, as well as many others.

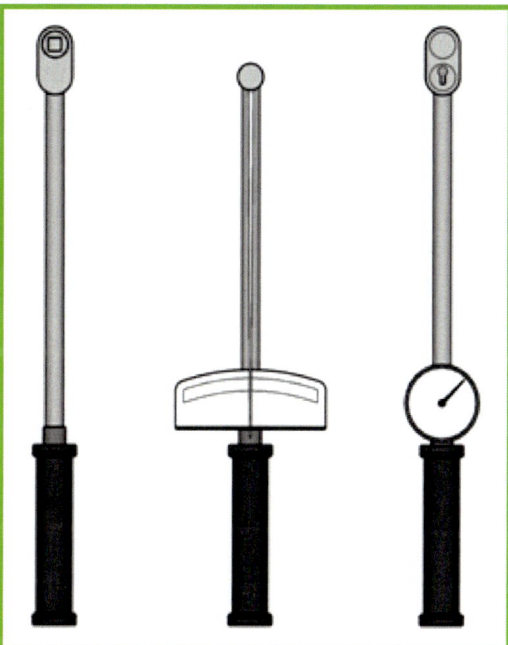

Figure 11.14 – Torque Wrenches

12   Heat Exchangers

An essential element of maintaining aquatic life is temperature control. Temperature is controlled by water chillers and heaters. A key component of temperature control units are heat exchangers. Heat exchangers work by using two fluids or gases at different temperatures and are not in direct contact to raise or lower the temperature. It is recommended to have isolation valves on both sides of heat exchanger vessels as well as flow meters to monitor any restriction or build-up.

12.1 Plate Exchangers

Plate heat exchangers (PHE) are a very efficient non-direct contact method of heating or cooling fluids on low or medium sized pressurized vessels. These units have the ability to add or subtract plates, which are used in pairs, depending on how much surface area/heat exchange is required. PHEs work by using a coolant or heated liquid (glycol, chilled/heated water from the facility's main building HVAC systems) to cool or heat another fluid. The two fluids flow in alternating directions between plates to maximize efficiency. The main components of these units are stainless steel or titanium plates, rubber gaskets and securing bolts. Titanium plates are more resistant to corrosion and provide an extra defense to cross contamination between process water and exhibit water. Even the highest quality of stainless may corrode in a saltwater exhibit. The ethylene propylene diene monomer (EPDM) gaskets are secured by glue or clips. Securing bolts should be coated with a protective anti-seize paste (especially in marine environments) to ensure they can be easily removed. PHEs require minimal space and are very efficient. In order to maintain efficient heat exchange rates, these plates should be broken down annually and cleaned. Heat exchangers are typically installed post filtration, with isolation valves on both inlets and outlets. When installing or cleaning plates, it is imperative that the order of the plates is re-installed correctly because plate A alternates with plate B until all of the designated plates are used. If plates A and B are mixed up, the separation of the two liquids will be compromised resulting in exhibit contamination.

Figure 12.1 – Plate Heat Exchanger

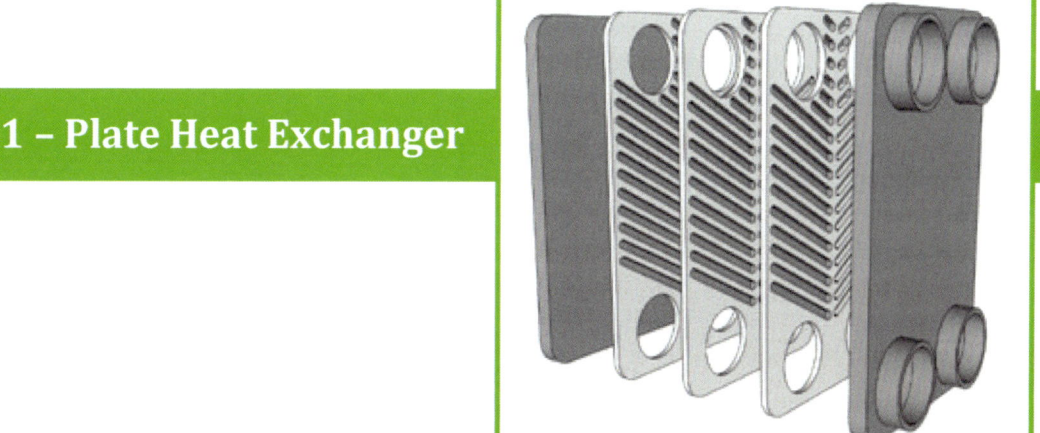

12.2 Shell and Tube Exchangers

Shell and tube heat exchangers use a pressurized vessel or a shell containing tubes or rods that are filled with heated or cooled fluids to cool a secondary fluid. The primary fluid (exhibit water) enters the vessel and flows in a helical pattern as it passes the rods. Examples of rod applications are seen in Figures 12.2 and 12.3. These vessels are common and typically found in zoological settings in the form of aquarium chillers. Rods should be cleaned annually and like PHEs, they should be installed with a flow meter and isolation valves to monitor any restrictions or build-up.

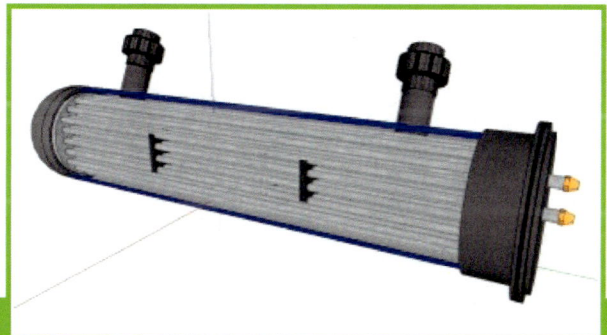

Figure 12.2 - Tube Heat Exchanger

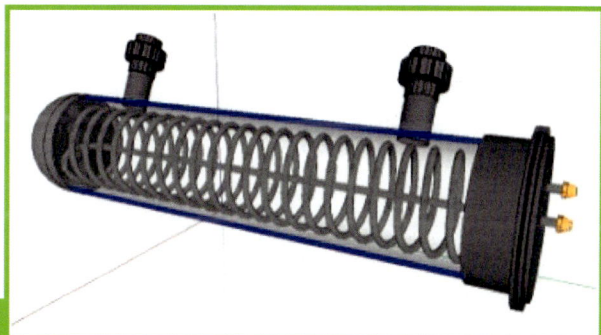

Figure 12.3 - Helical Heat Exchanger

The term, automation control systems, refers to any equipment that accomplishes monitoring and/or control of LSS equipment by an electronic device. This includes relay logic devices, PLCs, programmable automation controllers (PACs), distributed control systems (DCS), and SCADA. These systems are an invaluable means of ensuring safe and efficient operation of modern LSS installations. All controls systems, regardless of size, are comprised of the same general components. The inputs (sensors), the controller, and the outputs (controlled devices); together, they form the "control chain".

13.1 Control Chain

1. The controller – the device connected to inputs and outputs, which controls output devices so that desired system function is achieved.

2. The Field – everything else: the physical area where the controlled system and its equipment are located. The system inputs and outputs (I/O) are in the field.

3. HMI - (human machine interface) - HMI is not always required or present in automated control systems. HMIs provide a means by which operators may view and/or operate controlled equipment.

13.1.1 Controller

The controller in an automated system is the "brains" of the operation. There are many different types, makes, and models. Elements of hardware and software are common to all controllers. The hardware consists of a processor for computing and I/O modules for connecting to the inputs and outputs in the field. The software enables programming of the processor to perform the required operations. Some common programming types for automation system controllers include ladder logic, function block, instruction list, sequential function chart, structured text, as well as standard computer languages like C, C++, or python. A PLC is a well suited hardware option for use in LSS automation. Whatever the controller hardware type, it will usually be installed in a protective enclosure along with the various electrical components required to complete the system. Figure 13.1 identifies some common hardware found in a PLC control panel.

Figure 13.1 Control Panel

1.   Ethernet Switch - Many control panels have Ethernet switches for connecting PLCs, HMIs, networked I/O, and information systems.

2. PLC - This is the "brains" of the control panel. It reads inputs, executes code, and adjusts outputs accordingly.

3. I/O Modules - The field input and output devices connect to the controller at these

modules. The types and quantities of these modules are selected based on the type and quantity of field I/O circuits to be connected to the controller.

4. Wire Duct - Wire duct is used for housing the wires that interconnect the electrical components.

5. Power Line Filter - This device protects the PLC from surges and line noise in the incoming power that could cause mis-operation and damage.

6. Circuit Breakers - Circuit breakers protect loads from drawing too much current that could damage equipment or cause electrical fires.

7. Terminal Ground Blocks - A terminal block ground is usually internally grounded to the panel. They are often green or green/yellow for easy identification.

8. Relays - A relay is an electronically or magnetically operated switch. Power is applied to the coil which creates a magnetic field that switches the relay contacts. Relays control or turn on higher voltage equipment such as motors and actuators with a lower voltage.

9. Fuses - Fuses, like circuit breakers, protect loads from pulling too much current, but are only good for one use.

10. DC Power Supply - A DC power supply converts incoming AC or DC to a nominal operating DC voltage. This one converts 120 VAC to 24 VDC.

11. Convenience Receptacles - These are standard 120 VAC receptacles installed so that a system integrator may easily plug in a laptop and/or test equipment.

12. Terminal Blocks - Terminal blocks are connection points to tie wires together. Some are for internal connections and some are for connecting field components to the control system. These terminal blocks are specifically designed for analog sensors, and thus have 3 connection points on each side.

13. Terminal Blocks - These terminal blocks are the standard type, connecting one wire on each side.

Located outside of the control panel, the field inputs and outputs (I/O) or field devices make up the remainder of the automation system. I/O points are named by reference to the controller where INPUT represents a signal sent to the controller and OUTPUT represents a signal sent from the controller.

13.1.2 Inputs

There are two types of inputs: analog and digital. Analog inputs are also commonly called sensors. This component collects a specific measurement of the desired parameter in a repeatable way and provides the raw input for the control chain. The term analog, in this context, refers to a point that can hold a range of values such as a temperature or flow measurement. Examples of common sensors in the LSS field are temperature, pressure, flow, pH, and ORP. Each of these will convert a raw measurement response into an electrical signal suitable for evaluation by the controller. Common analog sensor signals use electrical currents, often 4 mA to 20 mA, or electrical voltage, often 0 VDC to 10 VDC to carry a signal to the controller. The controller is then responsible for evaluating the raw signal from the sensor in accordance with the programming logic.

The other input type is known as a digital input. Digital input devices are commonly referred to as switches or contacts. Unlike the analog inputs, which provide information within a range of values, digital inputs provide information limited to one of two states, ON or OFF. This "energized or not energized" state is used for data that can be understood in binary terms such as on/off, yes/no, high/low, made/not made, run/stop, etc., and is "seen" by the controller as either power/no power, entering the controller logic program as a 1 or a 0 respectively. Digital input circuits may be powered by either AC or DC and occur in various voltage levels of each. Never assume that a digital input circuit is safe, low voltage DC, because 120 VAC digital input modules are common. In digital input circuits, the field device is the "switch" that controls the on/off flow of electricity to the controller input which provides the electrical load portion of the circuit. An example of a digital input would be a circuit connected to the auxiliary contacts of a motor control contactor, providing the controller with the run status of a pump. Figure 13.2 illustrates a wiring diagram for a digital input.

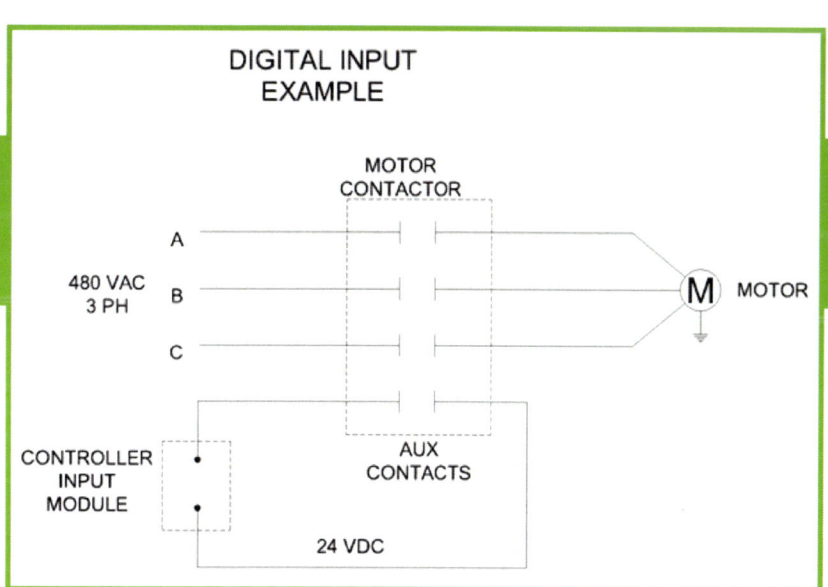

**Figure 13.2
Digital Input
Example Diagram**

13.1.3 Outputs

The final link in the control chain is the output, or controlled device. Outputs with respect to the controller, come in two types: digital and analog. Similar to the digital inputs, digital outputs are limited to the same two states ON or OFF. Based on its evaluation of the incoming data (inputs), the controller will perform the prescribed action with its outputs. If the outputs are digital, the controller will turn them ON or OFF by applying or removing power to the circuit. Digital output devices are the load part of the circuit and will usually take the form of a coil (such as a relay coil, solenoid coil, motor contactor coil, windings of a motor, or transformer) or resistive load such as a light or heating element. A controller's program will likely use 1 or 0 values when manipulating the digital outputs. The output module will then translate this state to the field circuit such that 1 = ON, and 0 = OFF (most commonly). Digital output modules are commonly used with both AC and DC power, in low to high voltages. Uses for digital outputs are numerous and could be as small as the activation of a signal light indicating either a nominal or alarm condition, or as large as the direct and automatic control of primary life support system equipment.

The other type of controller outputs are analog outputs. Just as with the analog inputs, an analog output is not limited to ON/OFF, and is capable of providing an output signal to a field device that conveys any desired value within a defined range. This analog output circuit from the controller will usually connect to the analog input terminals on devices and equipment in the field. In LSS applications, analog outputs may be used to provide the speed reference signal to variable frequency drives (VFDs), a position reference signal to a modulating control valve, or power output percentage reference signal to an ozone generator. It is helpful to think of the two types of controller outputs in the following way: the digital output can tell the pump to run; the analog output can tell the pump how fast to run. Similar to analog inputs, analog output circuits utilize a current or voltage type signal. Figure 13.3 illustrates a wiring diagram for a digit output.

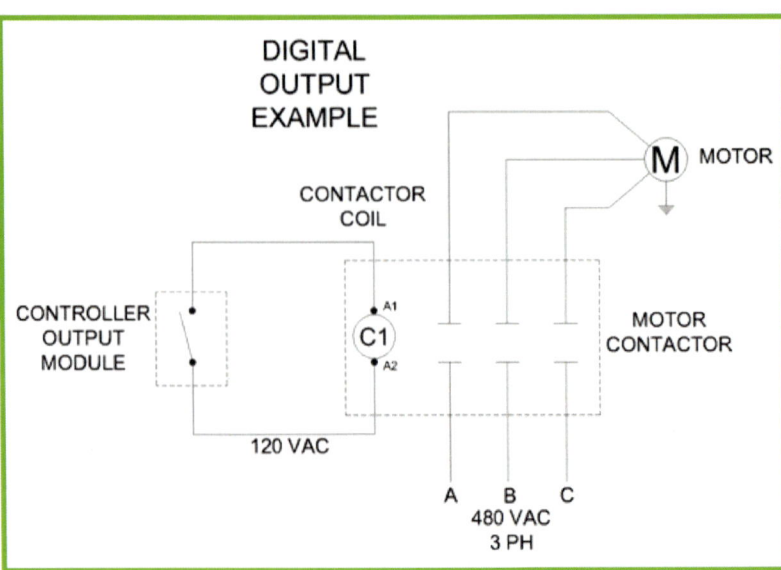

Figure 13.3 Digital Output Example Diagram

13.1.4 HMI

Many automation control systems utilize some form of HMI. The HMI may be a simple keypad, LCD display, graphic touch panel, computer, tablet, smartphone application, SCADA software, or any combination of these items that allow a human to interact with the system. Some commonly used terms synonymous with HMI are man machine interface (MMI), operator interface (OI), graphic user interface (GUI), and user interface (UI). HMIs are commonly used to display machine faults or machine status, allow an operator to monitor system parameters, or allow an operator to start or stop equipment or processes.

Figure 13.4 and 13.5 are screens from the touch panel type HMI located on the outside of the PLC control panel that was illustrated previously (Figure 13.1). The images shown are smartphone screen-captures, as this particular HMI may be viewed and controlled locally, from the touch panel in the field, or remotely, from any PC, tablet, or smartphone device. HMIs with far more advanced graphics and animations are common, and typically run on PC based software. Each has its advantages, and use of multiple HMIs is common.

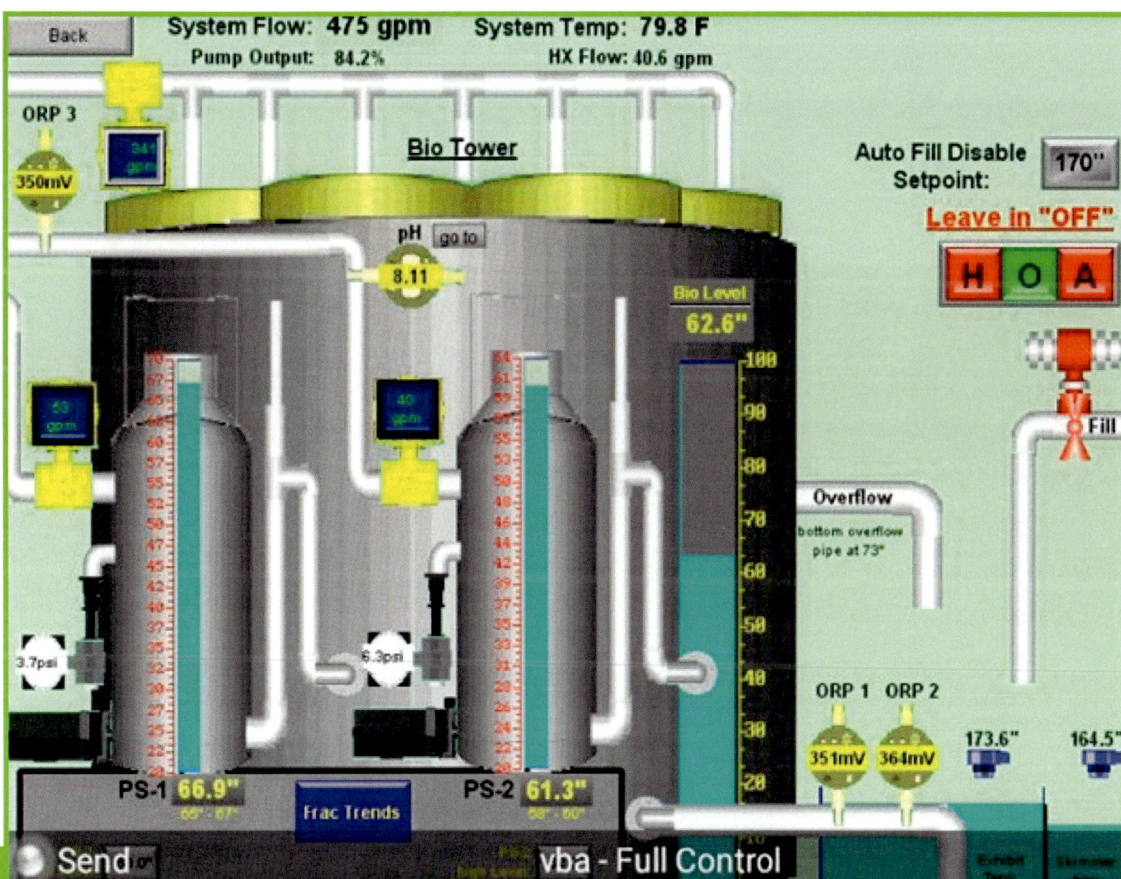

Figure 13.4 - Example of an HMI Screen

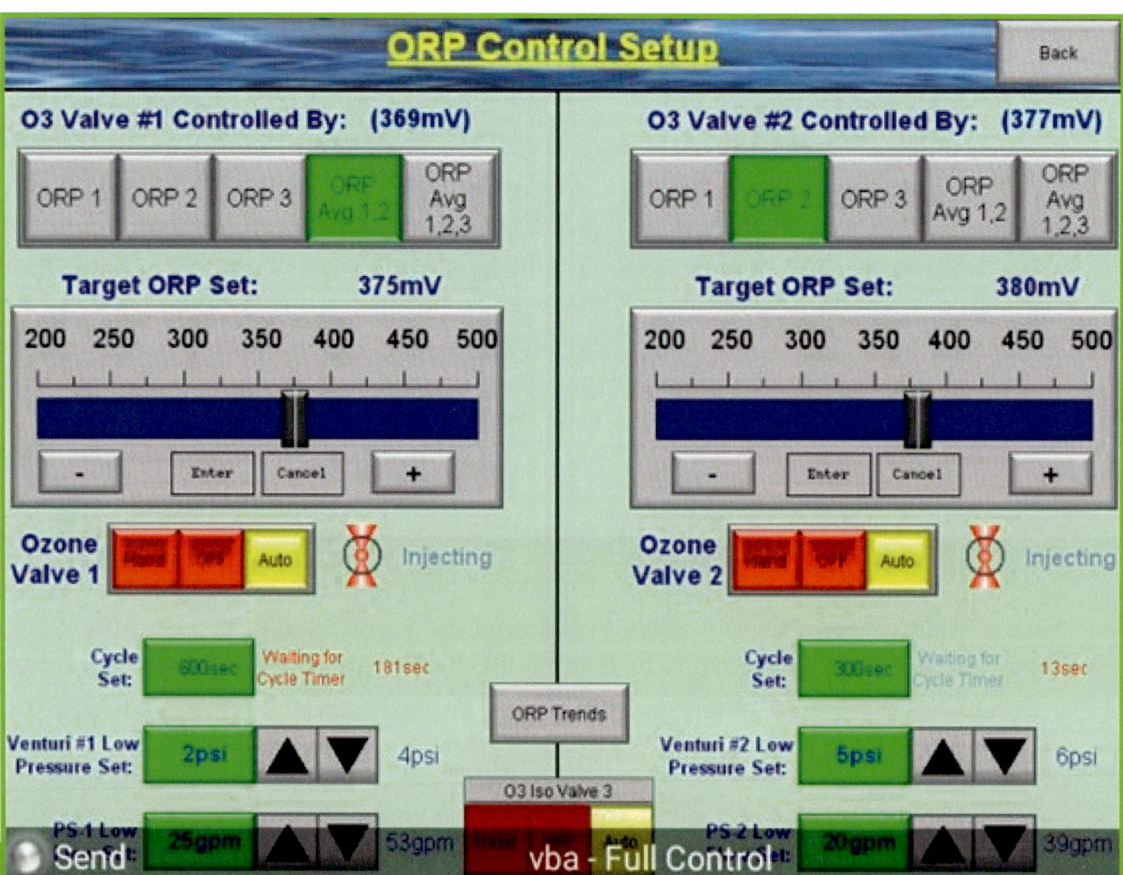

Figure 13.5 - Example of an HMI Screen

13.2 Common Application Examples in LSS

13.2.1 Measuring Water Level

Water level is commonly monitored by sensors using an ultrasonic transducer to bounce a soundwave off of the surface of the water and measure the time it takes to return to the sensor head. The electronics on board the sensor head will then convert the resulting signal into a standard current/voltage (for example, 4 mA to 20 mA) signal across the analog circuit connected to the controller. The 4 mA - 20 mA range in this example will be scaled to match the empty (4 mA) and full (20 mA) levels of the tank or basin being measured.

13.2.2 Measuring and Controlling Temperature

Water temperature is another common analog measurement. The amount of cooling or heating water flowing through a heat exchanger is controlled based on the reading from an immersion sensor. The sensor will generate an analog signal that will be read by the controller. The controller in turn will compare the input reading to the defined set point and determine whether to increase or decrease the amount of cooling or heating water passing through the heat exchanger in order to maintain the target set point. The adjustment to this flow rate will be achieved by modulating an actuated valve.

13.2.3 Controlling an Actuated Valve

In order to control complex devices it is necessary to bundle discrete (digital) points together. The control of a typical cam-on-shaft valve actuator is a good example, where the process of controlling an actuator intended for fully opened or closed operation only is described.

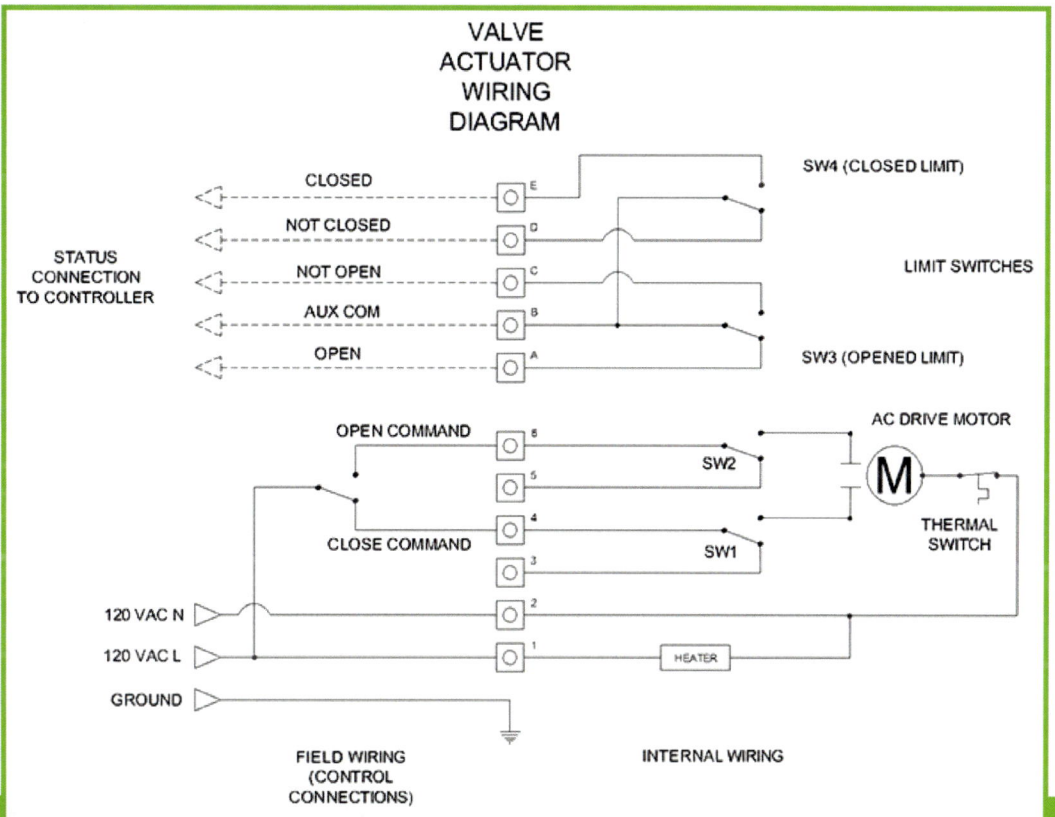

Figure 13.6 - Valve Actuator Wiring Diagram

This type of actuator can be controlled by bundling four points together: two digital output points (DO) and two digital input points (DI). The individual points are as follows:

- OPEN COMMAND (DO) Command to open valve sent by controller
  - Wired to terminal 4 activating SW1 inside the actuator
- CLOSE COMMAND (DO) Command to close valve sent by controller
  - Wired to terminal 6 activating SW2 inside the actuator

- OPENED STATUS (DI) Feedback from OPENED limit switch to controller
  - Wired to terminals A and B activated by SW3 inside the actuator
- CLOSED STATUS (DI) Feedback from CLOSED limit switch to controller
  - Wired to terminals D and E activated by SW4 inside the actuator

In normal operation, the controller sends a command to the actuator to open the valve resulting in the I/O hardware energizing the OPEN COMMAND circuit. The valve is then opened by the actuator, stopping when the OPENED limit switch is made thereby changing the state of the OPENED STATUS circuit. The controller then accepts that the command has been correctly executed and de-energizes the OPEN COMMAND circuit.

An actuated valve can be controlled using an analog output signal (a position reference) or using digital signals using a technique called pulse-width modulation (PWM). In the above example, the position of the valve can be fine-tuned by pulsing the open and close command circuits momentarily. This will be accomplished by comparing a measured flow rate to a defined flow set point and modulating the valve position in order to maintain that set point, allowing throttling.

13.2.4 Pump Protection by Monitoring Flow

Automated systems will typically use analog flow or pressure measurements or switches to monitor the operation of pumps. By monitoring the water flow and/or pressure associated with a pump, it can be protected from conditions that could result in pump damage. Automation can also be programmed to alert the operator to a potential pump fault by detecting a low or zero flow condition.

Since centrifugal pumps rely on water passing through them to regulate their temperature, lack of flow will damage a pump by causing heat buildup. In the event that a pump is running dry or in a dead-head condition (closed discharge valve), this heat buildup can result is severe damage to the pump and associated piping.

The control system can be programmed to interpret a low flow or low/high pressure value as either an incorrect valve lineup or failure of the pump. The control system will then automatically deactivate the pump run command, activate a system alarm, and often send a text or email to the operator.

13.2.5 Current Transducers

A transducer is a device that converts one form of energy to another. A current transducer (CT) is a device that takes advantage of the magnetic field created by the electricity flowing through an electric conductor and uses the principle of induction to generate a signal that is proportional to the amount of current flowing through the main conductor. This analog signal can be measured by a recording instrument or electronic controller. Some current transducers will take the form of a "current switch" that will have electronics incorporated into the device that will open or close, providing an on/off status that can be fed to a controller or other device.

Typical applications in an LSS installation include utility power status monitoring, energy metering, and equipment operation "proofing." In a utility power monitoring application, the CT is placed around the conductor(s) of the main electric supply or one of the branch circuits that supply electricity to the LSS. If the signal from the CT drops out, the controller will interpret this as a power failure and will take whatever programmed action is associated with a power outage, such as operator notifications and automated system shutdown routines. Additional functions may include automatic starting of emergency generators and standby power automatic transfer switch gear.

In an energy monitoring setup, the analog signal generated by the CT is logged continuously in order to calculate the total energy used by that circuit as a function of time. Normally this energy consumption will be measured in kilowatt-hours (KWH). Tracking energy usage by an LSS system can be used to reduce operating costs by changing the operational state of the system, minimizing electrical consumption during time of peak usage charges or by tracking electrical consumption as a means to monitor equipment health.

With an equipment proofing setup, the CT is used to verify that a piece of equipment that has been given a run command by the controller, has actually started. When a controller energizes the run command circuit for a pump, or other component, a CT attached to the conductors feeding the pump motor will detect if there is flow of electricity to the pump and verify that it has started. For a proofing setup, a current switch device is typically employed, instead of a CT giving an analog signal to the controller.

14 Construction and System Start Up

The design and construction of aquatic exhibits takes careful planning to ensure their performance supports animal, staff and guest needs. A wide variety of construction materials are readily available; however, many are not suited to aquatic exhibitry and careful consideration must be given to ensure appropriate materials are selected, prepared, and handled in the correct manner. Materials that may work in freshwater, may not be suitable for salt water, for example. The materials selection process is vital for the health of the animals exhibited and the structural integrity of the exhibit for the duration of the exhibit's lifetime.

14.1 Materials

The materials used in the design and construction of tanks used for holding aquatic specimens may vary according to the tanks intended purpose, such as systems used for quarantine, public display, and research. Many of the same materials can be used to construct a variety of systems. A list of commonly used aquarium construction materials and techniques are provided below.

14.1.1 Tank Construction

Glass and Acrylic

Glass and acrylic are commonly used materials in both the private and public aquarium industry. Glass has been used for the construction of both large and small aquarium exhibits for many decades with great success. It is easily acquired, inexpensive, does not easily scratch, and has high tensile strength. Acrylic can be formed into almost any desired shape and it has been used to build viewing panels capable of withstanding the pressure of millions of gallons of seawater. Acrylic provides greater viewing clarity and less distortion, compared to glass panels of the same dimension. Acrylic is much lighter in weight than glass and will not shatter if struck. Disadvantages of acrylic, when compared to glass, is the cost, its ability to easily scratch, and its expansion and contraction properties when exposed to certain temperatures.

Fiberglass

Fiberglass tanks and strut are fairly common due to their strength and customizability. These tanks are typically found in quarantine settings for their chemical resistance. Larger tanks have central I-beams or bracing around the tank to add strength. A drawback to fiberglass is the dust and volatile organic compounds (VOCs) they produce during initial construction.

Polyethylene

Pre-formed polyethylene holding systems come in a variety of shapes and sizes (size can be a limiting factor for larger systems). They are generally light in weight, cost efficient, easy to install, easily disinfected, and safe for housing marine and freshwater organisms.

Concrete

Concrete has been used in the construction of public aquarium exhibits with much success for many years. It is strong, readily obtainable, and relatively cheap. Inappropriate installation and preparation of the material can result in a multitude of issues for the facility both initially and many years after an exhibit in operation. The use of concrete for the construction of exhibit walls and some portions of theming elements requires embedded support materials. When possible, use non-metallic materials such as carbon fiber or glass fiber as the internal support materials for cement (Choromanski, 2004; Powell et al., 2004). While non-metallic materials are ideal, they may not be capable of providing the necessary support required by large systems and internal theming structures. In this case metallic reinforcing bar or "rebar" may be used. Rebar is the most commonly used support material and it should be installed at an appropriate depth of coverage to prevent corrosion. Coating rebar in a waterproofing protective agent such as epoxy prior to installation will enhance protection of the material. Ensure the depth of the support material and the ratio of water to cement is correct. If it is incorrectly installed, spalling may occur, where saltwater gains access to the metallic rebar and cause structural changes in the concrete. This is not only aesthetically displeasing, but it is also a hazard to the structural integrity of the exhibit and the aquatic organisms living within the exhibit. The importance of effectively waterproofing a structure intended to house aquatic life cannot be overstated. Waterproofing tanks prevents corrosion and leaks when correctly installed. Resins, polymers, liners, and other impermeable membranes are successfully used in many situations (Powell, Wisner and Rupp, 2004).

14.1.2 Acid Leaching and Pretreatment of Concrete

Acid leaching, also called acid etching, and pretreatment of concrete is also important when using this material for aquatic exhibit purposes. Cement is commonly used to construct tanks and theming and decor elements. Upon filing an exhibit constructed with cement components, there will often be a noticeable and dramatic rise in pH, compared to the source water. This pH increase is due to the alkalis leached from the cement. There are a number of ways to deal with this issue.

For example, the system can be filled up with freshwater and carefully dosed with hydrochloric (muriatic) acid over a period of days to establish a steady pH around 5 or 6, but no less than 4.5, as some undesirable changes may occur to the acrylic and some tank coatings. The display is then flushed to waste and replaced with clean, exhibit water. For freshwater systems, use dechlorinated freshwater of the desired pH and hardness. For marine systems, fill with clean sea water.

The idea behind the acid etching solution is to penetrate and saturate the porous exterior of the new decor to create a barrier layer just below the decor's surfaces that will limit the transfers of residual base ions into the water. Upon pH stabilization, the exhibit is drained and then filled with clean salt water to remove any residual compounds that might have been liberated from the concrete by the use of the acid (Choromanski, 2004). Once refilled, normal pH control methods can be applied to acidify the new incoming water if this is necessary. Unfortunately, there is no straightforward equation to specifically calculate the exact volume of acid to add to an exhibit.

To automate this process, a pH dosimeter can be setup to monitor pH and dose the acid as needed to maintain the water at a low pH to speed up the process of leaching. The control range of a pH controller can be set at 4.5 to 5.5 to achieve the maximum effectiveness of the treatment in the shortest amount of time. It is recommended that the acrylics manufacturer be consulted for pH levels that could cause issues with acrylic etching. For example, a low pH could cause damage to concrete surfaces and potentially rock work discoloration. Using an acid injection loop dilutes the acid before entering the water and reduces the risk of damage to any nearby acrylic or rockwork.

When the pH of the water in the exhibit reaches 5.5, the pH controller sends power to the dosing pump. This doses hydrochloric acid into the acid injection loop and then into the exhibit. This dosing continues until the pH controller reads 4.5 and then cuts off power to the dosing pump. This process can safely occur 24 hours a day, with little staff time needed. After about one to three weeks of automated dosing, the duration of pH stability between additions will get longer and longer. Acid dosing should be suspended and the pH allowed to rise to a stable value, to determine system stability. When the pH value rises to a pH of 9 or higher, it is a clear indicator that further leaching is still occurring and acid dosing should resume. When the controller reads a constant pH level of 7 - 8, it is an indication that the leaching process is nearly complete. After several weeks of constant acid dosing, the exhibit should be ready for a rinse and final fill. No further acid dosing should be needed.

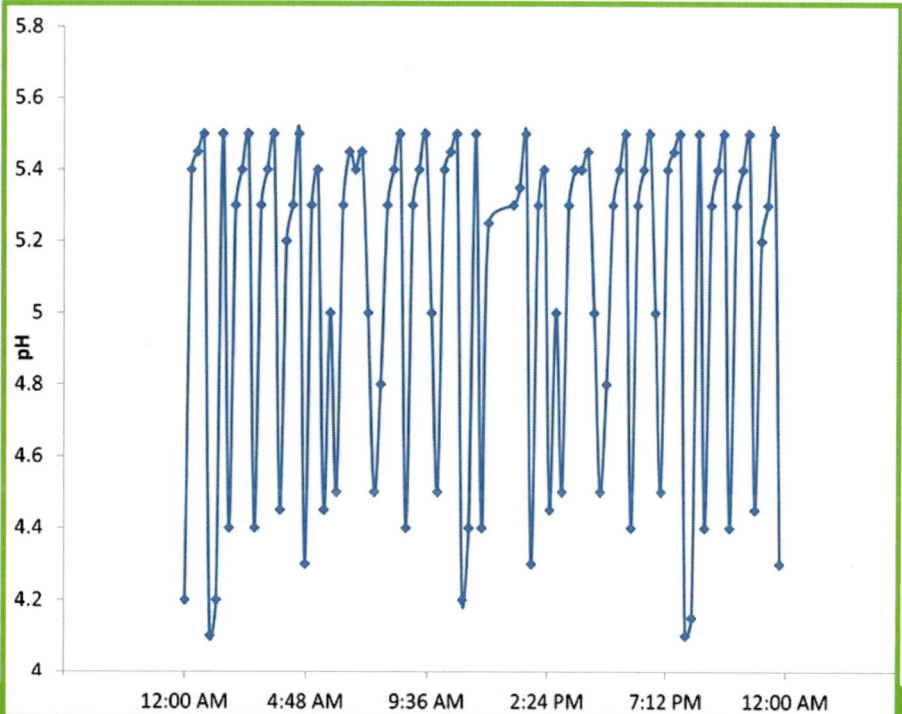

Figure 14.1 Twenty-four hours of pH readings on the Philippine Coral Reef Exhibit at the California Academy of Sciences. This data shows a rapid drop in pH after acid has been dosed, followed by a gradual increase as alkali leaches from concrete and rockwork.

14.1.3 Plumbing

PVC

Polyvinyl chloride (PVC) pipe is often used because of its reliability and cost effectiveness. It is readily available in two thicknesses: schedule 40 and schedule 80. Schedule 80 pipe and fittings are made with a thicker wall for higher pressure applications. Schedule 80 pipe has higher frictional losses than schedule 40 pipe due to having a smaller inner diameter. Schedule 80 tends to have a higher insulation rating than schedule 40.

HDPE

High density polyethylene (HDPE) is a form of plastic pipe that is used in aquarium and zoo settings. These pipes are connected through fusion welding or threaded connections. HDPE is fairly expensive due to its high chemical resistance and strength. It can be found mainly in laboratory settings and drain pipes. HDPE can also be used in underground settings because it has more flex than PVC. It is important to avoid flanged fittings in underground installations and use only welded connections. Once the pipe is above grade, a flanged fitting will be useful to convert to PVC piping.

ABS

Acrylonitrile butadiene styrene (ABS) is another type of thermoplastic pipe used in zoos and aquariums. ABS is connected similarly to PVC, but it does not require any primer to ensure a solid bond between fittings. It has a high impact strength but degrades in sunlight.

Primers

Primers, most commonly found in PVC applications, are used to treat and soften any surfaces prior to being glued. Different pipes have specific primers based on their chemical composition. It is important to always prime the surface prior to applying glue.

Glue

Glue or cement is the second solvent applied during the joining of two fittings, sometimes the only solvent depending on the type of pipe.

VOCs

A Volatile Organic Compound (VOC) is a general term used to describe a group of chemicals released as a gas from a multitude of commonly used construction and household products. Not only can these chemicals pose a health hazard to workers, they can also pose a serious threat to the health and wellbeing of many other living organisms including aquatic life. Many products will state if they are "low-VOC" or "VOC free." Methods for reducing exposure to VOCs include providing adequate ventilation, following all label precautions, and using the products according to the manufacturer's directions and not outside of their intended purposes (USEPA, 2017).

New LSS plumbing can be flushed to waste before the final fill of system water, as well as filtered over activated carbon for a week or more as an added precautions against contaminants from the LSS installation.

14.1.4 Structural Support

Wood

Wood is easily obtained and affordable, compared to many of the other materials used to construct aquarium stands, maintenance platforms, and other structures. If well maintained and allowed to dry, wood can last for years. Consideration should be given to the environmental stressors that the wood may exposed to. Products such as marine grade plywood are manufactured specifically for use in environments associated with high humidity such as boats and fishing docks. Other materials may require or come with additional preparation with some form of treatment or waterproof coating to prevent the structure from rotting, warping, or cracking and from developing mold and mildew. Some treatment may be toxic so care must be taken to ensure that drips or leaks across treated wood cannot gain access to life support systems or displays containing aquatic life.

Metal

Metal may seem to be an ideal material to use when designing structures to support and service aquatic exhibits due to its strength; however, the environmental stress this material will be exposed to in an aquatic facility should be carefully considered. Continuous exposure to salt water, in particular, may cause the structure to corrode and eventually fail. Products such as 316 stainless steel are specifically engineered to resist corrosion. When working with metal materials, it may be necessary to coat materials with some form of protectant, such as epoxy, acrylic, or powder coating to ensure the material retains its structural integrity for the duration of its use. Even after the appropriate measures have been taken to protect the material, routinely inspect the material for any signs of weakness or corrosion and address them immediately to prevent larger issues from developing. Leachates from metallic structures entering life support systems or displays may be toxic to aquatic life.

FRP

Fiberglass Reinforced Plastic (FRP), including "fiber grate", is chosen in many water and wastewater situations due to the material's extreme durability and long-term cost effectiveness. It can be formed to fit the individual's exact specifications. It is light in weight compared to similar structures that are primarily composed of metal and it is highly resistant to corrosion. Additionally, it is unaffected by temperature fluctuations. The two primary downsides to this material is its cost and the challenges associated with working with the material. The dust produced when cutting this material may cause eye, skin, and respiratory tract irritation; therefore, appropriate PPE should be worn to prevent these issues from occurring.

14.2 In-house LSS Design and Fabrication

The design phase of a new aquatic exhibit is commonly outsourced to engineers and architects. When the opportunity for in-house design does arise, it can present a valuable opportunity for life support operators. Proper construction and equipment planning is critical, as is communication with husbandry staff to ensure the needs of the animals in their care are met.

The location being considered for the system should be evaluated for the availability of space, power, water, and drains. Lack of necessary resources, especially electrical power, may require modifications to infrastructure. Long hoses can be used to service a system, but the extended use of electrical extension cords (more than 90 days) is not permissible by OSHA or the National Electrical Code (NEC).

Sketches may be all that is required to ensure design intentions are clear. In tight spaces and for complicated systems, even relatively small systems, the use of computer-aided design (CAD) software can be a powerful planning tool. CAD models, especially those with accurate details, can be used as aids in the construction process. 3D laser scanning technology can affordably create a model of an existing space to help integrate the new design and identify plumbing routes or potential conflicts.

A well thought out system will meet the needs of the animals, biologists, and operators. Equipment needs to be accessible for maintenance. Equipment requiring frequent maintenance should be isolatable by means of a bypass loop, allowing the equipment to be removed or serviced while the system is still operating.

Important considerations for choosing equipment are operability, cost, durability, and ease of maintenance. Balancing these factors can be difficult. The most durable equipment may be the most expensive, but the lowest cost equipment may not be repairable. Value engineering out important features, especially durability of materials, has a tendency to cause future problems in the long run. Seeking out types and brands of equipment that are already in use within the facility may be beneficial since operators will likely be familiar with its performance, reliability, and maintenance. This commonality can also help keep backup equipment and repair parts inventory simple. Trying new equipment can also be beneficial when the new equipment leads to improved conditions for the animals, energy or water savings, and/or maintainability. All equipment must be chosen based on the engineering requirements of the system. Consulting manufactures and other user within the industry can ensure the new equipment is appropriate for the application.

As with any new system, a detailed SOP should be developed for commissioning, operation, and maintenance of all equipment. Additionally, engineering notes can be included with the SOPs for added benefit. Once commissioned, all staff responsible for any parts of the system should be trained in its operation and maintenance.

14.3 Commissioning a New Life Support System

Commissioning a life support system is the process by which the system is brought into working condition and is made ready for the animals it was built for. This process involves leak testing, hydrostatic pressure testing, equipment startup, flow balancing, and establishing and stabilizing the chemical and biological aspects of the system to support the animals. It is recommended that a Standard Operating Procedure (SOP) be developed for commissioning new systems. A well thought out SOP will aid in preventing avoidable mistakes by outline each step of the commissioning process. For more on SOPs, see Section 15.1.

Leak testing is the process of verifying that the system will hold water. This process verifies the integrity of the exhibit, plumbing, and equipment such as filter vessels and heat exchangers. A thorough inspection of all equipment, unions, flanges, and valves can go a long way in preventing avoidable leaks. Typically, the exhibit is filled with freshwater and as much plumbing and equipment as possible is isolated by closing all valves. Once the exhibit is filled, portions of the plumbing are opened, exposing components to water in order of typical system operation. As each new section of plumbing is filled, all plumbing connections should be checked for leaks.

For some systems, such as those with LSS equipment above the exhibit, a static water test may not be possible in this manner. In those cases, pumps may be needed in order to expose all equipment and plumbing to water in order to check for leaks. Ensure that all pumps are installed in accordance to the manufacturer's recommendations. In the case of 3Ø (three-phase) motors, rotation should be checked and corrected if necessary, before bringing the pump up to working speed. As much air as possible should be vented from plumbing and equipment before turning on pumps. The pressure resulting from pump startup has the potential to cause catastrophic failures in plumbing and equipment that may not have occurred if air was properly vented. As pumps are brought online, air should be vented from equipment at the same time to avoid these types of failures. As air is vented and replaced with water, additional water may need to be added to the system in order to keep the system above the minimum operational water level. The additional pressure from pump start up may expose previously hidden leaks, so a full re-inspection of plumbing and equipment is recommended.

It should be noted that pressure testing plumbing with air can be extremely dangerous and is not recommended. Compressed air has the ability to release large amounts of energy in an explosive manner.

If possible, the system should be run without animals for an extended period to allow failures to manifest and be identified. During this time, automation and control systems can be tested and tuned, construction debris can be removed from the system, and flow rates can be balanced to equipment, all without risk of animal endangerment. Any important or helpful information discovered during the process should be recorded in the SOP.

An exhibit themed with unsealed concrete may result in an elevated pH that could be harmful to aquatic organisms. If elevated pH is observed, acid leaching may be required. Details on acid leaching an exhibit can be found in Section 14.1.2. It is recommended that a functioning biological filter be present before the addition of any aquatic animals. Details on seeding a biological filter can be found in Section 9.2.3.

14.4 Salt Water Reclamation Facilities

One of the largest challenges for maintaining large marine aquaria is the continuous need to source clean and chemically balanced seawater for water changes, filtration backwashes, and other maintenance purposes. While some facilities are located adjacent to natural supplies of seawater, other facilities must either transport pre-treated water from the coast or manufacture large quantities of saltwater in house.

Saltwater reclamation facilities allow public aquaria to conserve and reuse a portion or the entirety of the wastewater produced by their systems. These systems also allow the collection of wastewater that may require additional treatment before it can be disposed of due to local, state, or federal regulations. Mechanical, chemical, and biological filtration components should be incorporated into the design to ensure the wastewater is sufficiently treated for reuse in exhibits inhabited by marine life.

Preventing the transfer of pathogens and disease is of extreme importance. Many disinfection and sterilization methods are available to assist the life support operator with this task. Disinfection is the reduction of harmful pathogens and sterilization is the elimination of all pathogens (Sykes, 1965). Several agents can be used to perform these processes. They include ozone, chlorine, bromine, ultraviolet light, and foam fractionation among others. Appropriate treatment concentrations and contact times for the chemical agents mentioned above will be dependent upon the operator's objectives for the reclaimed water. Treatment of effluent water with ozone at concentrations of 8 mg/L for three minutes will eliminate most pathogens (Noga, 2010). Exposure to free chlorine levels of 60 ppm for 24 hours has been proven to prevent the hatching of eggs from the monogenean *H. okamotoi* and *C. irritans* cysts (Hirazawa, Goto, and Shirasu, 2003). Using mechanical filtration techniques with a filter size of 20 microns or less may also aid in the reduction of pathogen transmission. Sodium thiosulfate is commonly used to neutralize oxidants used to treat reclaimed water. Refer to section 10.0 Disinfection and Sterilization for further information.

	Chlorine	Ozone	Ultraviolet radiation
Microbial effectiveness	Effective at high concentrations	Effective in highly polluted water	Effective only in clear water
Equipment cost	Low	High	Moderate
Operating Cost	High	Low	Moderate
Disadvantages	Potential formation of chloramines and other disinfection byproducts. Staff exposure concerns.	Residual ozone needs to be removed before return to exhibit. Staff exposure concerns.	Must be cleaned and replaced frequently. Effectiveness may be blocked by particles.

Figure 14.2 - Comparison Disinfection Methods Used for Fish Culture

Figure 14.3 is an example of a recovery system design which incorporates the appropriate components to allow proper treatment and recovery of exhibit waste water.

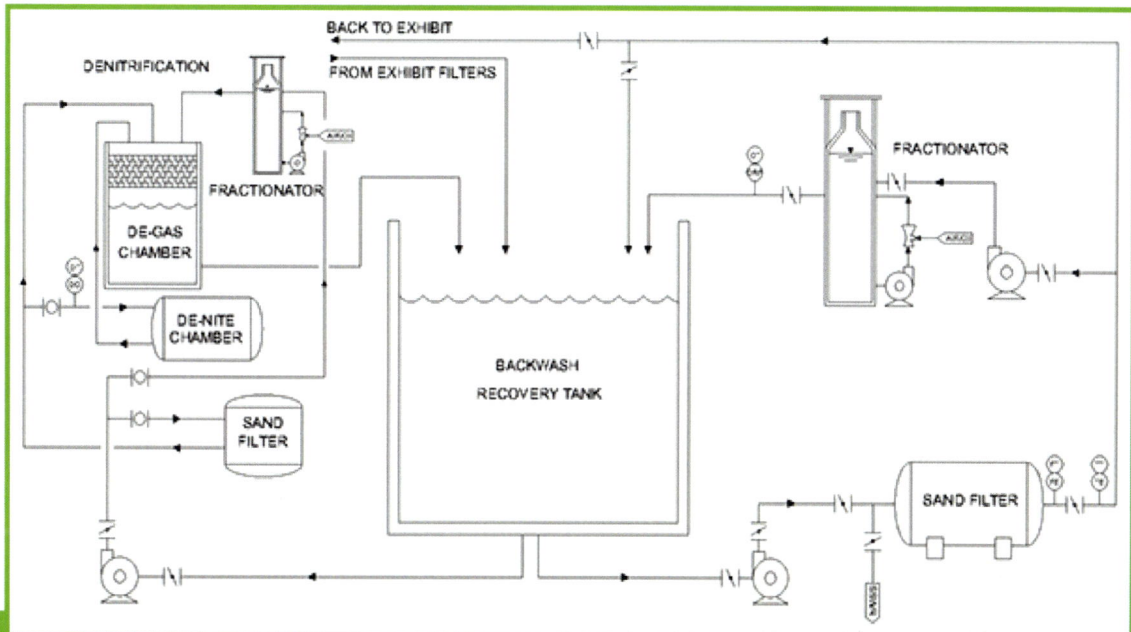

Figure 14.3 - Recovery System Design

14.5 Green Practices in LSS Operations: Water

From the early days of flow-through exhibits, aquatic life support systems in zoos and aquariums have made significant progress towards becoming less wasteful in their water usage. Design engineers and operators should seek ways to reduce water usage and make exhibits greener. Water use reductions are not only a benefit for the environment, but can also lower operating costs of zoos and aquariums.

14.5.1 Air Scour Backwashes

At many facilities, backwashing a sand filter is accomplished by reversing flow in the vessel. This process fluidizes the sand bed, releasing captured particulate. The waste containing water is sent to a reclamation basin to be reused or sanitary drain for disposal. With the addition of air to the backwash water, less water is required to achieve the same or better particulate removal. A rate of 2 - 3 SCFM/ft^2 (3 - 5 Nm^3/hr) of air and 3 - 5 GPM/ft^2 (120 LPM/m^2 - 200 LPM/m^2) of water is recommended. Due to the increased turbulence and fluidization of the sand bed, backwash time can be reduced, with the recommended time of around 2 minutes. Using this method can reduce water usage by 92.5% compared to a 4 minute backwash at 20 GPM/ft^2 (800 LPM/m^2). Typically, air scour backwashes are used on gravity sand filters (non pressurized), but can be used on pressurized sand filters with some considerations. When using an air scour backwash method, care needs to be taken in order to not over pressurize the vessel. Air should be vented during the operation if possible and the system completely vented before resuming sand filter operation.

14.5.2 Denitrification Systems

Artificial aquatic animal habitats need methods of reducing their accumulation of nitrogen (for more about nitrogen in aquatic habitats, see Section 5.1). A common way to reduce the nitrogen level is through water exchanges; however, this results in a significant volume of water to be discarded. Having a denitrification system built into a life support system can reduce or eliminate the need for water exchanges for nitrogen removal. For more information on denitrification systems, reference Section 9.2.2.

14.5.3 Reclaims

When backwashing a filter, wastewater is often sent to a sanitary drain; however, this water may be reclaimed to decrease water usage. Capturing backwash water in a designated basin allows for that water to be filtered, treated, and reused in the system. Reference Section 14.4 for details on reclamation system specifications and design. Reclaimed water may also be reused for non-LSS purposes, such as being used for watering plants and gardens at a facility after treatment.

14.5.4 Dive Activity Wastewater

When divers use a pump to remove debris, dive cleaning wastewater is often sent to a sanitary drain. Alternative methods can be investigated to reduce or eliminate sending this water to waste. If a system has a reclamation basin, dive cleaning wastewater can be sent to this basin to be filtered, treated, and reused in the system. If the filtration system has the capacity to treat the dive cleaning wastewater, it can be sent to the system sump for the filters to catch the debris. This method will increase the backwashes the filters need, but water may still be saved by not sending all the pump effluent water to a sanitary drain.

14.5.5 Backwashing Trigger Point

Operators can reduce water usage by performing backwashes based on performance conditions instead of a regular interval or schedule. This can be indicated by a reduced flow rate or an increase in the differential between the influent and effluent pressures on the filter. A flow rate of less than 75% of the nominal flow rate or a pressure differential between 10 psi to 12 psi may indicate that a filter should be backwashed. Reducing backwash frequency may decrease water usage, but may result in more nitrogenous waste build up in the system. Water quality should be monitored closely if using this method.

14.6 Green Practices in LSS Operations: Energy

For most facilities the design, fabrication, and installation of a new aquatic habitat is a significant investment. If not designed properly from the beginning, the long term operation of these systems can prove costly. The following section will touch on topics related to creating more energy efficient life support systems for aquatic displays.

14.6.1 Electricity

The pumps, heaters, chillers, lights, ozone generators, UV sterilizers, and automated operation/ monitoring systems that are key components of many modern life support systems require electricity to operate. The energy requirements of these components can be significant. A basic understanding of electrical terminology will help the operator understand how each component contributes to the overall energy demands of a system. For more information on motor terminology, see Section 7.3.2. Some of the most common electrical terms are defined below.

14.6.2 Electrical Terminology

The following terms and definitions are provided by the Occupational Safety and Health Association (OSHA, n.d.). A more extensive list can be found on the OSHA website at https://www.osha.gov/SLTC/etools/electric_power/glossary.html.

Ampere (A) or amp: The basic SI unit measuring the quantity of electricity. The unit for the electric current; the flow of electrons. One amp is 1 coulomb passing in one second. One amp is produced by an electric force of 1 volt acting across a resistance of 1 ohm.

Annual solar savings: The annual solar savings of a solar building is the energy savings attributable to a solar feature relative to the energy requirements of a non-solar building.

British thermal unit (Btu): The amount of heat energy required to raise the temperature of one pound of water from 60 degrees F to 61 degrees F at one atmosphere pressure.

Cable: A conductor with insulation, or a stranded conductor with or without insulation and other coverings (single-conductor cable), or a combination of conductors insulated from one another (multiple-conductor cable).

Cell: The basic unit of a photovoltaic system.

Central power: The generation of electricity in large power plants with distribution through a network of transmission lines (grid) for sale to a number of users. Opposite of distributed power.

Conductor: A wire or combination of wires not insulated from one another, suitable for carrying electric current.

Conversion efficiency (cell or module): The ratio of the electric energy produced by a photovoltaic device (under one-sun conditions) to the energy from sunlight incident upon the cell.

Electric current: A flow of electrons; electricity.

Electron volt: An energy unit equal to the energy an electron acquires when it passes through a potential difference of one volt; it is equal to 1.602×10^{-19} volt.

Energized (alive, live): Electrically connected to a source of potential difference, or electrically charged so as to have a potential significantly different from that of earth in the vicinity.

Gigawatt (GW): One billion watts. One million kilowatts. One thousand megawatts.

Heat pump: Similar to an air conditioner or refrigerator, a heat pump moves heat from one location to another. In the cooling mode, heat pumps reduce indoor temperatures in the summer by transferring heat to the ground. Unlike an air conditioning unit, however, a heat pump's cycle is reversible. In winter, a heat pump can extract heat from the ground and transfer it inside. The energy value of the heat thus moved can be more than three times the cost of the electricity required to perform the transfer process.

Kilowatt (kW): 1000 watts.

Kilowatt-hour (kWh): One thousand watts acting over a period of 1 hour. The kWh is a unit of energy. 1 kWh=3600 kJ.

Load: Anything in an electrical circuit that, when the circuit is turned on, draws power from that circuit.

Megawatt (MW): A unit of power, $= 10^6$ watts. MWe refers to electric output from a generator, MWt to thermal output from a reactor or heat source (for example, the gross heat output of a reactor itself, typically three times the MWe figure).

Photon: A particle of light that acts as an individual unit of energy.

Photovoltaic (Photovoltaic): Pertaining to the direct conversion of light into electricity.

Rated Voltage: The maximum voltage at which an electric component can operate for extended periods without undue degradation or safety hazard.

Semiconductor: Any material that has a limited capacity for conducting an electric current. Certain semiconductors, including silicon, gallium arsenide, copper indium diselenide, and cadmium telluride, are uniquely suited to the photovoltaic conversion process.

Thermal electric: Electric energy derived from heat energy, usually by heating a working fluid, which drives a turbogenerator.

Transformer: Converts the generator's low-voltage electricity to higher voltage levels for transmission to the load center, such as a city or factory.

Vmp: Voltage at maximum power

Volt (V): A unit of measure of the force, or 'push,' given the electrons in an electric circuit. One volt produces one ampere of current when acting on a resistance of one ohm.

Voltage: The effective (rms) potential difference between any two conductors or between a conductor and ground. Voltages are expressed in nominal values unless otherwise indicated. The nominal voltage of a system or circuit is the value assigned to a system or circuit of a given voltage class for the purpose of convenient designation. The operating voltage of the system may vary above or below this value.

Watt (W): The unit of electric power, or amount of work (J), done in a unit of time. One ampere of current flowing at a potential of one volt produces one watt of power.

14.6.3 Solar Energy

Harnessing the power of the sun is not a recent discovery. Records show that humans began intentionally capturing the sun's energy as early as the 7th century B.C. by concentrating the sun's rays to ignite fires (US Department of Energy, n.d.). It was not until 1839 that a French scientist by the name of Edmond Becquerel discovered the *Photovoltaic Effect*. This discovery served as the foundation for the development of the first solar cells further leading to the development of the solar panel (US Department of Energy, n.d.). The advantages and utilization of solar energy is becoming more common and is being adopted by many zoos and aquariums.

Solar panels use the Photovoltaic Effect; the process by which certain materials can absorb photons of light and release electrons, which are then captured creating an electrical current that can be used as electricity (Knier, n.d.).

The cost of installing a solar panel system will depend upon the number of solar panels needed to meet a building's energy demands, the quality of the panels and inverter purchased, the challenges associated with the specific installation, and location.

While the initial cost of these systems may deter an organization from further investigation, it is worth noting that a number of funding related opportunities may exist from a local, regional, and national level which can make the return on investment and long-term savings of these systems worth the investment.

14.6.4 Variable Frequency Drives

A variable frequency drive (VFD) controls the frequency and speed at which an electric motor operates. VFDs are also referred to as variable speed drives, adjustable speed drives, adjustable frequency drives, AC drives, microdrives, and inverters (Hartman, 2014).

VFDs can provide a multitude of benefits by improving efficiency and power factor. Using a VFD to lower the speed of the motor can bring the duty point closer to the best efficiency point of the pump, resulting in more efficient use of power. AC motors typically have a relatively low power factor, typically less than 0.8 at half load and 0.8 - 0.9 at full load (Peltola, 2003). A VFD can correct the power factor, bringing it closer to unity (Peltola, 2003). The increase in power factor can result in significant electrical cost savings. Additionally, operating a motor at a lowered speed, especially a 2-pole synchronous speed motor, results in decrease shaft deflection, heat and vibration. This leads to less friction on the mechanical seal, bearings, and rotational mass, which ultimately translates to a longer service life with less maintenance.

The benefits of VFD installation has been proven at many public aquariums and the return on investment has been rapid in many cases.

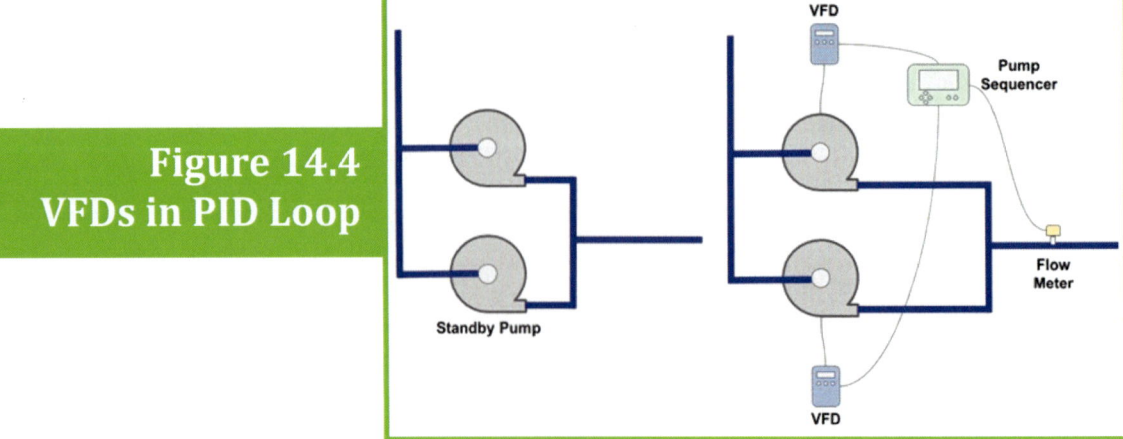

Figure 14.4 VFDs in PID Loop

14.6.5 LEDs

Proper illumination of both aquatic displays and public spaces not only impacts the display's inhabitants and overall aesthetic appeal; it can also affect the operational cost of these spaces. A multitude of lighting options are available for creating a well-lit exhibit however the focus of this section will relate to light emitting diodes (LEDs) and their efficiency from an energy conservation perspective.

Invented in 1962, LEDs produce light through the process of electroluminescence by passing an electrical current through a semiconductor. The color of light emitted is dependent upon the material the semiconductor is composed of (Energy Star, n.d.). When compared with incandescent, fluorescent, halogen, and metal halide type lights, LEDs typically have a higher lumen/watt ratio. This means that more light can produced with less power. In addition, LEDs have a long service life, which reduces the need for changing light bulbs and ultimately reduces the amount of hazardous waste produced from spent bulbs.

14.6.6 Temperature Regulation

The majority of live animal habitats rely upon chilling, and/or heating equipment to maintain the system within a desired temperature range. The energy required by these devices to operate can be significant; therefore, it is important to understand the variables that may affect the operational efficiency of these important components of modern day aquatic life support systems.

A number of factors can affect the efficiency of a chilling and/or heating system. Appropriately sizing the equipment for the system's requirements is the most important consideration. Equipment that is too small will run continuously and might not achieve the desired temperature range. Equipment that is too large will cycle frequently, drawing large amounts of power and contribute to premature equipment failure. Providing proper ventilation for the equipment is also important. If the unit is operating within a closed space, the ability of the equipment to transfer thermal energy may be impeded. Cooling or heating effects from other LSS components such as pumps or deaeration towers must also be taken into consideration when evaluating equipment size. Insulating pipes and components will help to stabilize the system temperature by reducing ambient influences.

14.7 Cathodic Protection

Cathodic protection is a process by which structural and system components of a life support system can be protected from the corrosive effects of seawater caused by electrolysis. When pool structures (such as iron reinforced concrete or steel sand filters) are installed, cathodic protection can be implemented to slow the corrosion process of these structures by connecting the easily oxidized iron/steel compounds to an even more easily oxidizable metal. Galvanic metals and alloys charts can be of assistance to correctly identify a higher corrosive potential. Metals plates such as zinc, magnesium, or aluminum can be inserted into the water to act as sacrificial anodes for the iron. Magnesium is the preferred choice due to animal health concerns and magnesium already exists in the makeup of seawater. Zinc anodes, though commonly used for cathodic protection on boat motors and oil rigs, produces zinc oxides during these processes that is toxic to biological filters, fish, invertebrates, and amphibians.

The desired level of protection does not always occur naturally. Cathodic protection can be forced through the use of DC power to both the cathode (the structural and system components themselves) and the anode (sacrificial metals such as zinc, magnesium, or aluminum). The diagram in Figure 14.5 shows the process of cathodic protection.

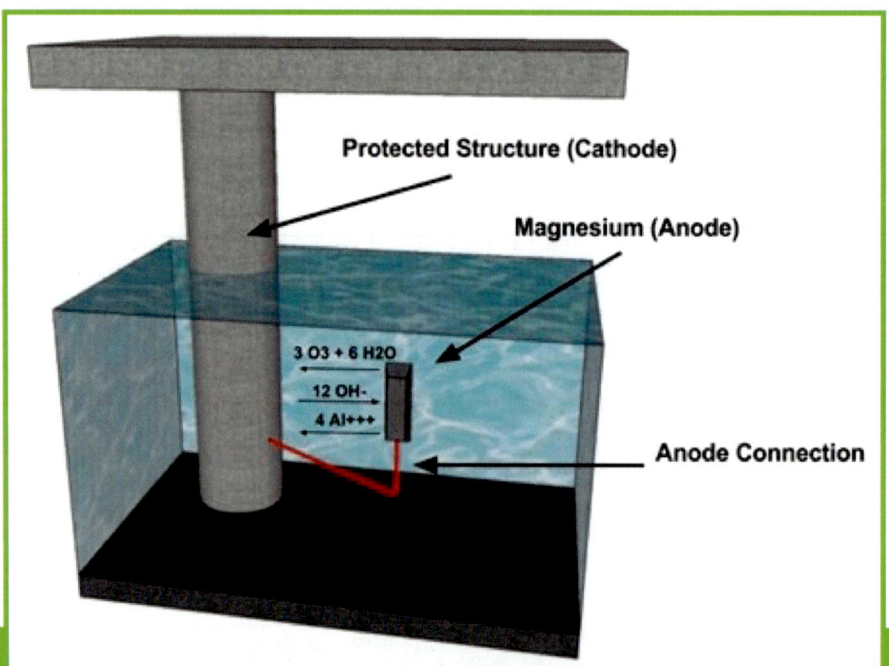

Figure 14.5 – Cathodic Protection

15 LSS Operational Standards

In order to maintain the proper environment for aquatic animals, LSS components and equipment are often combined into a complicated system that requires skilled LSS technicians to operate and maintain. Detailed instructions for maintenance procedures ensure that work is performed correctly and consistently and inform the operator. Plant rounds give operators the opportunity to ensure that all of the vital equipment needed to maintain a healthy environment for the animals is operating properly.

15.1 Standard Operating Procedures

SOPs are documents that lay out the step-by-step process to complete a specific task. Creating and following SOPs ensures that tasks are completed correctly, uniformly, and efficiently by all staff. They are particularly useful for training operators in the specific processes involved for an unfamiliar system. SOPs should describe individual systems and all of their associated tasks. Complete SOPs for each system should be compiled and made accessible to all staff. This should be done by keeping printed copies in a centrally located binder, which remains accessible even during power outages, as opposed to keeping solely digital copies. SOPs for individual tasks may also be posted in areas where the task would be completed. For example, a SOP for completing a sand filter backwash may be posted on a wall close by for quick reference. SOPs should be reviewed regularly by the operators performing the task outlined and it should be updated as necessary.

Complete SOPs for a system should include a system and equipment overview, desired water quality parameters, startup and shutdown procedures, maintenance procedures and schedules, record keeping protocols, and emergency procedures. SOPs for individual tasks should include a clear, step-by-step process with labeled pictures (if practical) and descriptions of each step, and any numerical data, such as flow rates and water quality parameters. A sample SOP for life support procedures can be found in Appendix 19.4.2.

15.2 LSS Rounds

LSS rounds, rounds, and system checks describe the process of ensuring that all equipment is functioning properly in a facility. Although automation has streamlined much of this process due to remote monitoring capabilities, rounds should still include physically checking equipment since automation can fail. Rounds give the operator a chance to recognize small issues before they become big problems. Rounds should be completed with the utmost care and attention to detail. Briefly looking over a system may save time in the moment, but could cost more in the future if some small symptom of a larger problem is missed. Investing time into rounds can save time and money in expensive repairs later.

Problem recognition can be enhanced by keeping written or digital records of numerical data. Tracking parameters such as temperature, ORP, flow rate, pressure, and tank levels, allows an operator to see major changes throughout the day and week. Written or digital records are also valuable for shift carryover and incident investigations. These values should be monitored for all applicable equipment including, pumps, sand filters, ozone systems, protein skimmers, heat exchangers, etc. Notes about out of the ordinary findings, like leaks, sounds, and smells, should be noted as well since they can be used to diagnose a problem. A sample rounds log sheet can be found in Appendix 19.5.

16 Applied Mathematics

Geometric and algebraic principles can aid an operator in performing everyday tasks. For example, when adding chemicals to a pool to reach a desired concentration, mathematical principles can be applied to figure out exactly how much to add. When an operator is asked to drain an aquarium, pool or tank mathematical principles can be applied to figure out just how long such a task would take. The following information can serve as a beginning to understanding these calculations, and how an operator can apply them.

There are some simple steps to use when approaching a problem that requires a mathematical equation (Smith, 1995). Start with gathering the important information:

Given or Known: What information is provided or what is already known?

Find: What is the answer or desired outcome of the problem?

Sketch: Sketch the problem to visualize the statement using what is given or known.

Equation: Which equation(s) is/are needed to find the solution?

Answer: Solve the equation(s) to get the answer.

Once an answer is obtained, then verify that the units are accurate to what is being asked, the math is correct is repeatable, and the answer makes sense.

16.1 Finding Surface Area

16.1.1 Rectangles

The area of a rectangle can be calculated by multiplying its length (x) and width (y).

$$\text{Area}_{\text{rectangle}} = x \times y$$

Examine the Figure 16.1:

30 ft

10 ft

Figure 16.1 - Surface Area of a Rectangle

The rectangle has a length of 30 ft and a width of 10 ft and by multiplying these together results in an area of 300 ft². Similarly, if the rectangle had a length of 30 m and a width of 10 m, the result would be 300 m². Area is always expressed in squared units.

16.1.2 Circles

To determine the area of a circle, consider the ratio of a circle's circumference to its diameter. This relationship is expressed as the symbol "π", which has an approximate value of 3.14.

$$\text{Area}_{\text{circle}} = \pi r^2$$

Examine the circle in Figure 16.2:

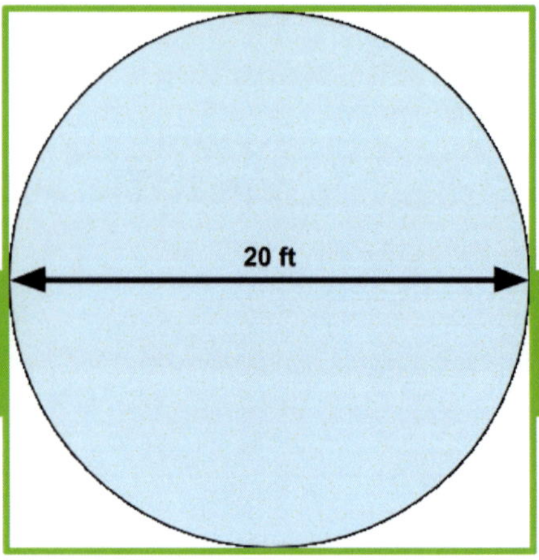

20 ft

Figure 16.2 - Surface Area of a Circle

The diameter of a circle is the length that spans the circle from one side to the other and transects the center of the circle into two equal parts. In the case of the circle above, the diameter is 20 ft. When solving for area, the radius of the circle is required. The radius of a circle is exactly half of the circle's diameter (In Figure 16.2, the radius would be 10 ft). For Figure 16.2, this would be solved by multiplying the square of 10 ft (100 ft^2) by π (3.14), yielding an area of 314 ft^2. If the diameter of the circle was 20 m, the radius would be 10 m and the equation would result in 314 m^2.

16.1.3 Triangles

The area of a triangle is a little less complicated. It helps to think of a triangle as half of a rectangle in which the length (b) × width (h) of the triangle is divided by 2:

$$\textbf{Area}_{\text{triangle}} = \textbf{½} \times \textbf{b} \times \textbf{h}$$

Consider Figure 16.3:

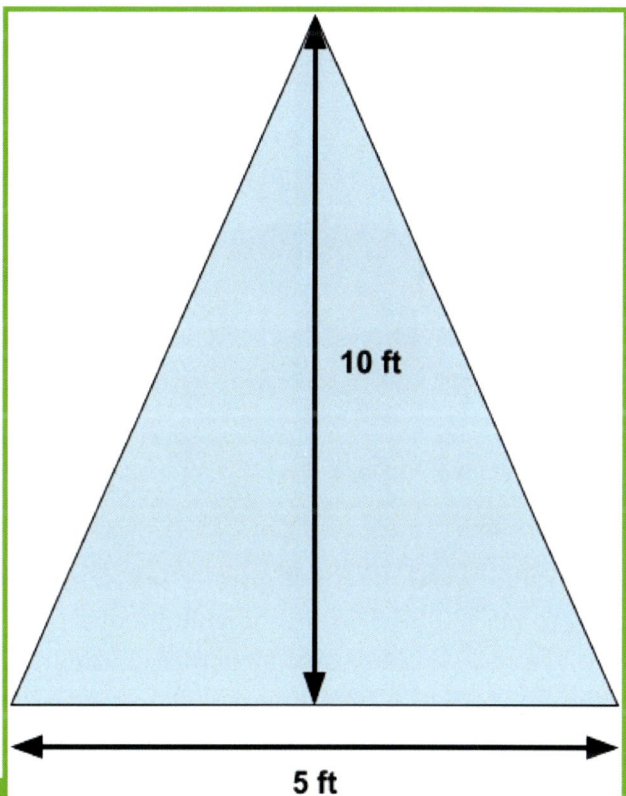

Figure 16.3 - Surface Area of a Triangle

The height of the triangle (10 ft) can be multiplied by the length of its base (5 ft), yielding a result of 50 ft^2. Divide that result by 2, and the area of the triangle is 25 ft^2. If the triangle was 10 m high and its base was 5 m long, the area of the triangle would be 25 m^2.

16.2 Finding Volume

Finding the volume of a three dimensional structure, such as a pool or tower, is just an additional step from area.

16.2.1 Volume of a Rectangular Prism

Consider Figure 16.4:

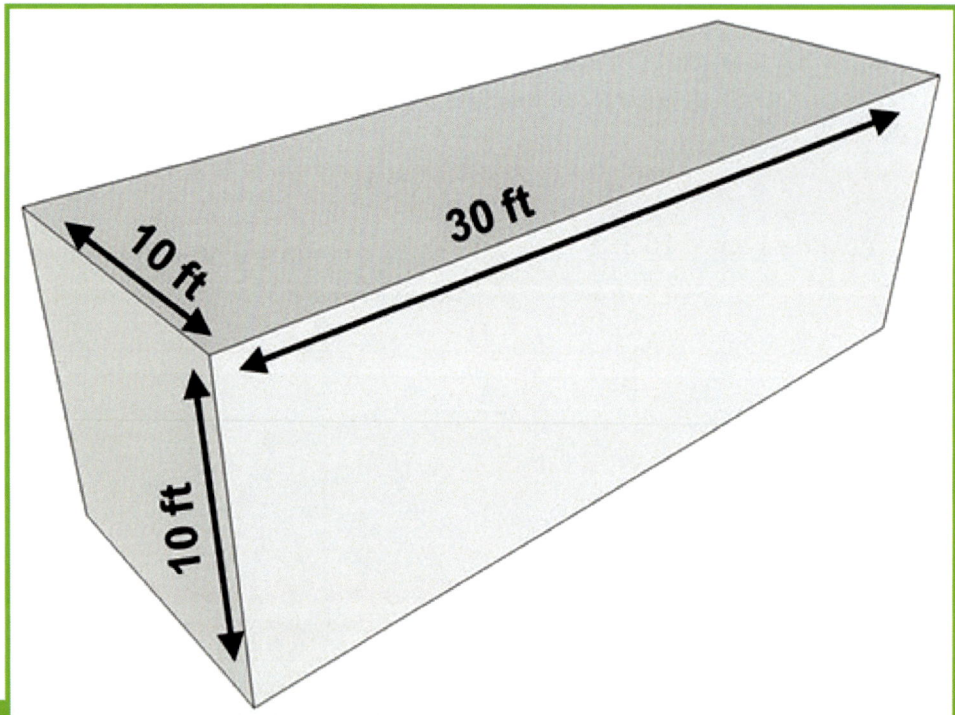

Figure 16.4 - Volume of a Rectangular Prism

As the length and width of this figure is the same as in Figure 16.1, we know the surface area to be 300 ft². To find the volume of a rectangular prism, simply multiply the surface area by the height of structure, in this example the height is 10 ft. The resulting volume is 3,000 ft³. Units of volume are expressed as cubed units, in this example, length in ft × width in ft × height in ft yields ft³. Cubic feet can then be converted to liquid units of volume. If this shape was measured in meters, the result would be in cubic meters which can also be easily converted into liters or milliliters. Conversion factors are found in Appendix 19.1.4. The conversion factor for cubic feet to gallons is 7.48 gallons/cubic foot. This means that 7.48 gallons of water would fill a box 1 foot long by 1 foot wide by 1 ft tall. For Figure 16.4, multiply the volume of the rectangular prism 3,000 ft³ by the conversion factor 7.48 gal/ft³. This yields a volume of 24,440 gallons of water.

$$\textbf{Volume}_{\text{rectangle}} = \textbf{l} \times \textbf{w} \times \textbf{h}$$

16.2.2 Volume of a Cylinder

Consider Figure 16.5:

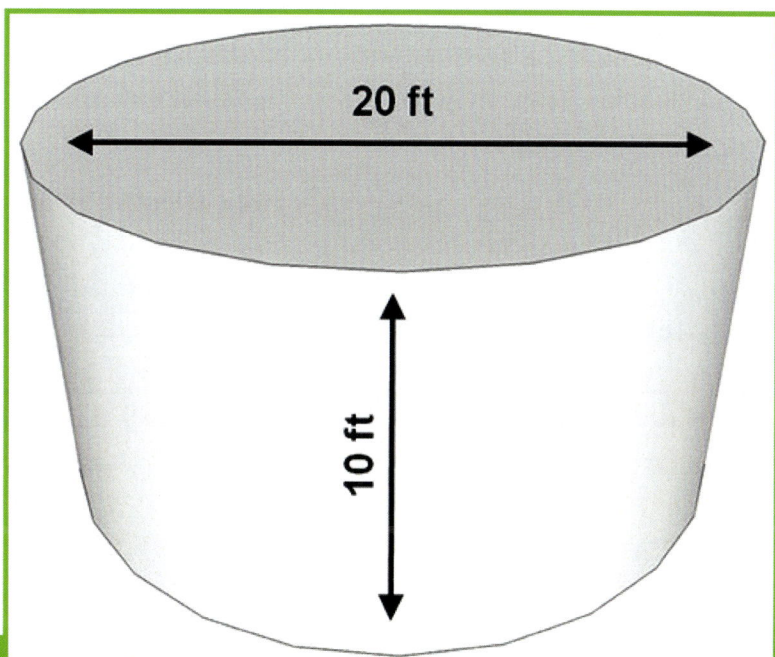

Figure 16.5 - Volume of a Cylinder

Finding the volume of a cylinder is performed in a similar way as a rectangular prism. The surface area in this example is the same as in Figure 16.2, 314 ft². To find volume, multiply the surface area of the circle (314 ft²) by the height of the vessel, in this example, 10 ft yields a volume of 3,140 ft³. To convert to gallons, multiply this result by the conversion factor of 7.48 gal/ft³ to yield a volume of 23,487.2 gallons.

$$\textbf{Volume}_{\textbf{cylinder}} = \boldsymbol{\pi r^2 \times h}$$

17 Applied Mathematics for Water Quality Technicians

Mathematics is a common requirement in the Water Quality Laboratory. It is used to calculate area, volume, ratios and conversions of units. Analytical chemistry is based upon mathematical relationships between detected signals and concentration of the analyte tested. Calculations may be handled automatically by the laboratory instrumentation or may necessitate manual tabulations. In either case, it is important to understand the mathematical relationships on which the equipment works, be able to determine volumes, dilutions, and dosing rates, know how to interpret and report significant figures, and understand the various units of measurement used and be able to convert between them.

17.1 Types of Units

Numerical results without accompanying units are meaningless. It is important to report the units of an analysis and especially when comparing data between institutions. There are often many ways to express the same result in water quality testing. Units that commonly cause confusion in the Zoo and Aquarium industry are ammonia, nitrite and nitrate, as they can be expressed as the ion (NO_3) or as Nitrogen (NO_3-N). For more information, please see section 5.1.2. For example, 100 mg/L as NO_3 is only 22.59 mg/L as NO_3-N; it means the difference between believing a tank is within acceptable limits or not.

The ability to accurately convert units between commonly used notations and equivalents is of the utmost importance. Appendix 19.1 has a thorough list of units and their equivalents for water quality and life support calculations.

SI units (derived from the French term, Systéme International), are used most often in the sciences and internationally; however, particularly in the United States, United States customary units (USCU) are often used.

Example: A colleague from Europe tells a lab technician to dose an exhibit at a concentration of 3 grams per liter. What is this dosing rate in grams per gallon? If the tank is 1,000 gallons, how many grams should the lab technician add?

1 liter = 0.264 gallons (equivalence given in Appendix 19.1.4)

$$\left(\frac{\textbf{3 grams}}{\textbf{1 liter}}\right) = \left(\frac{\textbf{3 grams}}{\textbf{0.264 gallons}}\right)$$

To solve for the amount needed to treat 1,000 gallons, multiply the dosing rate by the volume:

$$\left(\frac{\textbf{3 grams}}{\textbf{0.264 gallons}}\right)(\textbf{1000 gallons}) = \textbf{x grams}$$

The units for gallons cancel each other out, leaving an answer in grams:

$$\left(\frac{\textbf{3 grams}}{\textbf{0.264 gallons}}\right)(\textbf{1000 gallons}) = \textbf{11,400 grams}$$

x = 11,400 grams or 11.4 kilograms

Example: A technician reads that a tank should be kept at an alkalinity of 2.5 mEq/L but the test kit gives results in ppm as $CaCO_3$. What is the minimum acceptable level in ppm as $CaCO_3$?

1.0 mEq/L = 50 ppm as $CaCO_3$ (equivalence given in Appendix 18.1.4)
Set up a proportion to solve for x:

$$\left(\frac{\textbf{2.5 mEqL}^{-1}}{\textbf{1.0 mEqL}^{-1}}\right) = \left(\frac{\textbf{x}}{\textbf{50 ppm as CaCO}_3}\right)$$

x = 125 ppm as $CaCO_3$

While concentration is typically expressed in SI units of mg/L (ppm) or µg/L (ppb), percent composition is a common way of describing the concentration of a substance. Weight percent (w/w) is equal to the mass of solute divided by mass of solution or mixture multiplied by 100% and volume percent (v/v) is equal to the volume of solute divided by the volume of solution multiplied by 100% (Harris, 2001).

Weight percent (wt % or w/w) = (mass of solute/mass of total solution) × 100%

Volume percent (vol % or v/v) = (volume of solute/volume of total solution) × 100%

For example, a 25% w/w solution of methanol in water would be equal to: (25 grams of methanol/100 grams of solution) × 100%, with 75 grams of the solution attributed to water. A 25% v/v solution of methanol in water would be equal to: (25 mL of methanol/100 mL of solution) × 100%, with 75 mL of the solution attributed to water.

It is important to be able to convert between all of the different ways to express concentration in order to perform more advanced calculations and to convert data expressed in one set of units to another.

17.2 Significant Figures

Significant figures are needed to avoid ambiguity in reporting. When presenting data, only report digits that are known definitely, except the last digit, which may be in doubt (Rice et al., 1998). This is easily overlooked, since many times instruments will give more digits than are significant on their readout. The number of significant figures is the number of digits required to write a value in scientific notation. The number 138.2 has four significant figures, because it would be written as 1.382×10^2 in scientific notation.

The digit 0 can act either as a placeholder for a decimal point, or it can be part of a measured result. When a 0 is present at the end of a value, such as 150 mg/L, it is not clear if the 0 is significant or whether it is just needed to express the value. If a 0 is present for 0.150 mg/L, it is obvious that the 0 is significant, otherwise the result would be expressed as 0.15 mg/L. It is important to keep track of the correct number of significant figures when "ambiguous zeros" come into play; expressing these values in scientific notation eliminates the confusion. Zeros are significant when they occur in the middle of a number or at the end of a number on the right-hand side of a decimal point (Harris, 2001).

When rounding off data, if the digit is between 6 and 9, increase the preceding digit by 1 unit and if the digit is between 1 and 4, do not increase the preceding digit (for example, 2.7 should be rounded to 3 and 2.4 should be rounded to 2). If the digit to be dropped is 5, do not automatically round the value up. This introduces a bias in data. Instead, round off to the nearest even number (for example, 2.25 becomes 2.2 and 2.35 becomes 2.4) (Rice et al., 2012).

When reporting results, report to only to the fewest number of significant digits in the whole process. For example, if one is analyzing a sample on an instrument that should provide 3 significant figures, but measured the sample using a graduated cylinder only capable of measuring two significant figures, only report the final result with two significant figures. If the analysis requires a mathematical calculation, round the digits at the end of the calculation.

Simply put, the final result is limited by the value with the fewest significant figures. For example, 20.46675 + 15.226 + 10.9 = 46.59275, but we can only report 3 significant figures. With rounding off the data, we get 46.6. The exception to this rule is when adding or subtracting numbers with an equal number of digits, in which case the answer goes to the same decimal place as in the individual numbers (Harris, 2001). For example, 5.246 + 8.143 = 13.389. The result actually exceeds the original number of significant figures. Although there are several rules for performing arithmetic with significant figures, the real rule for significant figures is that the first uncertain figure of the answer is the last significant figure (Harris, 2001).

17.3 Calculating Chemical Dosing

The laboratory technicians in the water quality laboratory are generally the staff that handle the chemicals for a facility, because they maintain the inventory, storage and knowledge to safely handle the chemicals used. It is common for the laboratory technician to be asked to dose a tank or exhibit with a specific chemical. Knowing how to properly calculate the accurate amount of chemical needed is critical and could be potentially life threatening to the tank occupants if calculated incorrectly.

The information to calculate the amount of chemical needed is the volume of the tank in liters or gallons, and concentration of chemical required also known as the dose rate. Some chemicals come with a dose rate printed on the bottle in form of a ratio like 1 g/gal. Others are provided by the Veterinarian as a prescribed dose such as 5 mg/L which is the final concentration of chemical in the system. These calculations are determined in two different ways.

17.3.1 Calculating Dose Rate From a Solution

To calculate the amount of chemical needed from a ratio, start with what is required and what is known. The task is to neutralize a bleached tank with sodium thiosulfate so it can be prepared for the next occupant. This tank is 2,000 gallons and the dose rate is 1 gram of sodium thiosulfate per 50 gallons of water or 1 g/50 gal. The calculation is to divide 2,000 gallons by 50 which is 40 grams of sodium thiosulfate needed to neutralize this system.

$$2000 \text{ gallons} \left(\frac{1 \text{ gram}}{50 \text{ gallons}} \right) = x \text{ grams}$$

$$2000 \cancel{\text{ gallons}} \left(\frac{1 \text{ gram}}{50 \cancel{\text{ gallons}}} \right) = 40 \text{ grams}$$

17.3.2 Calculating From a Prescribed Dose

To calculate the amount of chemical needed from a prescribed dose, start with what is asked. The Veterinarian wants the quarantine tank to be dosed with Praziquantel to a concentration of 3 ppm for a continuous bath. The quarantine tank has a volume of 375 gallons. It is a standard conversion that 3 ppm is equal to 3 mg/L. What the unknown is: How many grams of Praziquantel is needed?

$$375 \text{ gallons} \left(\frac{3.785 \text{ liters}}{1 \text{ gallon}}\right) \left(\frac{3 \text{ mg}}{1 \text{ liter}}\right) \left(\frac{1 \text{ g}}{1000 \text{ mg}}\right) = x \text{ grams}$$

$$375 \text{ gallons} \left(\frac{3.785 \text{ liters}}{1 \text{ gallon}}\right) \left(\frac{3 \text{ mg}}{1 \text{ liter}}\right) \left(\frac{1 \text{ g}}{1000 \text{ mg}}\right) = 4.26 \text{ grams}$$

17.3.3 Redosing After a Water Change

This would be the same calculations used above, however the volume of water is not what the original volume was, but what the replacement volume is. A 25% water change on the 375 gallon quarantine system above would mean the redosing would be calculated on 93.75 gallons which is the 25% replacement volume. This is the calculation to redose the tank after a 25% water change to maintain the praziquantel level at 3 ppm.

375 gallons × 0.25 = 93.75 gallons (the replacement volume which needs to be redosed)

$$93.75 \text{ gallons} \left(\frac{3.785 \text{ liters}}{1 \text{ gallon}}\right) \left(\frac{3 \text{ mg}}{1 \text{ liter}}\right) \left(\frac{1 \text{ g}}{1000 \text{ mg}}\right) = x \text{ grams}$$

$$93.75 \text{ gallons} \left(\frac{3.785 \text{ liters}}{1 \text{ gallon}}\right) \left(\frac{3 \text{ mg}}{1 \text{ liter}}\right) \left(\frac{1 \text{ g}}{1000 \text{ mg}}\right) = 1.06 \text{ grams}$$

1.06 grams of praziquantel added to tank after the water change to maintain a 3 ppm dose

17.4 Stoichiometry

At the heart of stoichiometry is the concept of the mole. In chemistry, a mole is the SI base unit for the amount of a chemical substance, usually representing atoms, ions or molecules and is an astronomically large number because of the extremely small scale of these chemical building blocks.

1 mol = 6.022×10^{23} (Avogadro's Number)

The term molarity describes the concentration of moles per liter of solution and is expressed as mol/liter or simply as M.

Example: A solution contains 200 moles and has a volume of 2.3 liters. What is the molarity of the solution?

Molarity = moles / liter solution = 200 mol / 2.3 liters = 87 M

Example: A saltwater mix contains 2.7 grams of sodium chloride, NaCl, per 0.1 liter. What is the molarity of NaCl in the saltwater mix?

Use the molecular mass to convert between grams and moles: the molecular mass of NaCl is 22.99 (Na) + 33.45 (Cl) = 58.44 g/mol. The moles of NaCl in 2.7 g are:

$$(2.7 \text{ g}) \left(\frac{\text{mol}}{58.44 \text{ g}} \right) = 0.046 \text{ mol}$$

The molarity can now be determined:

$$\text{Molarity} = \left(\frac{\text{mol NaCl}}{\text{L of saltwater}} \right) = \left(\frac{0.046 \text{ mol}}{0.1 \text{ L}} \right) = 0.46 \text{ M}$$

Example:

A technician needs to prepare a stock solution of 0.25 M copper (II) sulfate pentahydrate ($CuSO_4 \cdot 5H_2O$) to dose an exhibit. If the technician needs to prepare 2 liters, how much copper (II) sulfate pentahydrate (in grams) does the technician need to dissolve into the solution?

$$(2 \text{ L solution}) \left(\frac{0.25 \text{ mol copper sulfate}}{\text{L solution}} \right) = 0.50 \text{ mol copper sulfate present in 2 L solution}$$

The formula mass of copper sulfate can be determined by adding the atomic weights of the components:

1 Copper (63.546 g/mol) + 1 Sulfur (32.065 g/mol) + 4 Oxygen (4 × 15.999 g/mol) = 159.607 g/mol

The formula mass of five water molecules can determined similarly:

10 Hydrogen (10 × 1.0079 g/mol) + 5 Oxygen (5 × 15.999 g/mol) = 90.076 g/mol

Therefore, the formula mass of $CuSO_4 \cdot 5H_2O$ is 249.69 g/mol.

Now that there is a conversion factor between grams of $CuSO_4 \cdot 5H_2O$ and moles of $CuSO_4 \cdot 5H_2O$, there is the ability to determine how many grams is equivalent to 0.5 moles:

$$(0.5 \text{ mol } CuSO_4 \cdot 5H_2O) \left(\frac{249.69 \text{ gram}}{\text{mol}} \right) = 124.84 \, CuSO_4 \cdot 5H_2O$$

17.5 Dilution Calculations

In dilution calculations, units types, siginificant figures, stoichiometry, and dosages may play a role. In a dilution, a target concentration is prepared from a more concentrated initial stock concentration. A concentrated form of a chemical is referred to as "stock". The concentration of solute in a solution is as important as understanding the solute and solvent's natural behavior and properties in this regard. Concentration of a solute is expressed in a variety of units, such as:

Molarity (M) = moles of solute / liter of solution
Normality (N) = equivalents of solute / liter of solution
Molality (m) = moles of solute / mass of solvent
Mass per volume (mg/L) = mass of solute / liter of solution
Weight % (Wt %) = [mass of solute / mass of solution] × 100%
Mole fraction, ( )= moles of solute / total moles

Dilute solution units: [moles of solute / volume of solution] $\times 10^x$
thousand, 10^3 (ppt) common major ions in seawater
million, 10^6 (ppm) nitrogen species and phosphates
billion, 10^9 (ppb) metals and organics
trillion, 10^{12} (ppt) trace metals and trace organics

Proper conversion of units is imperative to accurately dilute concentrations. A pre-prepared stock solution can help save time during preparation of working reagents and complex solutions. Stocks can be prepared and stored at a higher concentration and then diluted to lower concentration for routine use.

17.5.1 Dilution Fundamentals

It is important to understand some commonly used terms before performing dilutions:

Solution: a liquid mixture containing a soluble solute and a solvent.
Stock solution: a concentrated mixture which is diluted to lower concentrations for appropriate and immediate application.
Solute: is a dissolvable minimal component of a solution.
Solvent: is a substance that dissolves solutes, which results in a solution.
Dilution: A solution is considered diluted once more solvent is added to a mixture.
Diluent: A solution used to perform the dilution, usually deionized water.

An addition of more solute into a solution will increase the concentration of the solution; therefore the average distance between solute particles within the solvent has decreased. Hence, an addition of more solvent into a solution will decrease the concentration of the solution; therefore, the average distance between solute particles within the solvent has increased.

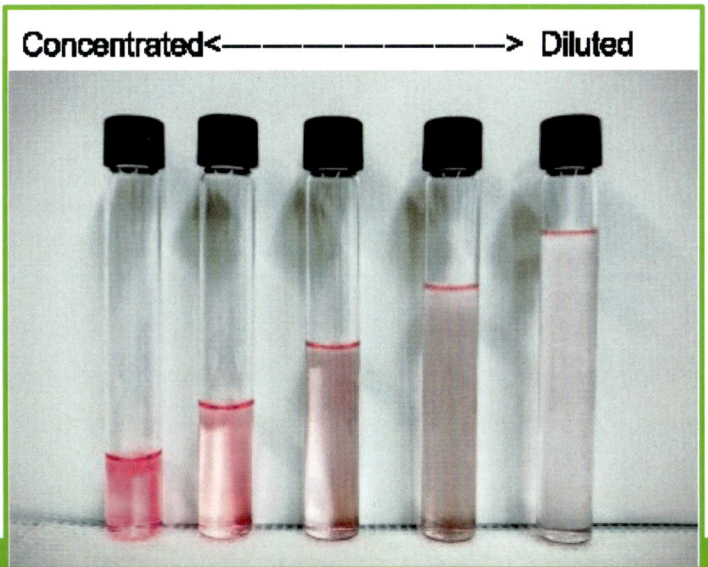

Concentrated <——————————————> Diluted

Photo 17.1 - Dilution with Distilled Water

When mixing a solution, it is imperative to be aware of the temperature of the solvent. This factor can cause the expansion and compression of the solvent and affect the accuracy of the results, even though proper additions were made. Typically, accuracy is guaranteed within a known margin of error at 20°C (68°F). Ensure that solutions are at room temperature prior to beginning the dilution process.

Volumetric laboratory glassware selection is very important when preparing dilutions. Class A volumetric glassware is the proper selection for analytical and quantitative laboratory work. Class B volumetric glassware is sufficient for liquid measurements in quantitative laboratories. Certified glassware is the best choice because it reduces errors and bias while preparing solutions.

When performing a dilution, moles should remain constant in this Concentration-Dilution complex. If there is an increase of a solution's volume, then the solute concentration of the solution will decrease; yet the moles of the concentrated and diluted solutions should remain the *same* in relation to the solute: solvent distribution ratio (Dahm et al, 2013).

Moles of solute in Concentrated solution = moles of solute in Dilute solution

Example: When the volume of a solution is increased by adding more diluent, the concentration must be increased by the same proportional relationship. For example, if a 50 mL solution with a concentration of 100 mg/L is diluted with the addition of 50 mL of deionized water. The total volume after dilution is doubled and increased to 100 mL; therefore the concentration is decreased to half of the initial concentration (100 mg/L ÷ 2 = 50 mg/L).

17.5.2 Converting Units using Scientific Notation

To make dilutions simple, all units should be converted to the same base unit. With practice, mathematical conversions can be easily performed quickly and with ease, especially while performing calculations involving molarity. See Appendix 19.1.5 for a chart to convert units using scientific notation.

17.5.3 The Dilution Equation

As mentioned earlier, in a dilution the amount of the solute remains the same, relatively, but the amount of the solvent changes. One can use this relationship to easily manipulate an equation.

Mathematically, this relationship can be described as:

Initial Concentration (C_1) × Initial Volume (V_1) = Final Concentration (C_2) × Final Volume (V_2)

$$(C_1 \times V_1 = C_2 \times V_2)$$

The units must be the same (consistency is key) in order for this equation to work appropriately.

Example: A stock solution of 16 N H_2SO_4 will be used to obtain a dilute solution of 2.25 N H_2SO_4. How much 16 N H_2SO_4 should be added to a 0.5L volumetric flask, to prepare the solution?

First identify the knowns; the given information of the equation.

Given a stock solution of 16 N H_2SO_4, prepare a 0.500 L solution of 2.25 N H_2SO_4.
C_1 (initial concentration) = 16 N H_2SO_4
C_2 (final concentration) = 2.25 N H_2SO_4
V_2 (final volume) = 0.500 L
V_1 (initial volume) = x

$$V_1 = \left(\frac{(0.5 \text{ L})(2.25 \text{ N } H_2SO_4)}{16 \text{ N } H_2SO_4} \right) = 0.070 \text{ L}$$

Therefore, 0.070 L of 16 N H_2SO_4, diluted to 0.500 L will accomplish the desired final concentration.

Overall, units and labels must cancel throughout this equation.

18 Applied Mathematics for Life Support Operators

Mathematics are also important for Life Support Operators. Various situations require calculations where certain values are given and, using formulas, one can obtain other information. Unit conversions/calculations must be taken into account at all times during the process.

18.1 Calculating Turnover Rate

In order to calculate turnover rate, the volume of the vessel and the flow rate through it must be known. For example, a sea lion system consists of 2 vertical high pressure sand filters, each producing a filter effluent flow of 150 gal/min. This places the total system flow at 300 gal/min. The formula for calculating turnover rate is:

$$\text{Turnover rate} = \left(\frac{\textit{pool volume (gallons)}}{\textit{total flow rate (gpm)}} \right)$$

$$\text{Turnover rate} = \left(\frac{\textit{pool volume (m}^3\text{)}}{\textit{total flow rate (m}^3\text{/min)}} \right)$$

So in the case described above, divide the volume of the pool (23,487 gallons) by the total system flow (300 gpm) to yield a turnover time of approximately 78 minutes. Then convert this into hours by dividing minutes by 60 min/hour to yield a turnover rate of 1.3 hours.

18.1.1 Mixing Model Turnover

Turnover time can also be calculated using a mixing model calculation. This model acknowledges that filtered water is mixed with unfiltered water as it circulates in a closed system. Since filtered and unfiltered water are constantly mixing, 100% of the water can never be considered filtered. This relationship can be described by using the following equation where x represents the percentage value of water considered filtered:

$$-\ln(1-x) = \text{purity coefficient}$$

99.99% of the water filtered can be considered sufficient in most cases (Escobal, 2000). The coefficient of 99.99% filtered water is found to be 9.2.

$$-\ln(1-0.9999) = 9.2$$

This coefficient is used in conjunction with the turnover calculation from Section 17.1 as seen below:

$$-\ln (1- x) \text{ x volume/flow rate}$$

For example, consider a 10,000 gallon or 10,000 liter system with a phytoplankton bloom that is equipped with a large UV sterilizer that kills 100% of the algae passing through it at 50 gpm/lpm. In order to find the time it takes for 99.99% of the water to pass through the UV sterilizer, consider the following:

$$(9.2 \times 10,000 \text{ gallons}) \left(\frac{\text{minute}}{50 \text{ gallons}}\right) = 1840 \text{ minutes} = 30.66 \text{ hours}$$

$$(9.2 \times 10,000 \text{ L}) \left(\frac{\text{minute}}{50 \text{ L}}\right) = 1840 \text{ minutes} = 30.66 \text{ hours}$$

By this calculation, it will take at least 30.66 hours to rid the system of most of the algae. Knowing this information can be helpful in sizing a piece of equipment so that it has a desired effect on the system in the desired time period. For example, to clear up the example tank in 6 hours, using the formula results in requiring a UV sterilizer that can kill the targeted algae at 255.55 gpm. The example is also given if the units were expressed in lpm:

$$\frac{(9.2 \times 10,000 \text{ gallons})}{6 \text{ hours} \times \left(\frac{60 \text{ minutes}}{1 \text{ hour}}\right)} = 255.55 \text{ gpm}$$

$$\frac{(9.2 \times 10,000 \text{ liters})}{6 \text{ hours} \times \left(\frac{60 \text{ minutes}}{1 \text{ hour}}\right)} = 255.55 \text{ lpm}$$

18.1.2 Half Time Turnover

Another way to factor filtered and unfiltered water mixing into a turnover calculation is to use the rule of half times. The rule of half times states that at one turnover (volume/flow rate), 50% of the water can be considered filtered. At two turnovers, 75% of the water can be considered filtered. At three turnovers 87.5%, at four turnovers 93.25%, and so on and so forth. This rule can be described by the following equation, where y equals the percentage of water filtered and x equals the number of turnovers (volume/flow rate):

$$y = 1 - 0.5^x$$

Basing a system's filtration on 9 turnovers gives similar results to the suggested 99.99% filtered in Section 18.1.1. Basing a system's filtration times on 9 turnovers gives:

$$1 - 0.5^9 = 0.9980$$

This means that after 9 turnovers, 99.80% of the water can be considered filtered. This rule is fairly close to the mixing model calculation at 9 turnovers with only a 0.19% difference in filtered water. Due to their similarities at 9 turnovers, thinking in terms of half times instead of doing a mixing model calculation can provide simpler means to a similar end.

In the example from Section 18.1.1, it took 30.66 hours to clean 99.9% of the water. Using the rule of half times at 9 turnovers, that time is 30 hrs.

18.2 Retention/Contact Time

Retention/contact time is how long water is retained in a vessel or how long it is exposed to a process such as ozonation or UV sterilization. It is found by dividing the volume of the vessel in question by the flow rate. For example, if one has a 200 gallon pressurized contact tank and a flow rate of 100 gpm, what is the contact time? Dividing 200 gallons by 100 gallons per minute equals 2 minutes of contact time.

18.3 Flow Unit Conversions

Converting units is often required to be able to plug figures into these equations. For example, if total system flow were given in cubic feet per second (ft^3/sec), first convert that into gallons per minute (gpm) before using the turnover formula. It is known that 1 cubic foot of water is equal to 7.48 gallons (see Appendix 19.1.4). There are 60 seconds in a minute.

To convert, 3 ft^3/sec into gpm, start with the volume. Multiply cubic feet (3) by the conversion factor (7.48 gal/ft^3) to yield 22.44 gallons. This expression represents flow in gallons per second. There are 60 seconds in a minute, therefore multiply the gallons per second (22.44) by 60 seconds per minute to attain an end result of 1,346.4 gpm.

$$\left(\frac{3 \text{ feet}^3}{1 \text{ second}}\right)\left(\frac{7.48 \text{ gallons}}{1 \text{ foot}^3}\right)\left(\frac{60 \text{ seconds}}{1 \text{ minute}}\right) = \frac{1346.4 \text{ gallons}}{1 \text{ minute}}$$

If system flow was given in cubic meters (m^3/hr) and was needed in liters per minute (lpm), start by multiplying m^3 by 1000 L/m^3, then divide this number by 60 minutes/hour to get to lpm.

To convert 10 m³/hr to lpm, multiply by 1000 L/m³ and divide by 60 min/hr to get 166.66 lpm.

$$\left(\frac{10 \text{ m}^3}{1 \text{ hour}}\right)\left(\frac{1000 \text{ liter}}{1 \text{ m}^3}\right)\left(\frac{1 \text{ hour}}{60 \text{ minutes}}\right) = \frac{166.66 \text{ liters}}{1 \text{ minute}}$$

18.4 Velocity

Velocity is often used to describe water movement in various situations. To convert velocity into a flowrate, the diameter of the pipe must be known since pipes of different diameters can have the same velocity of water flowing through them. For example, convert 3 feet per second (fps) in a 1 inch diameter pipe to gallons per minute. First, use the equation for the surface area of a circle to find the surface area of a cross section of the pipe. This produces a cross section surface area of 0.785 in². Then convert 3 fps to inches per second by multiplying by 12 inches per foot, producing 36 inches per second. Now multiply the cross section surface area, 0.785 in², by 36 inches per second, producing 28.26 in³ per second. Divide this number by 231 in³ per gallon and multiple by 60 seconds per minute, producing the flow rate of 7.34 gallons per minute.

$$\left(3.14 \times (0.5 \text{ inches}^2)\right)\left(\frac{3 \text{ feet}}{1 \text{ second}}\right)\left(\frac{12 \text{ inches}}{1 \text{ foot}}\right)\left(\frac{60 \text{ seconds}}{1 \text{ minute}}\right)\left(\frac{1 \text{ gallon}}{231 \text{ inches}^3}\right) = \frac{7.34 \text{ gallons}}{1 \text{ minute}}$$

To convert this flow rate back into a velocity, do the reverse.

$$\left(\frac{7.34 \text{ gallons}}{1 \text{ minute}}\right)\left(\frac{231 \text{ inches}^3}{1 \text{ gallon}}\right)\left(\frac{1 \text{ minute}}{60 \text{ seconds}}\right)\left(\frac{1 \text{ foot}}{12 \text{ inches}}\right)\left(\frac{1}{3.14 \times (0.5 \text{ inches}^2)}\right) = \frac{3 \text{ feet}}{1 \text{ second}}$$

Velocities for metric pipe sizes can be calculated in a similar way. For example, convert 1.2 m/s in a 40 mm pipe to m³/hr. Convert the radius from millimeters to meters by dividing by 1000, then multiply by the radius squared, 3.14 (pi), velocity, and 3600 s/hr to get m³/hr.

$$\left(3.14 \times (0.02\text{m}^2)\right)\left(\frac{1.2 \text{ m}}{1 \text{ second}}\right)\left(\frac{3600 \text{ seconds}}{1 \text{ hour}}\right) = \frac{5.42 \text{ m}^3}{1 \text{ hour}}$$

To convert flow to velocity, run the process in reverse.

18.5 Fluid Dynamics - Calculating Head Pressures

Head pressure or head is a term used in fluid dynamics to describe the pressure that a fluid exerts on the reference point. The center of the impeller of a centrifugal pump is used as the reference point in this section. Head is most commonly expressed in linear units of length (such as feet or meters).

18.5.1 Suction Head

Suction head can be described as the height of the water that exists before the reference point. For example, a pump is placed at ground level, and is fed from a reservoir behind it. The water in the reservoir is 10 feet deep. At this instance, the suction head at the point of reference is -10 ft.

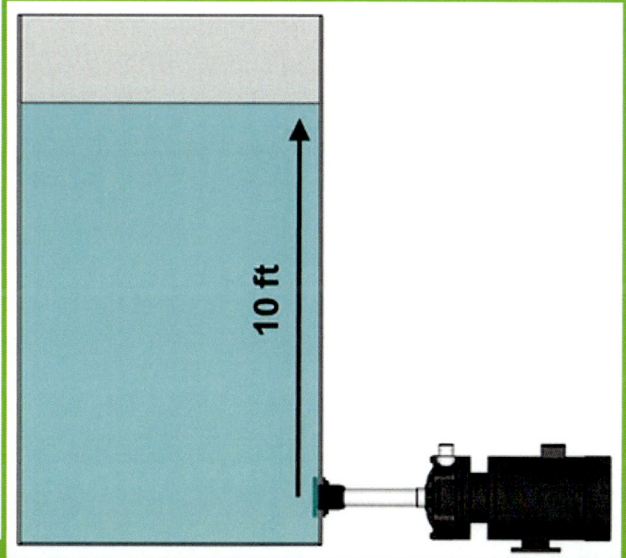

Figure 18.1 - Suction Head

If the reservoir were in the ground, and the suction pipe from the pump extended down to its bottom, at 10 feet, then the suction head in this instance would be 10 feet.

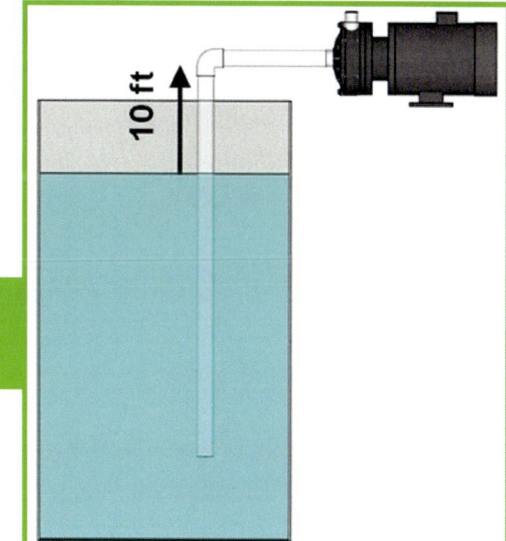

Figure 18.2 - Suction Lift

18.5.2 Discharge Head

Discharge head is the height that the water must reach after the reference point. If the pipe that extends from the centrifugal pump reaches a height of 25 feet, the discharge head at the reference point would be 25 feet.

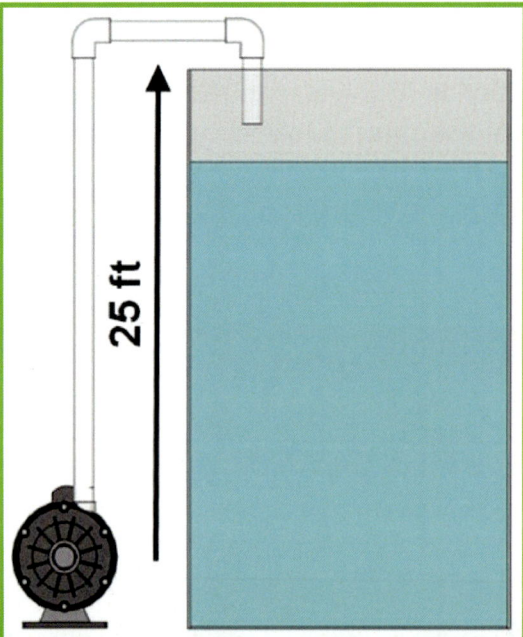

25 ft

Figure 18.3 - Discharge Head

18.5.3 Total Static Head

Total static head (TSH) is the sum of the suction head and discharge head.

Consider Figure 18.4:

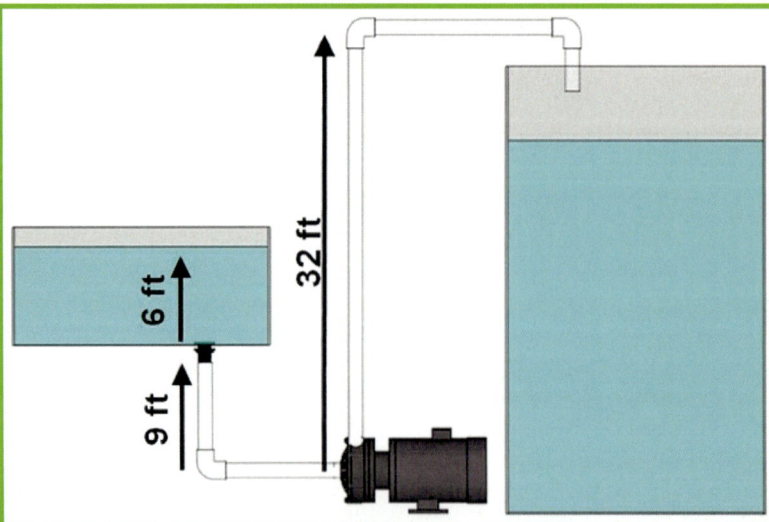

6 ft

32 ft

9 ft

Figure 18.4 – Total Static Head

The suction head at this instance is the sum of the vertical rise of the pipe behind the pump (9 ft) and the height of the fluid in the reservoir (6 ft) which is equal to 15 feet. The discharge head in this instance is 32 ft (the vertical rise after the reference point). The suction head in this example is negative due to the fact that the water sits at an altitude above the reference point, thus the sum of the discharge head and the suction head (TSH) is 17 feet.

18.5.4 Friction Loss

Friction loss is the loss of head due to fluid flowing through a piping system. Friction loss can occur in straight pipe, but it is more significant through obstructions, diameter transitions, directional changes, etc. This causes turbulence within the fluid and would require more energy to overcome. Friction loss is often shown in equivalent feet to simplify head calculations. For reference, see friction loss charts in Appendix 19.8.

To calculate friction loss, the length of pipe needs to be measured, and the number and types of fittings need to be counted. The number of fittings are then converted to equivalent feet of straight pipe, and this is added to the actual length of pipe present. This number is then divided by 100 and multiplied by the number found on the table in Appendix 19.8 next to the flow rate through the pipe. The resulting number is the equivalent added discharge head to the system For example, a run of SCH80 3" pipe that is 25 feet long with 6 90° elbows and 2 45° elbows is equivalent to 80.4 feet of straight pipe. 80.4ft/100 is 0.84. If this pipe flows at 100 gpm, the chart gives a value of 2.9ft/ 1.3 psi. Multiplying by 0.84 gives us 2.44ft/0.25 psi of equivalent added discharge head.

18.5.5 Total Dynamic Head

Total dynamic head (TDH) is a sum of the total static head at the reference point and any losses in energy due to friction (also expressed in feet). For example, if the friction loss of the pipe in Figure 18.4 were calculated to be the equivalent of 12 feet of head, those 12 feet must be added to the total static head. This would yield a TDH of 29 feet.

18.5.6 Converting Head to Pressure

Essentially, head is pressure expressed in distance. Calculating the pressure that a gauge would read is just a matter of conversion:

For example, a gauge placed at the bottom of the suction pipe for the system in Figure 18.1 above would read at about 6.5 psi. This figure represents the height of the water (15 ft) multiplied by the conversion factor (0.433 psi/ft). Inversely, if just the gauge pressure were given (say 10 psi), multiply by the conversion factor (2.31 ft/psi) to get the height of water in the column (23.1 feet). If using metric units of meters and bar, a height of 15 m would be divided by 10.2 m/bar to equal approximately 1.47 bar.

18.5.7 Flow

Fluid flow is often measured in units of volume over time, for example, gallons per minute (gpm) or liters per minute (lpm). It can also be measured using velocity, for example, feet per second (fps) or meters per second (mps).

Common meters used to measure flow include mechanical flow meters and pressure-based flow meters. Both of these types require contact with the water for them to provide an output measurement. Non-contact flow meters can include ultrasonic flow meters and magnetic flow meters.

18.5.8 Pressure Differential

Pressure differential can be used to determine many characteristics of fluid, such as flow and level. Pressure measurements taken before and after a component such as a sand filter can be an effective way to monitor filter performance.

Water level can be determined by measuring pressure differential across the top and bottom of a column of water. A change in this level will result in a corresponding change in differential pressure.

19 Appendices

19.1 Formulas and Conversions

19.1.1 Basic Formulas

Radius (r) of a circle	$r = (½) \times Diameter (D)$
Area of a Rectangle	$A = Length (L) \times Width (W)$
Area of a Triangle	$A = (½) \times Base (B) \times Height (H)$
Area of a Circle	$A = (\pi) \times (r^2)$
Volume of a Rectangular Prism	$V = Length (L) \times Width (W) \times Height (H)$
Volume of a Cylinder	$V = (\pi) \times (r^2) \times Height (H)$
Volume of a Sphere	$V = (4/3)(\pi)(r^3)$
Turnover Rate	$Turnover\ Rate = \dfrac{Volume\ (gallons)}{Flow\ (gpm)}$
Total Static Head	$TSH = Suction\ Lift\ (ft) + Discharge\ Head\ (ft)$
Total Static Head	$TSH = Discharge\ head\ (ft) - Suction\ Head\ (ft)$
Total Dynamic Head	$TDH = Total\ Static\ Head\ (ft) + Friction\ Loss\ (ft)$
PSIA	$PSIA = PSIG + 14.7$
Hydraulic or Water Horsepower (Whp)	$Whp = \dfrac{Flow\ (gpm) \times Head\ (ft)}{3960}$
Brake Horsepower (Bhp)	$Bhp = \dfrac{Flow\ (gpm) \times Head\ (ft)}{3960 \times Pump\ Efficiency}$
Motor Horsepower (Mhp)	$Mhp = \dfrac{Flow\ (gpm) \times Head\ (ft)}{3960 \times Pump\ Eff. \times Motor\ Eff.}$
Motor Horsepower (Metric Horsepower)	$Mhp = \dfrac{Flow\ (lpm) \times Head\ (m)}{4500 \times Pump\ Eff. \times Motor\ Eff.}$

Pump Power (kW)	$P (kW) = \dfrac{Flow\ (m3/hr) \times Head\ (m)}{367 \times Pump\ Eff. \times Motor\ Eff.}$
Pump Efficiency	$Pump\ Efficiency = \dfrac{Water\ hp}{Brake\ hp} \times 100\%$
Torque	$Torque = Force\ (lbs,\ ounces,\ newtons) \times Radius\ (inches,\ feet,\ centimeters,\ meters)$
Horsepower	$HP = Torque\ (T) \times Speed\ (S)Constant$
Horsepower when Torque is in foot pounds and speed is in RPM	$HP = (T \times S)/5{,}252$
Horsepower when Torque is in inch pounds and speed is in RPM	$HP = (T \times S)/63{,}025$
Horsepower when Torque is in inch ounces and speed is in RPM	$HP = (T \times S)/1{,}000{,}000$
Metric Horsepower when Torque is in newton meters and speed is in RPM	$HP\ (metric) = T \times S \times 2\pi/60$
BTU/Hr	$BTU/Hr = \dfrac{(Weight\ of\ water\ (lbs))(Temperature\ increase\ (F))}{(24\ Hours)(Efficiency)}$
1 KCal	$1\ KCal\ raises\ 1\ kg\ of\ water\ 1\ °C$
Chemical Additions to reach a desired concentration (in lbs of 100% pure chemical)	$Pounds\ of\ chemical = \dfrac{(Desired\ ppm) \times (Weight\ of\ pool\ water\ lbs)}{1{,}000{,}000}$ $Pounds\ of\ chemical = \dfrac{(Volume\ of\ pool\ (L)) \times (desired\ mg/L)}{453{,}592\ mg/lb}$
PPM Result of adding a known quantity of chemical	$PPM = \dfrac{(1{,}000{,}000) \times (Pounds\ of\ chemical)}{Weight\ of\ Pool\ Water\ (lbs)}$ $mg/L = \dfrac{(Pounds\ of\ chemical) \times (453{,}592\ mg/lb)}{Volume\ of\ Pool\ (L)}$
Diluted Chemical Addition	$Pounds\ of\ diluted\ chemical = \dfrac{(Pounds\ of\ chemical\ needed\ (pure)}{\%\ Solution}$

19.1.2 Units of Measure for Water Quality

Unit	Notation
one part per thousand	ppt; $^0/_{00}$
one part per million	ppm; 10^{-6}
one part per billion	ppb; 10^{-9}
gram per liter	g/L
milligram per liter	mg/L
microgram per liter	µg/L
milligram per kilogram	mg/kg
milliliter per liter	mL/L

19.1.3 Parts per Million and Parts per Billion Equivalents

Unit	Equivalent	Equivalent	Equivalent
ppm	g/kL	mg/L	µg/mL
ppm	mg/kg	µg/g	ng/mg
ppm	mL/kL	µL/L	nL/mL
ppb	mg/kL	µg/L	ng/mL
ppb	µg/kg	ng/g	pg/mg
ppb	µL/kL	nL/L	pL/mL

19.1.4 Basic Conversions

Unit	Equivalent
1 mL	1 cm^3 (cc)
1 mL	0.034 fl oz (US)
1 mL	0.203 tsp (US)
1 mL	0.068 tbsp (US)

1 mL	20 drops
1 gal (US)	4 qt (US) or 8 pints (US)
1 gal (US)	3.785 L
1 gal (US)	16 cup (US)
1 gal (US)	128 fl oz (US)
1 gal (US)	231 in^3
1 gal freshwater	8.34 lbs
1 gal saltwater	8.55 lbs
1 liter freshwater	1.000 kg
1 liter saltwater	1.024 kg
1 L	0.264 gal (US)
1 m^3	1000 L
1 tbsp (US)	3 tsp (US)
1 ft^3	7.48 gallons
12 inches	1 foot
1 yard	3 feet
1 cm	0.394 in
1 m	3.281 ft
1 m	1.094 yd
1 km	0.621 mil
1 km	0.540 nautical mile
1 lb	453.59 grams
1 kg	2.205 pounds
1 kg	35.274 oz
1 ton	2000 pounds

1 ton of refrigeration	12,000 BTU/hr
°F	(1.8 x °C) + 32°
°C	(°F - 32°) / 1.8
1 mEq/L alkalinity	50 ppm as $CaCO_3$
1 mEq/L alkalinity	2.8 dKH
1 psi	2.31 ft. of water column (Head)
1 psi	6.895 kPa
1 bar	100 kPa
1 ft. of water column (Head)	0 .433 psi
1 bar	10.2 m H_2O
1 Horsepower	0.746 Kilowatts
1 Metric Horsepower	0.736 Kilowatts
1 Metric Horsepower	75 kg-m/sec
1 kWh	1 Kilowatt for 1 hour
1 kWh	3412.14 BTU/hr
1 kW	1 Newton-meter (N-m)
1 kW	6118.3 kg-m/min
1 kW	859.85 kCal
1 KCal	4184 Joules
1 KCal	3.965 BTU
1 RPM	2π/60 rads/sec
1 BTU	1°F increase in 1 lb. of water in 24 hours
1 mol	6.022×10^{23}
π	3.14
Specific Gravity	Pure water = 1.00 (at 39.2°F) Seawater = 1.025 (at 77°F)

19.1.5 Converting Units using Scientific Notation

Prefix	Symbol for Prefix	--	Scientific Notation
exa	E	1 000 000 000 000 000 000	10^{18}
peta	P	1 000 000 000 000 000	10^{15}
tera	T	1 000 000 000 000	10^{12}
giga	G	1 000 000 000	10^{9}
mega	M	1 000 000	10^{6}
kilo	k	1 000	10^{3}
hecto	h	1 00	10^{2}
deka	da	1 0	10^{1}
--	--	1. 00	10^{0}
deci	d	0. 1	$10^{(-1)}$
centi	c	0. 01	$10^{(-2)}$
milli	m	0. 001	$10^{(-3)}$
micro	μ	0. 000 001	$10^{(-6)}$
nano	n	0. 000 000 001	$10^{(-9)}$
pico	p	0. 000 000 000 001	$10^{(-12)}$
femto	f	0. 000 000 000 000 001	$10^{(-15)}$
atto	a	0. 000 000 000 000 000 001	$10^{(-18)}$

19.2 Common Chemicals

Chemical Name	Common Name / Synonym	Chemical Formula
Acetic acid	Vinegar (5% acetic acid)	$C_2H_4O_2$

Ammonium chloride	Salmiac	NH_4Cl
Ammonium molybdate tetrahydrate	Hexaammonium molybdate	$(NH_4)_6Mo_7O_{24} \bullet 4H_2O$
Ascorbic acid	Vitamin C	$C_6H_8O_6$
Boric acid	Boracic acid	H_3BO_3
Calcium carbonate	Limestone	$CaCO_3$
Calcium chloride	Calcium dichloride	$CaCl_2$
Calcium hydroxide	Lime	$Ca(OH)_2$
Carbon rock	GAC; Granular activated carbon charcoal	C
Citric acid	--	$C_6H_8O_7$
Cobalt sulfate (heptahydrate)	--	$CoSO_4 \bullet 7 H_2O$
Copper sulfate	Copper	$CuSO_4$
Ethyl alcohol	Ethanol; Alcohol	CH_3CH_2OH
Ferric Oxide	GFO; Granular ferric oxide	Fe_2O_3
Formaldehyde 37%	Formalin	$HCHO$
Glycerin	Glycerol	$C_3H_5(OH)_3$
Hydrochloric acid	Muriatic acid	HCl
Hydrogen sulfate	Sulfuric acid	H_2SO_4
Iodine	Lugol's solution	I_2
Isopropyl alcohol	2-Propanol	C_3H_8O
Lanthanum chloride	Phosphate remover	$LaCl_3 \bullet 7 H_2O$
Magnesium chloride	--	$MgCl_2$
Magnesium sulfate	--	$MgSO_4$
Manganese sulfate hydrate	--	$MnSO_4 \bullet 1 H_2O$
Ozone	Ozone gas	O_3

Potassium chloride	Electrode storage solution	KCl
Potassium hydroxide	--	KOH
Potassium iodide	--	KI
Quinhydrone	Ozone calibration powder	$C_{12}H_{10}O_4$
Sodium bicarbonate	Baking soda	$NaHCO_3$
Sodium carbonate	Soda ash; Washing soda	Na_2CO_3
Sodium chloride	Salt	NaCl
Sodium hydroxide	Lye; Caustic soda	NaOH
Sodium hypochlorite	Bleach	NaOCl
Sodium molybdate	Disodium molybdate	$Na_2MoO_4 \bullet 2\ H_2O$
Sodium nitrate	Chile saltpeter	$NaNO_3$
Sodium nitrite	--	$NaNO_2$
Sodium thiosulfate	Sodium hyposulfite	$Na_2S_2O_3$
Strontium chloride	Strontium dichloride	$SrCl_2 \bullet 6\ H_2O$
Tricaine methanesulfonate	MS-222	$NH_2C_6H_4COOC_2H_5 \bullet CH_3SO_3H$
Zinc sulfate (heptahydrate)	White vitriol	$ZnSO_4 \bullet 7\ H_2O$

19.3 Salt Mixes

19.3.1 Ratios of Salts Found in Natural Seawater

Chemical	Spotte,1973	Hovanec and Coshland, 2004	MBARI data Johnson et al., 2014
Aluminum	0.16 - 1.9 mg/L	0.270 µg/L	0.16 µg/L
Antimony	-	0.146 µg/L	0.20 µg/L
Arsenic	0.003 - 0.024 mg/L	-	1.50 µg/L

Barium	0.05 mg/L	-	0.02 µg/L
Beryllium	-	0.0002 µg/L	0.0001 µg/L
Boron	4.6 mg/L	-	4.42 mg/L
Bromide	65 mg/L	67.3 mg/L	69 mg/L
Bromine	-	-	
Cadmium	-	0.079 µg/L	0.06 µg/L
Calcium	400 mg/L	412 mg/L	409 mg/L
Chloride	18,980 mg/L	19,353 mg/L	19,793 mg/L
Chromium	-	0.208 µg/L	0.15 µg/L
Cobalt	0.1 µg/L	0.001 µg/L	0.003 µg/L
Copper	0.001 - 0.09 mg/L	0.254 µg/L	0.06 µg/L
Fluoride	1.4 mg/L	1.3 mg/L	1.39 mg/L
Iodide	0.05 mg/L	-	0.04 mg/L
Lead	0.004 - 0.005 mg/L	0.002 µg/L	0.002 µg/L
Lithium	0.1 mg/L	-	0.175 mg/L
Magnesium	1,272 mg/L	1,284 mg/L	1,323 mg/L
Manganese	1.0 µg/L	0.027 µg/L	0.03 µg/L
Mercury	0.3 µg/L	-	0.14 µg/L
Molybdenum	-	10.0 µg/L	9.6 µg/L
Nickel	0.1 - 0.5 µg/L	0.470 µg/L	0.0050 µg/L
Potassium	380 mg/L	399 mg/L	410 mg/L
Rubidium	0.2 mg/L	-	0.130 mg/L
Selenium	4 µg/L	-	4 µg/L
Silver	-	0.0027 µg/L	0.0019 µg/L
Sodium	10,560 mg/L	10,781 mg/L	11,008 mg/L

Strontium	13 mg/L	7.94 mg/L	7.80 mg/L
Sulfate	2,560 mg/L	2,712 mg/L	2,777 mg/L
Thallium	-	0.012 µg/L	0.014 µg/L
Uranium	0.15 - 1.6 µg/L	-	3.2 µg/L
Vanadium	-	2.0 µg/L	1.6 µg/L
Zinc	5 - 14 µg/L	0.392 µg/L	0.35 µg/L

19.3.2 Chemicals Used in Artificial Salt Mixes

Chemical Name	Chemical Formula
Major Compounds	
Sodium chloride	$NaCl$
Magnesium sulfate	$MgSO_4 \bullet 7\ H_2O$
Magnesium chloride	$MgCl_2 \bullet 6\ H_2O$
Calcium chloride	$CaCl_2$
Potassium chloride	KCl
Sodium sulfate	Na_2SO_4
Minor Compounds	
Sodium bicarbonate	$NaHCO_3$
Sodium carbonate	Na_2CO_3
Sodium tetraborate	$Na_2B_4O_7 \bullet 10\ H_2O$
Boric acid	H_3BO_3
Strontium chloride	$SrCl_2 \bullet 6\ H_2O$
Manganese sulfate	$MnSO_4 \bullet 1\ H_2O$
Sodium phosphate	$Na_2HPO_4 \bullet 7\ H_2O$
Potassium bromide	KBr

Lithium chloride	LiCl
Sodium molybdate	$Na_2MoO_4 \bullet 2\ H_2O$
Aluminum sulfate	$Al_2(SO_4)_3$
Calcium gluconate	$C_{12}H_{22}CaO_{14}$
Trace Compounds	
Rubidium chloride	RbCl
Cobalt sulfate	$CoCO_4 \bullet 7\ H_2O$
Potassium iodide	KI
Zinc sulfate	$ZnSO_4 \bullet 7\ H_2O$
Vanadium pentoxide	V_2O_5
Copper sulfate	$CuSO_4 \bullet 5\ H_2O$

19.3.3 Example of Artificial Salt Recipe Used at the Steinhart Aquarium

Chemical Name	Chemical Formula	per 75 cubic meters	per 20,000 gallons
Sodium chloride	NaCl	2,001 kg	4,412 lbs
Magnesium blend	$MgSO_4$ & $MgCl_2$	454 kg	1,000 lbs
Calcium chloride	$CaCl_2$	89 kg	196 lbs
Potassium chloride	KCl	56 kg	124 lbs
Sodium bicarbonate	$NaHCO_3$	11.3 kg (varies)	25 lbs (varies)
Boric acid	H_3BO_3	1,875 g	1,875 g
Strontium chloride	$SrCl_2$ x 6H2O	1,150 g	1,150 g
Potassium iodide	KI	11.33 g	11.33 g
Zinc sulfate	$ZnSO_4$ x $7H_2O$	5.23 g	5.23 g
Cobalt sulfate	$CoCO_4$ x $7H_2O$	3.92 g	3.92 g
Sodium molybdate	Na_2MoO_4 x $2H_2O$	2.16 g	2.16 g

19.3.4 Common Method Preservation and Holding Times

Determination	Preservation	Holding Time
pH	Analyze Immediately	15 minutes
Alkalinity	Cool, 4°C	14 days
Salinity		6 months
Temperature	Analyze Immediately	15 minutes
Nitrogen		
Ammonia	Analyze Immediately or Cool, 4°C, H_2SO_4 to pH<2	28 days
Nitrite	Analyze Immediately or Cool, 4°C	48 hours
Nitrate	Analyze Immediately or Cool, 4°C	48 hours
Chlorine, Total, residual	Analyze Immediately	15 minutes
Chlorine, Free, residual	Analyze Immediately	15 minutes
Bromine	Analyze Immediately	15 minutes
Iodine	Analyze Immediately	15 minutes
Metals		
Copper	HNO_3 to pH < 2	6 months
Chromium VI	Cool, 4°C	24 hours
Iron	HNO_3 to pH < 2	6 months
Manganese	Analyze Immediately or HNO_3 to pH < 2	24 hours
Fecal Coliform	Cool, 4°C	8 hours
Turbidity	Analyze Immediately; store is dark, Cool, 4°C	48 hours
Hardness	HNO_3 or H_2SO_4 to pH <2	6 months
Calcium Hardness	HNO_3 or H_2SO_4 to pH <2	6 months
Magnesium	HNO_3 or H_2SO_4 to pH <2	6 months

Hardness		
Phosphate	Analyze Immediately or Cool to 4°C	48 hours
Oxygen, Dissolved, Probe	Analyze Immediately	15 minutes
Ozone	Analyze Immediately	15 minutes
Silica	Cool, 4°C	28 days

Adapted from *Standard Methods for the Examination of Water & Wastewater* (Rice et al., 2012).

19.4 SOP

19.4.1 Water Quality SOP Template

AALSO WATER QUALITY EDUCATION COMMITTEE SOP TEMPLATE	SOP #	101
	Current Version	1.0
	Previous Version	NA
SOP Owner: Lab Manager Name	Date Modified	1 January 2017

NAME OF TEST AND DEVICE USED

1.0   SCOPE AND APPLICATION
    1.1   Describe what this method is used to test

2.0   SUMMARY OF METHOD
    2.1   Describe how this test works

3.0   QUALITY CONTROL
    3.1   List any standards used

4.0   PREVENTION OF INTERFERENCES
    4.1   List of interferences
    4.2   Describe how to compensate for interferences

5.0   SAFETY
    5.1   List all safety requirements

6.0   APPARATUS AND MATERIALS
    6.1   List all equipment used

7.0   STANDARDS AND REAGENTS
    7.1   List all reagents used

8.0 CALIBRATION AND MAINTENANCE
8.1 List any calibration or maintenance needed

9.0 SAMPLE COLLECTION, PRESERVATION, AND HANDLING
9.1 Describe how are samples collected, in what container and how are they stored

10.0 PROCEDURE
10.1 Step by step procedures for running the test

11.0 WASTE DISPOSAL
11.1 Describe methods for waste disposal

12.0 CALCULATIONS
12.1 Describe all calculations used

19.4.2 Life Support SOP Template

AALSO LIFE SUPPORT EDUCATION COMMITTEE SOP TEMPLATE		SOP #	101
		Current Version	1.0
		Previous Version	NA
SOP Owner:	LSS Manager Name	Date Modified	1 January 2017

NAME OF SYSTEM AND PROCEDURE

1.0 SYSTEM LOCATION
1.1 Describe where the system is located

2.0 WATER QUALITY PARAMETERS
2.1 Describe normal water quality parameters for system

3.0 STARTUP/SHUTDOWN PROCEDURES
3.1 System commissioning
3.2 Normal system startup
3.3 Normal system shutdown

4.0 MAINTENANCE PROCEDURES
4.1 Describe maintenance procedures
4.2 Maintenance schedule

5.0 RECORD KEEPING
5.1 List all safety requirements

6.0 EMERGENCY PROCEDURES
6.1 Describe likely emergencies and their solutions
6.2 Emergency contact information

19.5 Life Support Rounds Example

		Rounds #	1975
AALSO Life Support Education Committee Rounds Sample		Current Version	1983
		Previous Version	1978
		Date Modified:	July 22, 1983

System Name: Jaws

	Sunday	Monday	Tuesday	Wednesday	Thursday	Friday	Saturday
Date							
Time							
Operator Initials							
SF Pump							
Influent Pressure (psi)							
Effluent Pressure (psi)							
Oil Level							
Sand Filter							
Influent Pressure (psi)							
Effluent Pressure (psi)							
Flow (gpm)							
Ozone Contactor							
Venturi Influent (psi)							
Venturi Effluent (psi)							
Venturi (psi)							
Ozone Contact Pump							
Influent Pressure (psi)							
Effluent Pressure (psi)							
Strainer Basket Clean							
Heat Exchanger							
Influent Temp (F)							
Effluent Temp (F)							
Influent Pressure (psi)							
Effluent Pressure (psi)							
HMI Values							
Water Level (inches)							
Water Temp (F)							
O3 Contactor ORP (mV)							
DAT ORP (mV)							
Exhibit Return ORP (mV)							

Expected Values

SF Flow Rate	Water Temperature (F)	Exhibit Return ORP (mV)	DAT ORP (mV)
275 - 300	76 - 77 F	300 - 350 mV	400 - 450 mV

O3 Contactor ORP (mV)
<600 mV

19.6 Water Quality Data Sheet Example

Tank ID	pH	Temp (C)	Salinity (ppt)	Ammonia (mg/L)	Nitrite (mg/L)	Nitrate (mg/L)
PGN10	8.03	18.2	33.4	ND	0.01	33.4
ARF10	7.02	26.4	ND	0.01	0.01	15.4
CCE10	8.01	11.3	33.5	ND	ND	8.9
RLE10	8.05	25.1	32.5	ND	0.01	37.9
CRE10	8.1	25.2	34.6	ND	ND	12.3
SWE10	7.82	25.5	ND	0.01	0.01	13.4
AFE10	7.15	24.9	ND	ND	0.01	53.5

19.7 Motor Reference Charts

19.7.1 Three Phase Frame Sizes for ODP Motors

RPM	3600			1800			1200			900		
NEMA Rating	Original	1952	1964	Original	1952	1964	Original	1952	1964	Original	1952	1964
1 HP	N/A	N/A	N/A	203	182	143T	204	184	145T	225	213	182T
1.5 HP	203	182	143T	204	184	145T	224	184	182T	254	213	184T
2 HP	204	184	145T	224	184	145T	225	213	184T	254	215	213T
3 HP	224	184	145T	225	213	182T	254	215	213T	284	254U	215T
5 HP	225	213	182T	254	215	184T	284	254U	215T	324	256U	254T
7.5 HP	254	215	184T	284	254U	213T	324	256U	254T	326	284U	256T
10 HP	284	254U	213T	324	256U	215T	326	284U	256T	364	286U	284T
15 HP	324	256U	215T	326	284U	254T	364	324U	284T	365	326U	286T
20 HP	326	284U	254T	364	286U	256T	365	326U	286T	404	364U	324T
25 HP	364S	286U	256T	364	324U	284T	404	364U	324T	405	365U	326T
30 HP	364S	324US	284TS	365	326U	286T	405	365U	326T	444	404U	364T
40 HP	365S	326US	286TS	404	364U	324T	444	404U	364T	445	405U	365T
50 HP	404S	364US	324TS	405S	365US	326T	445	405U	365T	504	444U	404T
60 HP	405S	365US	326TS	444S	404US	364T	504	444U	404T	505	445U	405T
75 HP	444S	404US	364TS	445S	405US	365T	505	445U	405T	N/A	N/A	444T
100 HP	445S	405US	365TS	504S	444US	404T	N/A	N/A	444T	N/A	N/A	445T
125 HP	504S	444US	404TS	505S	445US	405T	N/A	N/A	445T	N/A	N/A	
150 HP	505S	445US	405TS	N/A	N/A	444T	N/A	N/A	N/A	N/A	N/A	
200 HP	N/A	N/A	444TS	N/A	N/A	445T	N/A	N/A	N/A	N/A	N/A	
250 HP	N/A	N/A	445TS	N/A	N/A	N/A	N/A	N/A	N/A	N/A	N/A	

19.7.2 Three Phase Frame Sizes for TEFC Motors

Three Phase Frame Sizes for Totally Enclosed Fan Cooled Motors											
RPM	**3600**			**1800**			**1200**			**900**		
NEMA Program	Original	1952	1964	Original	1952	1964	Original	1952	1964	Original	1952	1964
1 HP	N/A	N/A	N/A	203	182	143T	204	184	145T	225	213	182T
1.5 HP	203	182	143T	204	184	145T	224	184	182T	254	213	184T
2 HP	204	184	145T	224	184	145T	225	213	184T	254	215	213T
3 HP	224	184	182T	225	213	182T	254	215	213T	284	254U	215T
5 HP	225	213	184T	254	215	184T	284	254U	215T	324	256U	254T
7.5 HP	254	215	213T	284	254U	213T	324	256U	254T	326	284U	256T
10 HP	284	254U	215T	324	256U	215T	326	284U	256T	364	286U	284T
15 HP	324	256U	254T	326	284U	254T	364	324U	284T	365	326U	286T
20 HP	326	286U	256T	364	286U	256T	365	326U	286T	404	364U	324T
25 HP	365S	324U	284TS	365	324U	284T	404	364U	324T	405	365U	326T
30 HP	404S	326US	286TS	404	326U	286T	405	365U	326T	444	404U	364T
40 HP	405S	364US	324TS	405	364U	324T	444	404U	364T	445	405U	365T
50 HP	444S	365US	326TS	444S	365US	326T	445	405U	365T	504	444U	404T
60 HP	445S	405US	364TS	445S	405US	364T	504	444U	404T	505	445U	405T
75 HP	504S	444US	365TS	504S	444US	365T	505	445U	405T	N/A	N/A	444T
100 HP	505S	445US	405TS	505S	445US	405T	N/A	N/A	444T	N/A	N/A	445T
125 HP	N/A	N/A	444TS	N/A	N/A	444T	N/A	N/A	445T	N/A	N/A	N/A
150 HP	N/A	N/A	445TS	N/A	N/A	445T	N/A	N/A	N/A	N/A	N/A	N/A

19.7.3 NEMA Standard Frame Dimensions

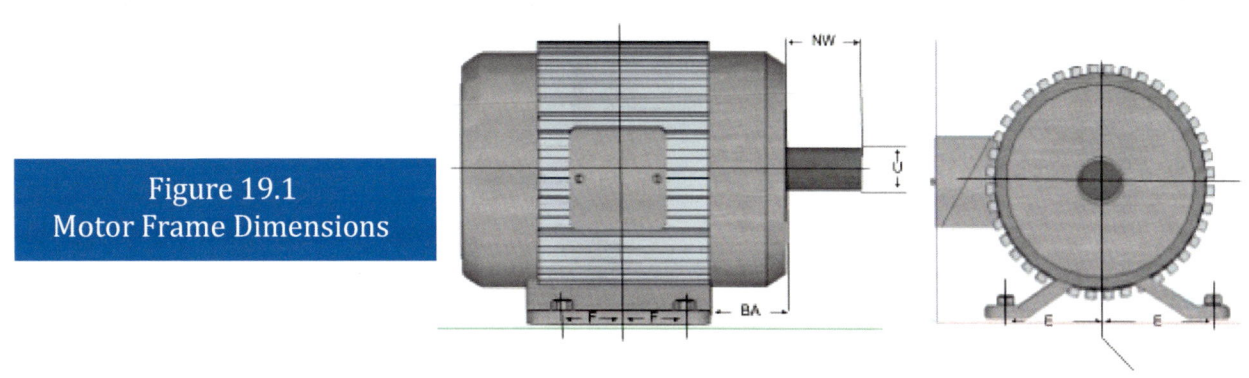

Figure 19.1
Motor Frame Dimensions

NEMA Standard Frame Dimensions						
NEMA Frame	D	E	2F	U	V	BA
42	$2 - \frac{5}{8}"$	$1 - \frac{3}{4}"$	$1 - \frac{11}{16}"$	$\frac{3}{8}"$	$1 - \frac{1}{8}"$	$2 - \frac{1}{16}"$
48	$2 - \frac{1}{8}"$	$2 - \frac{1}{8}"$	$2 - \frac{3}{4}"$	$\frac{1}{2}"$	$1 - \frac{1}{2}"$	$2 - \frac{1}{2}"$
56	$3 - \frac{1}{2}"$	$2 - \frac{7}{16}"$	$3"$	$\frac{5}{8}"$	$1 - \frac{7}{8}"$	$2 - \frac{3}{4}"$
56H						
143T	$3 - \frac{1}{2}"$	$2 - \frac{3}{4}"$	$4"$	$\frac{7}{8}"$	$2 - \frac{1}{4}"$	$2 - \frac{1}{4}"$
145T			$5"$			
182	$4 - \frac{1}{2}"$	$3 - \frac{3}{4}"$	$4 - \frac{1}{2}"$	$\frac{7}{8}"$	$2 - \frac{1}{4}"$	$2 - \frac{3}{4}"$
184			$5 - \frac{1}{2}"$			
182T			$4 - \frac{1}{2}"$	$1 - \frac{1}{8}"$	$2 - \frac{3}{4}"$	
184T			$5 - \frac{1}{2}"$			
213	$5 - \frac{1}{4}"$	$4 - \frac{1}{4}"$	$5 - \frac{1}{2}"$	$1 - \frac{1}{8}"$	$3"$	$3 - \frac{1}{2}"$
215			$7"$			
213T			$5 - \frac{1}{2}"$	$1 - \frac{3}{8}"$	$3 - \frac{3}{8}"$	
215T			$7"$			
254U	$6 - \frac{1}{4}"$	$5"$	$8 - \frac{1}{4}"$	$1 - \frac{3}{8}"$	$3 - \frac{3}{4}"$	$4 - \frac{1}{4}"$
256U			$10"$			
254T			$8 - \frac{1}{4}"$	$1 - \frac{5}{8}"$	$4"$	
256T			10			
284U	$7"$	$5 - \frac{1}{2}"$	$9 - \frac{1}{2}"$	$1 - \frac{}{8}"$	$4 - \frac{7}{8}"$	$4 - \frac{3}{4}"$
286U			$11"$			
284T			$9 - \frac{1}{2}"$	$1 - \frac{7}{8}"$	$4 - \frac{5}{8}"$	
286T			$11"$			
284TS			$9 - \frac{1}{2}"$	$1 - \frac{5}{8}"$	$3 - \frac{1}{4}"$	

286TS			11"			
324U	8"	6 - $\frac{1}{4}$"	10 - $\frac{1}{2}$"	1 - $\frac{7}{8}$"	5 - $\frac{5}{8}$"	5 - $\frac{1}{4}$"
326U			12"			
324T			10 - $\frac{1}{2}$"	2 - $\frac{1}{8}$"	5 - $\frac{1}{4}$"	
326T			12"			
324TS			10 - $\frac{1}{2}$"	1 - $\frac{7}{8}$"	3 - $\frac{3}{4}$"	
326TS			12"			
364U	9"	7"	11 - $\frac{1}{4}$"	2 - $\frac{1}{8}$"	6 - $\frac{3}{8}$"	5 - $\frac{7}{8}$"
365U			12 - $\frac{1}{4}$"			
364T			11 - $\frac{1}{4}$"	2 - $\frac{3}{8}$"	5 - $\frac{7}{8}$"	
365T			12 - $\frac{1}{4}$"			
364TS			11 - $\frac{1}{4}$"	1 - $\frac{7}{8}$"	3 - $\frac{3}{4}$"	
365TS			12 - $\frac{1}{4}$"			
404U	10"	8"	12 - $\frac{1}{4}$"	2 - $\frac{3}{8}$"	7 - $\frac{1}{8}$"	6 - $\frac{5}{8}$"
405U			13 - $\frac{3}{4}$"			
404T			12 - $\frac{1}{4}$"	2 - $\frac{7}{8}$"	7 - $\frac{1}{4}$"	
405T			13 - $\frac{3}{4}$"			
404TS			12 - $\frac{1}{4}$"	2 - $\frac{1}{8}$"	4 - $\frac{1}{4}$"	
405TS			13 - $\frac{3}{4}$"			
444U	11"	9"	14 - $\frac{1}{2}$"	2 - $\frac{7}{8}$"	8 - $\frac{5}{8}$"	7 - $\frac{1}{2}$"
445U			16 - $\frac{1}{2}$"			
444T			14 - $\frac{1}{2}$"	3 - $\frac{3}{8}$"	8 - $\frac{1}{2}$"	
445T			16 - $\frac{1}{2}$"			
447T			20"			

449T			25"		
444TS			14 - $\frac{1}{2}$"		
445TS			16 - $\frac{1}{2}$"	2 - $\frac{3}{8}$"	4 - $\frac{3}{4}$"
447TS			20"		
449TS			25"		

19.7.4 NEMA Shaft Keyseat Dimensions

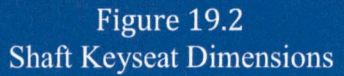

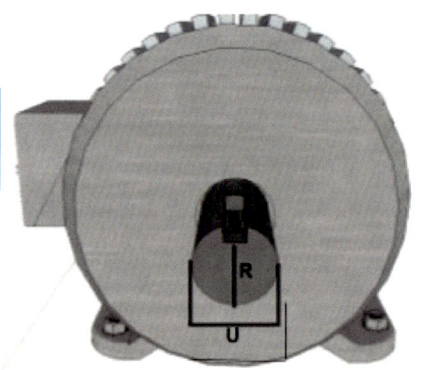

Figure 19.2
Shaft Keyseat Dimensions

NEMA Shaft Keyseat Dimensions					
Shaft	**Keyseat Dimensions**		**Shaft**	**Keyseat Dimensions**	
Diameter (U)	R	S	Diameter (U)	R	S
$\frac{3}{8}$"	$\frac{21}{64}$"	Flat	**1 - $\frac{7}{8}$"**	1 - $\frac{19}{32}$"	$\frac{1}{2}$"
$\frac{1}{2}$"	$\frac{29}{64}$"	Flat	**2 - $\frac{1}{8}$"**	1 - $\frac{27}{32}$"	$\frac{1}{2}$"
$\frac{5}{8}$"	$\frac{33}{64}$"	$\frac{3}{16}$"	**2 - $\frac{3}{8}$"**	2 - $\frac{1}{64}$"	$\frac{5}{8}$"
$\frac{7}{8}$"	$\frac{49}{64}$"	$\frac{3}{16}$"	**2 - $\frac{1}{2}$"**	2 - $\frac{3}{16}$"	$\frac{5}{8}$"
1 - $\frac{1}{8}$"	$\frac{63}{64}$"	$\frac{1}{4}$"	**2 - $\frac{7}{8}$"**	2 - $\frac{29}{64}$"	$\frac{3}{4}$"
1 - $\frac{3}{8}$"	1 - $\frac{13}{64}$"	$\frac{5}{16}$"	**3 - $\frac{3}{8}$"**	2 - $\frac{7}{8}$"	$\frac{7}{8}$"
1 - $\frac{5}{8}$"	1 - $\frac{13}{32}$"	$\frac{3}{8}$"	**3 - $\frac{7}{8}$"**	3 - $\frac{5}{16}$"	1"

19.8 PVC Friction Loss and Flow Velocities

19.8.1 ½" PVC Friction Loss and Flow Velocities

Volume Flow (gal/min)	Velocity (ft/sec)*	Friction Head (ft/100ft)*	Friction Loss (psi/100ft)*
1	1.1/1.5	2.1/4.0	1.9/1.7
2	2.3/3.0	4.2/8.0	1.8/3.5
5	5.6/7.4	23.4/45.2	10.5/19.6
7	7.9/10.3	43.1/83.1	18.6/36.0
10	11.3/	82.0/	35.5/

*Sch. 40/ Sch. 80

19.8.2 ¾" PVC Friction Loss and Flow Velocities

Volume Flow (gal/min)	Velocity (ft/sec)*	Friction Head (ft/100ft)*	Friction Loss (psi/100ft)*
1	0.6/0.7	0.5/0.9	0.2/0.4
2	1.3/1.6	1.0/1.7	0.4/0.7
5	3.⅔.9	5.7/9.7	2.5/4.2
7	4.4/5.5	10.5/11.8	4.6/7.7
10	6.3/7.8	20.0/33.8	8.7/14.7
15	9.5/11.8	42.5/71.7	18.4/31.1
20	12.7/	72.3/	31.3/

*Sch. 40/ Sch. 80

19.8.3 1" PVC Friction Loss and Flow Velocities

Volume Flow (gal/min)	Velocity (ft/sec)*	Friction Head (ft/100ft)*	Friction Loss (psi/100ft)*
2	0.8/0.9	0.6/0.9	0.2/0.4
5	1.9/2.3	1.7/2.6	0.8/1.2

7	2.7/3.3	3.2/5.0	1.4/2.2
10	3.9/4.7	6.0/9.6	2.6/4.2
15	5.8/7.0	12.8/20.4	5.5/8.8
20	7.7/9.4	21.8/34.7	9.4/15.0
25	9.7/11.7	32.9/52.4	14.2/22.7
30	11.6/14.0	46.1/73.5	20.0/31.8

*Sch. 40/ Sch. 80

19.8.4 1 ¼" PVC Friction Loss and Flow Velocities

Volume Flow (gal/min)	Velocity (ft/sec)*	Friction Head (ft/100ft)*	Friction Loss (psi/100ft)*
2	0.4/0.5	0.1/0.2	0.1/0.1
5	1.1/1.3	0.4/0.7	0.2/0.3
7	1.6/1.8	0.8/1.2	0.4/0.5
10	2.2/2.6	1.6/2.3	0.7/1.0
15	3.3/3.9	3.3/4.9	1.4/2.1
20	4.4/5.2	5.6/8.3	2.4/3.6
25	5.5/6.5	8.5/12.6	3.7/5.4
30	6.6/7.8	11.9/17.9	5.1/7.6
35	7.7/9.1	15.8/23.4	6.8/10.1
40	8.8/10.4	20.2/30.0	8.7/13.0
45	9.9/11.7	25.1/37.3	10.9/16.1
50	11.1/13.0	30.5/45.3	13.2/19.6

*Sch. 40/ Sch. 80

19.8.5 1 ½" PVC Friction Loss and Flow Velocities

Volume Flow (gal/min)	Velocity (ft/sec)*	Friction Head (ft/100ft)*	Friction Loss (psi/100ft)*
2	0.3/0.4	0.1/0.1	0.03/0.04
5	0.8/0.9	0.2/0.3	0.1/0.1
7	1.1/1.3	0.4/0.6	0.2/0.2
10	1.6/1.9	0.7/1.0	0.3/0.5
15	2.4/2.8	1.5/2.2	0.7/1.0
20	3.2/3.8	2.6/3.8	1.1/1.6
25	4.0/4.7	4.0/5.7	1.7/2.5
30	4.9/5.6	5.0/8.0	2.4/3.4
35	5.7/6.6	7.4/10.6	3.2/4.6
40	6.5/7.5	9.4/13.6	4.1/5.9
45	7.3/8.4	11.7/16.9	5.1/7.3
50	8.1/9.4	14.3/20.5	6.2/8.9
60	9.7/11.3	20.0/28.7	8.7/12.4

*Sch. 40/ Sch. 80

19.8.6 2" PVC Friction Loss and Flow Velocities

Volume Flow (gal/min)	Velocity (ft/sec)*	Friction Head (ft/100ft)*	Friction Loss (psi/100ft)*
5	0.5/0.6	0.07/0.1	0.03/0.04
7	0.7/0.8	0.1/0.2	0.05/0.07
10	1.0/1.1	0.2/0.3	0.09/0.1
15	1.5/1.7	0.5/0.6	0.2/0.3
20	2.0/2.2	0.8/1.1	0.3/0.5
25	2.4/2.8	1.2/1.6	0.5/0.7
30	2.9/3.4	1.6/2.3	0.7/1.0

35	3.4/3.9	2.2/3.0	0.9/1.3
40	3.9/4.5	2.8/3.8	1.2/1.7
45	4.4/5.0	3.4/4.8	1.5/2.1
50	4.9/5.6	4.2/5.8	1.8/2.5
60	5.9/6.7	5.8/8.1	2.5/3.5
70	6.8/7.8	7.8/10.8	3.4/4.7
75	7.3/8.4	8.8/12.3	3.8/5.3
80	7.8/8.9	9.9/13.8	4.3/6.0
90	8.8/10.1	12.4/17.2	5.4/7.5
100	9.8/11.2	15.0/20.9	6.5/9.1

*Sch. 40/ Sch. 80

19.8.7 3" PVC Friction Loss and Flow Velocities

Volume Flow (gal/min)	Velocity (ft/sec)*	Friction Head (ft/100ft)*	Friction Loss (psi/100ft)*
5	0.2/0.3	0.02/0.02	0.01/0.01
7	0.3/0.4	0.02/0.03	0.01/0.01
10	0.4/0.5	0.03/0.04	0.01/0.02
15	0.7/0.8	0.07/0.09	0.03/0.04
20	0.9/1.0	0.1/0.2	0.05/0.07
25	1.1/1.3	0.2/0.2	0.07/0.1
30	1.3/1.5	0.2/0.3	0.1/0.1
35	1.6/1.7	0.3/0.4	0.1/0.2
40	1.8/2.0	0.4/0.5	0.2/0.2
45	2.0/2.2	0.5/0.7	0.2/0.3
50	2.2/2.5	0.6/0.8	0.3/0.4
60	2.7/3.0	0.9/1.1	0.4/0.5

70	3.1/3.5	1.1/1.5	0.5/0.7
75	3.3/3.7	1.3/1.7	0.6/0.7
80	3.5/4.0	1.4/1.9	0.6/0.8
90	4.0/4.5	1.8/2.4	0.8/1.0
100	4.4/5.0	2.2/2.9	0.9/1.3
125	5.5/6.2	3.3/4.4	1.4/1.9
150	6.6/7.5	4.6/6.2	2.0/2.7
175	7.7/8.7	6.2/8.3	2.7/3.6
200	8.8/10.0	7.9/10.6	3.4/4.6
250	11.0/12.5	11.9/16.0	5.2/6.9

*Sch. 40/ Sch. 80

19.8.8 4" PVC Friction Loss and Flow Velocities

Volume Flow (gal/min)	Velocity (ft/sec)*	Friction Head (ft/100ft)*	Friction Loss (psi/100ft)*
20	0.5/0.6	0.03/0.04	0.01/0.02
25	0.6/0.7	0.04/0.06	0.02/0.03
30	0.8/0.9	0.06/0.08	0.03/0.04
35	0.9/1.0	0.08/0.1	0.04/0.05
40	1.0/1.2	0.1/0.1	0.05/0.06
45	1.2/1.3	0.1/0.2	0.06/0.07
50	1.3/1.4	0.2/0.2	0.07/0.09
60	1.5/1.7	0.2/0.3	0.1/0.1
70	1.8/2.0	0.3/0.4	0.1/0.2
75	1.9/2.2	0.3/0.5	0.2/0.2
80	2.1/2.3	0.4/0.5	0.2/0.2
90	2.3/2.6	0.5/0.6	0.2/0.3
100	2.6/2.9	0.6/0.8	0.3/0.3

125	3.2/3.6	0.9/1.2	0.4/0.5
150	3.8/4.3	1.2/1.6	0.5/0.7
175	4.5/5.0	1.6/2.2	0.7/0.9
200	5.1/5.7	2.1/2.8	0.9/1.2
250	6.4/7.2	3.2/4.2	1.4/1.8
300	7.7/8.6	4.4/5.8	1.9/2.5
350	9.0/10.0	5.9/7.8	2.6/3.4
400	10.2/11.5	7.5/9.9	3.3/4.3

*Sch. 40/ Sch. 80

19.8.9 6" PVC Friction Loss and Flow Velocities

Volume Flow (gal/min)	Velocity (ft/sec)*	Friction Head (ft/100ft)*	Friction Loss (psi/100ft)*
50	0.6/0.6	0.02/0.03	0.01/0.01
60	0.7/0.8	0.03/0.04	0.01/0.02
70	0.8/0.9	0.04/0.05	0.02/0.02
75	0.8/0.9	0.05/0.06	0.02/0.03
80	0.9/1.0	0.05/0.07	0.02/0.03
90	1.0/1.1	0.06/0.08	0.03/0.04
100	1.1/1.3	0.08/0.1	0.04/0.04
125	1.4/1.6	0.1/0.2	0.05/0.07
150	1.7/1.9	0.2/0.2	0.07/0.1
175	2.0/2.2	0.2/0.3	0.1/0.1
200	2.3/2.5	0.3/0.4	0.1/0.2
250	2.8/3.1	0.4/0.6	0.2/0.2
300	3.4/3.8	0.6/0.8	0.3/0.3
350	3.9/4.4	0.8/1.0	0.3/0.5
400	4.5/5.0	1.0/1.3	0.4/0.6
450	5.1/5.6	1.3/1.7	0.6/0.7

500	5.6/6.3	1.5/2.0	0.7/0.9
750	8.4/9.4	3.3/4.3	1.4/1.8
1,000	11.2/12.5	5.5/7.2	2.4/3.1

*Sch. 40/ Sch. 80

19.8.10 8" PVC Friction Loss and Flow Velocities

Volume Flow (gal/min)	Velocity (ft/sec)*	Friction Head (ft/100ft)*	Friction Loss (psi/100ft)*
125	0.7/0.9	0.03/0.05	0.01/0.02
150	0.8/1.1	0.04/0.05	0.02/0.02
175	1.0/1.3	0.04/0.08	0.02/0.03
200	1.1/1.4	0.06/0.09	0.02/0.04
250	1.3/1.8	0.07/0.1	0.03/0.06
300	1.6/2.1	0.1/0.2	0.05/0.09
350	1.9/2.5	0.2/0.3	0.07/0.1
400	2.3/2.9	0.2/0.3	0.09/0.2
450	2.6/3.2	0.3/0.4	0.1/0.2
500	2.9/3.6	0.3/0.5	0.1/0.2
750	3.2/5.4	0.4/1.1	0.2/0.5
1,000	4.9/7.1	0.9/1.8	0.4/0.8
1,250	6.5/8.9	1.5/2.8	0.6/1.2
1,500	8.1/10.7	2.2/4.0	1.0/1.7

*Sch. 40/ Sch. 80

19.8.11 10" PVC Friction Loss and Flow Velocities

Volume Flow (gal/min)	Velocity (ft/sec)*	Friction Head (ft/100ft)*	Friction Loss (psi/100ft)*
200	0.8/0.9	0.03/0.04	0.01/0.02
250	1.0/1.1	0.04/0.05	0.02/0.02
300	1.2/1.4	0.05/0.07	0.02/0.03

350	1.4/1.6	0.07/0.09	0.03/0.04
400	1.6/1.8	0.09/0.1	0.04/0.05
450	1.9/2.0	0.1/0.1	0.05/0.06
500	2.1/2.3	0.1/0.2	0.06/0.07
750	3.1/3.4	0.3/0.4	0.1/0.2
1,000	4.1/4.5	0.5/0.6	0.2/0.3
1,250	5.1/5.7	0.7/0.9	0.3/0.4
1,500	6.2/6.8	1.0/1.3	0.4/0.6
2,000	8.2/9.1	1.7/2.2	0.7/1.0
2,500	10.3/11.3	2.6/3.3	1.1/1.4

*Sch. 40/ Sch. 80

19.8.12 12" PVC Friction Loss and Flow Velocities

Volume Flow (gal/min)	Velocity (ft/sec)*	Friction Head (ft/100ft)*	Friction Loss (psi/100ft)*
350	1.0/1.1	0.03/0.04	0.01/0.02
400	1.2/1.3	0.04/0.05	0.02/0.02
450	1.3/1.4	0.05/0.06	0.02/0.03
500	1.5/1.6	0.06/0.07	0.03/0.03
750	2.2/2.4	0.1/0.2	0.05/0.07
1,000	2.9/3.2	0.2/0.3	0.09/0.1
1,250	3.6/4.0	0.3/0.4	0.1/0.2
1,500	4.3/4.8	0.4/0.6	0.2/0.2
2,000	5.8/6.4	0.7/0.9	0.3/0.4
2,500	7.2/8.0	1.1/1.4	0.5/0.6
3,000	8.7/9.6	1.6/2.0	0.7/0.9

3,500	10.1/11.2	2.1/2.7	0.9/1.2
4,000	11.1/12.8	2.7/3.4	1.2/1.5

*Sch. 40/ Sch. 80

19.8.13 PVC Fitting Friction Loss

Friction Loss - Equivalent Length (feet of straight pipe)												
	PVC Pipe											
Fitting	**½"**	**¾"**	**1"**	**1 ¼"**	**1 ½"**	**2"**	**3"**	**4"**	**6"**	**8"**	**10"**	**12"**
90° Ell	1.5	2.0	2.5	3.8	4.0	5.7	7.9	11.4	16.7	21.0	26.0	32.0
45° Ell	0.8	1.1	1.4	1.8	2.1	2.6	4.0	5.1	8.0	10.6	13.5	15.5
Tee - Run	1.0	1.4	1.7	2.3	2.7	4.0	6.1	7.9	12.3	14.0	17.5	20.0
Tee - Branch	3.8	4.9	6.0	7.3	8.4	12.0	16.4	22.0	32.7	49.0	57.0	67.0

19.9 Valves Pros/Cons for Different Use

Valve Type	Pros	Cons	Applications
Ball Valve	· Easy to replace and install	· Can be expensive	· Common in aquaria
	· Least restrictive to flow	· Typically found ≤ 6" pipe size	· Found in Smaller applications
Butterfly Valve	· Easy to replace and install	· Requires flanges for installation, adding cost	· Large Diameter pipe
	· Limited flow loss	· Should be used in > 4"pipe size	
Globe Valve	· Flow regulation	· Expensive	· City water mains
		· Reduces flow significantly	
		· Plugs eventually wear	
Gate Valve	· Flow restriction	· Poor flow regulation	· On/off applications
	· Inexpensive	· Wears out quickly	· Discharge of Protein skimmers
Diaphragm Valve	· Fine adjustments	· Cannot be used in high pressure applications	· Actuators
	· Can be used to redirect flow	· Causes more turbulence in water flow	· Pneumatics
	· Can be used in on/off applications		

19.10 Dial Indicator Shaft Alignment Worksheet

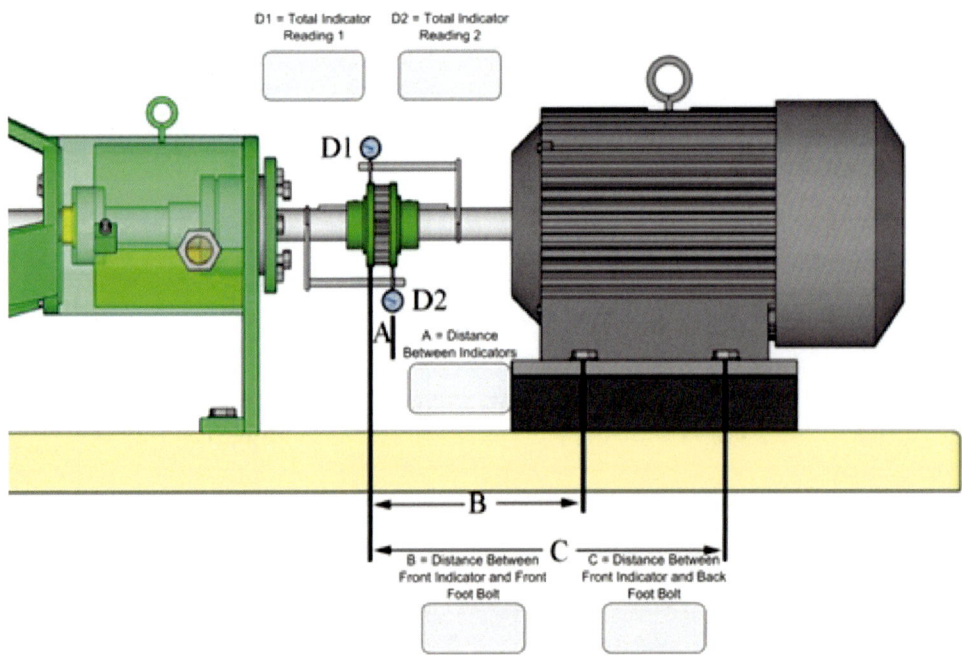

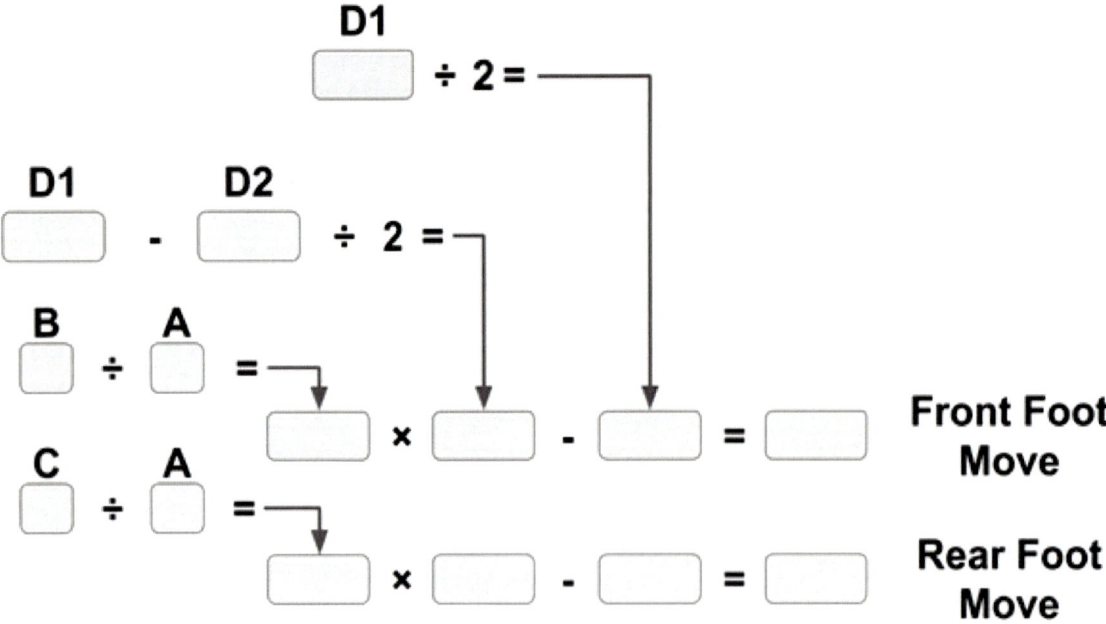

20   AALSO Exam Handbook

Introduction

This Exam Handbook is your guide to preparing for the AALSO Certification Exams.

AALSO members are the water quality and mechanical system professionals that move the water, design and maintain the systems, develop and distribute the products to manage the daily requirements for animals in our care at hundreds of facilities across the world. We care for the systems that make animal care possible. We are a 501(c)(6) non-profit organization focusing on the education and training of aquatic life support operators around the world. Formed in 1994, we are supported by the entire industry.

AALSO offers a multi-level competency acknowledgment program for life support operators and water quality technicians based on test scores received from exams administered by the AALSO certification committee. AALSO believes that the proficiency program's recognition criteria is based on practical, on-the-job applications and encourages Zoo and Aquarium institutions to incorporate this training into their employee development program.

Code of Ethics

AALSO expects high level of standards and professionalism from members and certificate holders that are fitting for institutions with live animals in their care and to instill confidence in the public that living collections are being cared for with competence and integrity. AALSO members and certificate holders are expected to follow all symposium testing rules, conduct themselves honestly, and not engage in any activities that could jeopardize the integrity of the certification exams.

Exam Rules and Security

In order to secure the integrity of the certification exams, all work and notes taken during the examination must be turned in with the exam. Test candidates are encouraged to use the examination itself to work out the problems, before filling out the answer sheet. Both the examination packet and the answer sheets must be returned to the certification committee members before leaving the testing site. You will be able to use the AALSO Field Guide, an AALSO approved calculator, and any notes taken during the study period at the symposium. Candidates who do not follow these rules may have their membership or certifications disqualified.

Exam Availability

Levels one, two, and three exams for both life support operator and water quality technician are available at the annual symposium. To qualify for subsequent level exams, you must have successfully fulfilled the requirements and passed the supporting examination of the previous level(s). For each AALSO life support or water quality status level, you must have successfully fulfilled the requirements and scored a 70% or better on the corresponding examination in order to qualify for that level, as defined by AALSO. It is also possible to take the level one exams after attending one of AALSO's Education and Training (EaT) courses. These courses bring an AALSO instructor directly to a facility in order to train and certify operators and technicians who cannot make it to the annual symposium.

Exam Eligibility

To qualify for the level 2 or level 3 exams, you must be involved in the function or sales of life support operations, water quality, or be a student in an aquarium based program, and be an AALSO member in good standing.

Level one is available for industry members as well as for those looking to transition into roles from related industries or educational programs, and be an AALSO member in good standing. Associate Memberships are available for individuals who are not currently employed in the aquatic animal care industry.

Level two and/or three are awarded to any zoo or aquarium life support operator and/or water quality technician with relevant experience who successfully passed the corresponding exam covering set recognition criteria for that level.

The life support operator certification acknowledges general operator proficiency with tasks ranging from basic routine operations to advanced applications and theory, covering topics such as: sand filtration, biological filtration, chemical filtration, USDA regulations, cathodic protection, turbidity, safety, pump curves, trouble shooting, pool volume calculations, filter surface area calculations, and pool turnover rate calculations.

The water quality technician certification acknowledges general operator proficiency with task ranging from basic laboratory techniques to advanced applications and theory, covering topics such as: laboratory safety, laboratory equipment and measurements, quality assurance and assessment, nitrification, denitrification, basic microbiology monitoring, understanding stoichiometry and chemical reactions and dilutions.

Test Results Scoring

All tests are scored carefully by certification committee members. Committee members do not discuss the results with test candidates or other AALSO members. Test scores are kept confidential. A score of 70% or higher is considered passing for each level.

Test Results Notification

Certificates are handed out during the symposium's certification banquet and scores are posted privately to the member's accounts after the symposium.

Test Format

The Life Support exams are available in two formats: United States based exams with English units, or international versions with SI units. The water quality exams are universal and use SI units.

Life Support Operator Exam I

- 60 minutes for level I
- 25 Multiple Choice Questions
  - 15 Operational Questions
  - 5 Safety and Regulatory Questions
  - 5 Mathematical Calculations

Life Support Exam II

- 60 minutes for level II
- 25 Multiple Choice Questions
  - 14 Operational Questions
  - 4 Safety and Regulatory Questions
  - 7 Mathematical Calculations

Life Support Exam III

- 90 minutes for level III
- Approximately 25 Questions

Water Quality Exam I

- 60 minutes for level I
- 25 Multiple Choice Questions
  - 10 Water Quality Testing Theory Questions
  - 5 Safety and Regulatory Questions
  - 4 Analytical Equipment Questions
  - 5 Quality Control/Quality Assurance Questions
  - 1 Mathematical Calculation

Water Quality Exam II

- 60 minutes for level II
- 25 Multiple Choice Questions
  - 8 Water Quality Testing Questions
  - 6 Chemistry Questions
  - 4 Safety and Regulatory Questions
  - 9 Mathematical Calculations

Water Quality Exam III

- 90 minutes for level III
- Approximately 25 Questions

Accommodations for Those with Physical or Learning Disabilities

In compliance with the Americans with Disabilities Act, reasonable accommodations can be provided for individuals who provide a physician's certificate documenting a physical or psychological disability that may affect the individual's ability to complete the certification examination. Written requests must be made no later than four weeks before the symposium.

Preparing for your Test

Individuals are responsible for preparing for their certification test. The AALSO Field Guide is a useful study tool and covers many of the topics that are on the examinations. The majority of content from the level I examinations can be found in the AALSO Field Guide. There is the potential for some content and knowledge to be acquired from on-the-job experience. The level II examinations also contain a majority of content from the field guide; however, more deductive reasoning, expanded calculations and deeper comprehension of the topics may be required. The level III examinations draw on theoretical and practical applications that may not be discussed fully in the field guide and require an advanced knowledge of the subject material. It may be necessary to consult additional, in-depth texts to ensure the mastery of life support and water quality needed to pass a level III exam.

20.1 AALSO Water Quality Technician Level 1 Practice Exam

1. Salinity is commonly measured using which unit?

   A. CFU
   B. NTU
   C. mEq/L
   D. ppt

2. How would you prepare 100 mL of 0.0400 M KCl from 0.200 M KCl stock solution?

   A. Withdraw 10.0 mL of 0.200 M KCl, place it in a partially filled 100 mL volumetric flask and add water until the final volume is 100 mL.
   B. Withdraw 20.0 mL of 0.200 M KCl, place it in a partially filled 100 mL volumetric flask and add water until the final volume is 100 mL.
   C. Withdraw 40.0 mL of 0.200 M KCl, place it in a partially filled 100 mL volumetric flask and add water until the final volume is 100 mL.
   D. Withdraw 50.0 mL of 0.200 M KCl, place it in a partially filled 100 mL volumetric flask and add water until the final volume is 100 mL.

3. Which of the following is not considered Laboratory Personal Protective Equipment (PPE)?

   A. Safety Glasses
   B. Hair Tie
   C. Face Shield
   D. Lab Coat

4. Which of the following is a concern after a chemical spill?

   A. Environmental release
   B. Adequate engineering controls or PPE to protect staff during cleanup
   C. Slip or Trip Hazard
   D. All of the above

5. Where should flammable liquids be stored?

   A. In a fume hood
   B. In a locked cabinet
   C. In the bed of a pickup truck
   D. In an approved flammable liquid storage cabinet

6. If a water quality laboratory technician records data incorrectly, how should they respond?

   A. Erase the misprint so it cannot be misinterpreted by husbandry staff
   B. Draw a single line through the entry making sure that the inaccurate information is still legible. Initial and date the entry. State the reason for the error. Document the correct information.
   C. Re-record the worksheet so the data is easy to read
   D. Do not make any alterations to the record

7. Why should you never add water to acid?

   A. The exothermic reaction could possibly splash the content (acid) out of the container.
   B. The endothermic reaction could freeze the container causing it to shatter.
   C. It would neutralize the acid too much to render it useless.
   D. Nothing would happen. There is no difference if you add water to acid or acid to water.

8. Which of the following is not a disinfection byproduct of chlorine disinfection?

   A. Sodium hypochlorite
   B. Trihalomethane compounds
   C. Haloacetic acids
   D. Chloroform

9. What is an alternative way to indirectly measure the amount of dissolved ozone in an aquarium?

   A. DPD test for chlorine or bromine
   B. Specific Conductance
   C. pH
   D. Stray Voltage

10. Which of the following disinfection methods has a low potential for creating disinfection byproducts?

    A. Ozone
    B. UV
    C. Chlorine
    D. Bromine

11. What is the best definition of alkalinity?

    A. The measurement of the amount of metals in water
    B. The measurement of the amount of cations in water
    C. The measurement of the pH buffering capacity in water
    D. Any liquid with a pH greater than 7

12. A solution with a pH of 7 is considered to be:

    A. Acidic
    B. Neutral
    C. Basic
    D. Strongly Acidic

13. List, in order of nitrification, the major compounds associated with the nitrogen cycle as it pertains to aquatic system health.

    A. Ammonium, Nitrate, Nitrite
    B. Ammonia, Nitrate, Nitrite
    C. Ammonium, Nitrite, Nitrate
    D. Ammonia, Nitrite, Nitrate

14. Which of the following is true about NH_3-N?

    A. This form of ammonia is the unionized component
    B. The measurement includes contributions from nitrite
    C. The NH_3-N form uses the molecular weight of only the nitrogen atoms
    D. This formula expresses ammonium

15. Which of the following do not contribute to Conductivity/Salinity?

    A. Sulfates
    B. Oxygen
    C. Chlorides
    D. Carbonates

16. What wavelength is considered part of the Visible Spectrum?

    A. 10 nm
    B. 5000 nm
    C. 500 nm
    D. 200 nm

17. What is the volume of water in this graduated cylinder?

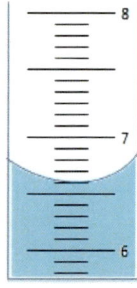

    A. 6.5 mL
    B. 6.6 mL
    C. 6.7 mL
    D. 6.8 mL

18. When analyzing ammonia, a technician analyzed spiked a sample containing 0.05 ppm ammonia as N with a standard, adding 0.10 ppm ammonia as N. When she reads the value of her LFM on the spectrophotometer, she sees a result of 0.05 ppm. Her LFB was spiked with 0.10 ppm ammonia as N and her result was 0.09 ppm ammonia as N. What corrective action is appropriate?

    A. Analyze another LFB
    B. Re-prepare both LFM and LFB
    C. Re-prepare LFM and if it still fails, consider using a different method
    D. Discard secondary reference solution.

19. The veterinary staff indicated an elevated presence of goiters in your saltwater fish tank. He/she indicated that this is due to the reduced amount of iodine in the water. What could be the cause of the problem?

    A. Ozonation disinfection
    B. Nitrogen Gas Saturation
    C. pH and alkalinity
    D. UV

20. When a measurement is repeatable and consistent it is said to have:

    A. High Precision
    B. High Accuracy
    C. High Significance
    D. High Quality

21. Which of the following errors can be traced to defective equipment?

    A. Gross Errors
    B. Systematic Errors
    C. Random Errors
    D. Significant Errors

22. A freshwater system with a carbon filter is tested weekly for chlorine, with a normal result of 1.0ppm pre-filter and n/d post-filter. A DPD test today shows a value of 0.8ppm post-filter. After performing a retest and getting a similar result, what is the next thing you should do?

    A. Check the date the carbon in the filter was last changed
    B. Perform a total organic carbon analysis of the water
    C. Test the alkalinity of the incoming water
    D. Nothing, that value indicates no reason for further investigation

23. SDS is short for:

    A. Safest Defensive Strategy
    B. Simple Dissolved Substance
    C. Safety Data Sheet
    D. Safe Data Set

24. What is the preferred glassware to use when doing a dilution?

    A. Erlenmeyer Flask
    B. Graduated Cylinder
    C. Volumetric Flask
    D. Beaker

25. What should be added to a sample taken from a chlorinated mammal pool for coliform testing?

    A. Sodium citrate
    B. Sodium hypochlorite
    C. Sodium thiosulfate
    D. Sodium bicarbonate buffer

20.2 AALSO Life Support Operator Level 1 Practice Exam

1. A positive displacement pump that utilizes a set of rollers that compress and rotate across an elastomeric tube to pump a fluid is a:

    A. Flexible impeller pump
    B. Diaphragm pump
    C. Centrifugal pump
    D. Peristaltic pump

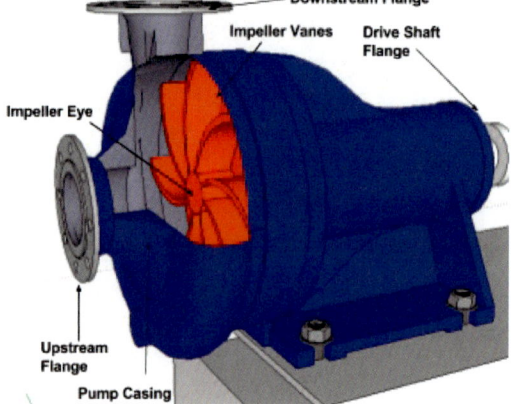

2. According to the diagram, which part of the centrifugal pump does the motor connect to?

    A. Pump casing
    B. Impeller
    C. Volute
    D. Drive shaft flange

3. Which of the following life support system components could be categorized as mechanical filtration?

    A. Ultraviolet sterilizer
    B. Ozone contact tank
    C. Rotating drum filter
    D. None of the above

4. Which of the following life support system components uses high flow rates and higher pressures to mechanically filter water?

    A. Ultraviolet sterilizer
    B. Carbon filter
    C. High pressure sand filter
    D. None of the above

5. A _____ valve uses the guillotine action of a solid wall to control the flow of water:

    A. Butterfly
    B. Ball
    C. Gate
    D. Globe

6. A globe valve uses _____ to control the flow of water:

    A. Wafer-like articulating disk
    B. Guillotine action of a solid wall
    C. Plug and baffle
    D. Spherical articulating disk

7. Which condition can decrease foam fractionator efficiency?

    A. Consistent flow rate through the fractionator
    B. Large disruptive bubbles in the reaction column
    C. Uniform bubble size in the reaction column
    D. Higher salinity (such as full strength seawater)

8. Before entering a confined space, one should do all of the following EXCEPT:

    A. Lock out/tag out all mechanical equipment
    B. Ensure adequate ventilation
    C. Test oxygen levels and dangerous gases
    D. Securely tie a rope around one's waist to ensure rescue if necessary

9. Which of the following is a type of chemical filtration?

    A. Degas tower
    B. Carbon filter
    C. Sand filter
    D. Bag filter

10. Channeling in a sand filter can be caused by

    A. Improper backwashing frequency
    B. Broken lateral
    C. Low filtering flow rates
    D. Both A & B

11. What is the media flow rate range for a sand filter during normal operation?

    A. 5-10 Gal/min/ft^2
    B. 10-15 Gal/min/ft^2
    C. 15-18 Gal/min/ft^2
    D. 18-20 Gal/min/ft^2

12. What is the appropriate way to dispose of burnt-out fluorescent bulbs that contain mercury?

   A. Recycle
   B. Compost
   C. Landfill
   D. Hazardous waste

13. An aquarium to be used as a sump tank is 6ft long, 2ft wide, and 2ft deep. While normally operating the sump will be 1/3 full. How many gallons will the sump hold when normally operating? (Round answer to the nearest gallon)

   A. 120 gallons
   B. 24 gallons
   C. 179 gallons
   D. 60 gallons

14. OSHA requires SDS be in a central location that is readily accessible unless:

   A. They are secured in a locked office or file
   B. They are on or near the door to the room where the chemicals are used
   C. There are no exceptions
   D. The chemicals are only being stored, not used

15. A technician needs to refill a tank, which contained 10,000 gallons of water before 25% was removed during a water exchange. The technician can fill at rate of 3,600 gph. How long will it take to refill the tank?

   A. 41.66 minutes
   B. 31.66 minutes
   C. 60.66 minutes
   D. 66.66 minutes

16. A pump suction line pulls from a circular tank that sits 10 feet below the pump and discharges to the display aquarium 100 feet above on the fourth floor. What is the total static head at the pump?

   A. 110 ft
   B. 10 ft
   C. 90 ft
   D. 1,000 ft

17. Which condition decreases foam fractionator efficiency?

   A. Too little air injected into the foam fractionator
   B. Dirty riser tube/chimney, and collection cup
   C. Inconsistent flow rates and varying water level within the fractionator column
   D. All of the above

18. A 68,000 gallon Hippo exhibit has 4 recirculation pumps rated at 340 gpm each. What is the turnover time in minutes for this system?

   A. 90 minutes
   B. 50 minutes
   C. 39.5 minutes
   D. 200 minutes

19. If a pump is rated for 960 gpm, how many cubic feet per second (cfs) would that be?

   A. 1.92 cfs
   B. 128.34 cfs
   C. 2.14 cfs
   D. 16 cfs

20. Hazard(s) associated with UV bulbs:

   A. Contain mercury
   B. Sharp when broken
   C. High voltage when operating
   D. All of the above

21. The effectiveness of disinfection of potentially pathogenic waterborne micro-organisms through the use of the ozone is influenced the most by which of these factors?

   A. Temperature
   B. Concentration
   C. Salinity
   D. pH

22. What does LOTO stand for?

   A. Lock out, tell operator
   B. Leave open, take off
   C. Lock out, tag out
   D. Your retirement plan

23. The tank material, HDPE is also known as?

     A. Hyper dense polyethylene
     B. High density proethane
     C. High density polyethylene
     D. Hyper dense proethane

24. Which of the following can change when powerheads are used?

     A. ORP increases
     B. ORP decreases
     C. Water temperature can increase
     D. Water temperature can decrease

25. What is a common cause of dead heading a pump?

     A. Pump cavitation
     B. The suction side of the pump is closed
     C. The valve(s) directly down-stream from the pump is (are) closed
     D. Increasing water temperature

20.3 Answers to Practice Exams

20.3.1 Answers for Water Quality Practice Exam

1. D
2. B
3. B
4. D
5. D
6. B
7. A
8. A
9. A
10. B
11. C
12. B
13. D
14. C
15. B
16. C
17. B
18. C
19. A
20. A
21. B
22. A
23. C
24. C
25. C

20.3.2 Answers for Life Support Practice Exam

1. D
2. D
3. C
4. C
5. C
6. C
7. B
8. D
9. B
10. D
11. B
12. D
13. D
14. C
15. A
16. A
17. D
18. B
19. C
20. D
21. B
22. C
23. C
24. C
25. C

Aiken, A. (1995). *Use of Ozone to Improve Water Quality in Aquatic Exhibits.* International Zoo Yearbook, 34, 106 – 114.

Aiken, A., & Smith, M. (2015). *Management and Application of Ozone in Aquatic Life Support Systems.* AZA 2015 Annual Conference. Retrieved from https://be36b7be-a-62cb3a1a-s-sites.googlegroups.com/site/aqualitysymposium/Ozone%20Management%20for%20Aquatic%20Life%20Support%20Systems.pdf?attachauth=ANoY7crBjPW1r1EbOcofFjqqnq8F-ldLRpCzTqFcmOmiWsscUOsSkCTykfIWKPJCOWnOkjPBsR2FSScXKO3YXUBvAoYepvjs4CkzPYYe if_sg5RZpR4aCGWbQbL7FsvNTCYUJZO7y02jtYArD6_jJDvjAagAH3hGYn4ZKk-AYHtNsYXW DIu9DF7HuK_cUwvw40XP57HOZGdGdMNylbwmaFSsnfOpfb843sXy7WDeYb0ClacosHduF3uG m8LkQyF039_bdOMaQdo3AXQv_mEicB6WvAI77Pm-Rw%3D%3D&attredirects=0

Amand, W. (1993). *Infectious Disease Reviews.* American Association of Zoo Veterinarians. Media, Pennsylvania, USA.

Bower, C.E., & Bidwell, J.P. (1978). *Ionization of Ammonia in Seawater: Effects of Temperature, pH and Salinity* Journal of the Fisheries Board of Canada, 1978, 35 (7), 1012-1016.

Brady, J.E., Russell, J.W., & Holum, J.R. (2000). *Chemistry Matter and Its Changes.* New York: John Wiley & Sons, 881 pp.

Carlson, G., & Kirkbride, T. (2005). *Supersaturation and Gas Bubble Disease – Why Measure Total Dissolved Gas?* Retrieved from https://www.in-situ.com/wp-content/uploads/2015/01/Supersaturation-and-Gas-Bubble-Disease-%E2%80%93-Why-Measure-Total-Dissolved-Gas-Tech-Note.pdf

Chappell, J.A. (2008). *Nitrite Poisoning or "Brown Blood Disease" - A Preventable Problem.* Retrieved from http://www.aces.edu/dept/fisheries/aquaculture/documents/BrownBlood.pdf

Chester, R., & Jickells, T. (2012). *Marine Geochemistry.* West Sussex, UK: Blackwell Publishing.

Choromanski, J. M. (2004). Quarantine and Isolation Facilities for Elasmobranchs: Design and Construction. In M. Smith, D. Warmolts, D. Thoney, and R. Hueter (Eds.), *Elasmobranch Husbandry Manual: Captive Care of Sharks, Rays, and their Relatives.* Retrieved from https://sites.google.com/site/elasmobranchhusbandry/manual

Choromanski, J. (2004). *Acid Leaching and Concrete Pretreatment* [PowerPoint Slides]. Retrieved from https://be36b7be-a-62cb3a1a-s-sites.googlegroups.com/site/aquality symposium/23.%20Acid%20Leaching%20and%20Concrete%20Pretreatment%20%28PPT%2 9.pdf?attachauth=ANoY7crPed8HcmgRsttFbfGKwDgwWSYWl5pEeC0P1v914NtQ3mTUD8swoj EOLJRM8Re2nTZnZ238fh-VpqnEAdVuw9DGWozAbCbfQG2EDDPOCqbsHeknoav20YKe7p8 fejbvhhYuNgEVx_YqOH9pLAM_tmZc_G0nTyh4cPK1lU4Au7mmXlfZnRQHeFDrVpDMUQUrm6LL bqrQeUsD-zIP6j8PMnILRZERDzHTDdKFlBpSLWMkQtTXSp32MQj8xUQ4Q7_LTl-kkR2uOL08SV zvwSxQsw98O3X10w%3D%3D&attredirects=0

Coakley, J., & Crawford, R.L. (1998). *Marine Mammal Water Quality: Proceedings of a Symposium*, United States Department of Agriculture, Animal and Plant Health Inspection Service, Technical Bulletin No. 1868.

Colt, J. (1984). *Computation of Dissolved Gas Concentrations in Water as Functions of Temperature, Salinity, and Pressure.* Special Publication No. 14. Bethesda, MD: American Fisheries Society.

Cowern, E. (n.d.). C*owern Papers.* Retrieved from http://www.baldor.com/mvc/Download Center/Files/PR2525

Crowder, J.; Charanda, T. (2004) *Development and application of a method to detect and quantify praziquantel in seawater.* 1st AQuality Symposium, April 2-7, 2004, Oceanario de Lisboa, Portugal.

Curtis, R. (1999). *Controlling Pipette Performance in the Real World.* National Conference of Standards Laboratories. 1999 NCSL Workshop and Symposium. Session 3B.

Dahm, D.J., & Nelson, E.A. (2013). *Calculations in Chemistry: Dilutions.* New York: W. W. Norton & Company.

Deckwer, W., Cottrell, V., & Field, R. W. (1992). *Bubble column reactors.* Chichester: J. Wiley and Sons.

Delong, D. P. & Losordo, T. M. (2012). *How to Start a Biofilter.* Southern Regional Aquaculture Center. Publication Number 4502. Retrieved from http://fisheries.tamu.edu/files/2013/09/ SRAC-Publication-No.-4502-How-to-Start-a-Biofilter.pdf

DeSilva, F. J. (1999). *Essentials of Ion Exchange.* Paper presented at the 25th Annual Water Quality Association Conference (p. 5). Lisle: Resintech.

D'Aoust, B.G. (2016). *A Brief Discussion of Gas Bubble Disease, Dissolved Gases and Techniques for Measurement.* Point Four TGP Meter Instruction Manual. Retrieved from http://smhttp.29106. nexcesscdn.net/80C113/pentairaes/media/docs/Point-Four-Tracker-PortableTGP-Meter-Manual.pdf

Emerson Process Management (2008). *Fundamental of ORP Measurement.* Retrieved from http://www2.emersonprocess.com/siteadmincenter/PM%20Rosemount%20Analytical%20Documents/Liq_ADS_43-014.pdf)

Energy Star. (n.d.). Learn About LED Lighting. Retrieved from https://www.energystar.gov/products/lighting_fans/light_bulbs/learn_about_led_bulbs

Escobal, P. R. (2000). *Aquatic Systems Engineering: Devices and How They Function* (2nd ed.). CA: Dimensions Engineering Press.

Fossa, A. S. & Nilsen, A.J. (1996). *The Modern Coral Reef Aquarium* (1st ed.) Bornheim: Schmettkamp

Georg Fischer (2009). *Signet pH and ORP Buffer Solutions. Retrieved from* http://spectechind.com/Documents/signet-ph-orp-buffer-data.pdf

Gosse, P.H. (1854). *The Aquarium: An Unveiling of the Wonders of the Deep Sea.* London: J. Van Voorst.

Gottschalk, Christiane, et al. *Ozonation of Water and Waste Water: a Practical Guide to Understanding Ozone and Its Applications.* Second ed., Wiley-VCH, 2010.

HACH Company (2008). *Water Analysis Handbook, Fifth Edition.* Loveland, CO: Hach Company.

HACH Company (2016). *Application: Drinking Water Analysis, The Importance of Measuring Total Organic Carbon.* Retrieved from www.hach.com

HACH Company (2018). *What do the Units NH3-N Mean? Document ID TE149.* Retrieved from https://support.hach.com/app/answers/answer_view/a_id/1000078/~/what-do-the-units-nh3-n-mean%3F-

Harris, D.C. (2001). *Exploring Chemical Analysis, 2nd Edition.* New York, NY: W.H. Freeman and Company.

Hartman, C. (2014). What is a Variable Frequency Drive? Retrieved from https://www.vfds.com/blog/what-is-a-vfd

Hirazawa, N., Goto, T., & Shirasu, K. (2003). *Killing effect of various treatments on the monogenean Heterobothrium okamotoi eggs and oncomiracidia and the ciliate Cryptocaryon irritans cysts and theronts.* Aquaculture, 223, 1–13.

Hovanec, T. A. (2015). *An Introduction to Nitrification in Aquaria.* 2015 Aquatic Animal Life Support Operators 21st Annual Symposium Newport Aquarium. Retrieved from https://members.animalprofessional.com/conf/aalso/aalso2015/Pages/wqc.aspx

Hovanec, T. A. & Coshland, J. L. (2004). *A Chemical Analysis of Select Trace Elements in Synthetic Sea Salts and Natural Seawater.* Advanced Aquarist Online Magazine, 3: 9. Retrieved from http://www.advancedaquarist.com/2004/9/aafeature

Johnson, K., Johnson, B. & Johnson, H. (2014). *Periodic Table of Elements in the Ocean: MBARI Chemical Sensor Program*, Retrieved from http://www.mbari.org/chemsensor/pteo.htm

Jones, R. (2014). *The Nitrogen Cycle & Biofiltration* [Webinar]. In *World Aquatic Veterinary Medical Association Webinar Series.* Retreived from www.wavma.org/Webinars/B-1001-Jones-Nitrogen-Cycle-Biofiltration

Kellner, R., Mermet, J.-M., Otto, M., Valcarcel M. & Widmer, H.M. (2004). *Analytical Chemistry A Modern Approach to Analytical Science, 2nd Edition.* Germany: WILEY-VCH Verlag GmbH & Co. KGaA Weiheim.

Kerri, K. D., Dendy, B.B., Brady, J., & Crooks,W. (2008). *Operation of Wastewater Treatment Plants, A Field Study Training Program Seventh Edition, Volume I and II.* Sacramento: Office of Water Programs, California State University Sacramento.

Knier, G. (n.d.). *How do photovoltaics work?* Retrieved from https://science.nasa.gov/science-news/science-at-nasa/2002/solarcells/

LaBonne, D. L. & Rozenblum, D. (2004). *Design Considerations for Water Recovery Systems* [PowerPoint Slides]. Retrieved from https://be36b7be-a-62cb3a1a-s-sites.googlegroups.com/site/aqualitysymposium/12.%20Design%20Considerations%20for%20Water%20Recovery%20Systems%20%28PPT%29.pdf?attachauth=ANoY7cqRESKbTHO90BbLOVqKEBpoBacQZPOB6D1Q27aNGm6eoUlNetEvf6J-oRFzyUOLtLFSQyFRGpT2u0GnkdhUpvPeYJQ4Cu6-pscDcYyr2yP4-KwmfDdlk9mSByMv6eGDj5usNajdK-EHt69-u3sqUqbrnMLyML8xh9gaJgMfRfy4DVmTDySJ5xhvtpQAqDKoKAuN5kb1lSLFTd9wzrC6RKA2OHlvTEHpPkqLNeDo2lj8AGIsXAD7T4p2p0NbcFmYmn4v2CmY6G1Xv2EFwp-oo86-EuwcXIQj2npMso-U-V9OyrHM4ps%3D&attredirects=0

Lampe, D.G. & T.C. Zhang (1996). *Evaluation of sulfur-based autotrophic denitrification.* In Proceedings of the HSRC/ WERC Joint Conference on the Environment. Great Plains/ Rocky Mountain Hazardous Substance Research Center. Retrieved from http://www.engg.ksu.edu/HSRC/96Proceed/lampe.pdf

Lekang, O. (2013). *Aquaculture engineering.* Chichester, West Sussex, UK: John Wiley & Sons Ltd.

Lewis, E.L. (1980). *The practical salinity scale 1978 and its antecedents.* IEEEJ. Oceanic Eng. OE-5:50.

Lytle, D.A., Copeland, R.C., & James, C.N. (2004). *Relationship between Oxidation-Reduction Potential, Oxidant, and pH in Drinking water.* WQTC Conference: American Water Works Association (pp5-6).

McCosker, J. (1999). *The History for Steinhart Aquarium: A Very Fishy Tale.* Virginia Beach, VA: The Donning Company/Publishers.

Morris, A.L., Hamlin, H.J., Francis-Floyd, R.,Sheppard, B.J., & Guillette, L.J. (2011). *Nitrate-induced goiter in captive whitespotted bamboo sharks Chilosryllium plagiosum. Journal of Aquatic Animal Health*, 23(2):92-9.

National Research Council (2011). *Prudent Practices in the Laboratory: Handling and Management of Chemical Hazards, Updated Version.* Washington, DC: The National Academies Press.

Noga, E. J. (2010). *Fish Disease Diagnosis and Treatment* (2nd ed.) Daryagani, New Delhi: Wiley India Pvt. Ltd.

Occupational Safety and Health Administration (OSHA) (n.d.). *Electric Power eTool: Glossary of Terms.* Retrieved from https://www.osha.gov/SLTC/etools/electric_power/glossary.html

Occupational Safety and Health Administration (OSHA) (n.d.). *Flammable Liquids 29 CFR 1910.106.* Retrieved from: https://www.osha.gov/dte/library/TrngandMatlsLib_FlammableLiquids.pdf

Occupational Safety and Health Administration (OSHA) (2012). *Injury and Illness Prevention Programs White Paper.* Retrieved from https://www.osha.gov/dsg/InjuryIllnessPrevention ProgramsWhitePaper.html

Occupational Safety and Health Administration (OSHA) (2012). *Hazard Communication Standard: Safety Data Sheets.* Retrieved from https://www.osha.gov/Publications/ OSHA3514.html

Oxidation Technologies (2017). *Ozone Production from UV.* Retrieved from https://www. oxidationtech.com/ozone/ozone-production/uv-lamp.html

Pang, F., Christison, T. (2017) *Determination of Nitrite and Nitrate in Wastewater Using Capillary IC with UV Detection.* Retrieved from www.thermofisher.com/IC

Partain, J. (2014). *Breakpoint Chlorination.* Retrieved from http://texaswateroperators.com /break-point-chlorination/

Pentair. (2014). *Chiller Installation and Sizing.* Tech Talk 59. Retrieved from https://pentairaes .com/learn-about-aquaculture/chiller-installation-and-sizing-tt59/

Pentair. (2014, May 12). *AES Chiller Sizing Chart* [table]. Retrieved from https://pentairaes.com /learn-about-aquaculture/chiller-installation-and-sizing-tt59/

Peltola, M. (2003). *Power Factor Improved by Variable Speed AC Drives.* Retrieved from www04.abb.com/GLOBAL/seitp/seitp202.nsf/viewunid/57D1C4FC9FB087F885256D420065A F11/$file/Power Factor Improved Via AC Drives - Release.pdf.

Powell, D. C., Wisner, M. & Rupp, J. (2004). *Design and Construction of Exhibits for Elasmobranchs.* In M. Smith, D. Warmolts, D. Thoney, and R. Hueter (Eds.), *Elasmobranch Husbandry Manual: Captive Care of Sharks, Rays, and their Relatives.* Retrieved from https://sites.google.com/site/elasmobranchhusbandry/manual

Rice, E.W., Baird, R.B., Eaton, A.D., Clesceri, L.S., Eaton, A.D., Clesceri, L.S., Greenberg, A.E., & Franson, M.A. H., (2012). *Standard methods for the examination of water and wastewater, 22nd Edition.* Washington, DC: American Public Health Association., American Water Works Association., & Water Environment Federation.

Reclos, G.C., Tsamis, T., & Illiopoulos, A. (2004). *Skim the Cream.* Retreived from www.mchportal .com/fishkeeping-mainmenu-60/systems-the-structure-main-menu-78/572-skim-the-cream .html

Rogers, G. (2005). *Total Gas Saturation Considerations for Recirculating Aquatic Systems.* International Journal of Recirculating Aquaculture, Volume 6. Retrieved from https:// ejournals.lib.vt.edu/ijra/article/view/1400/1926

Shimadzu (2014). *Shimadzu Total Organic Carbon Analyzer TOC-L Brochure.* Retrieved from: www.shimzadzu.com/an/

Simkiss, K. (1964). *Phosphates and Crystal Poisons of the Calcification.* Biological Reviews of the Cambridge Philosophical Society. 39. 487-505.

Skoog, D. A., Holler, F .J., & Crouch, S. R. (2007). *Principles of Instrumental Analysis, Sixth Edition.* Belmont, CA: Thomson Brooks/Cole.

Smith, R. K. (1995). *Water and Wastewater Laboratory Techniques.* Water Environment Federation. Alexandria, VA: Water Environment Federation.

Spotte, S.H. (1973). *Marine Aquarium Keeping: The Science, Animals and Art.* New York: John Wiley & Sons, 171 pp.

Spotte, S. H. (1991). *Sterilization of Marine Mammal Pool Waters: Theoretical and Health Considerations*, United States Department of Agriculture, Animal and Plant Health Inspection Service, Technical Bulletin No. 1797.

Spotte, S.H. (1992). *Captive Seawater Fishes: Science and Technology.* New York: John Wiley & Sons.

Steininger, J.M., & Pareja, C. (1996). *ORP Sensor Response in Chlorinated Water.* NSPI Series, Volume I.

Suslow, T.V. (2004). *Oxidation-Reduction Potential (ORP) for Water Disinfection Monitoring, Control, and Documentation.* University of California Division of Agriculture and Natural Resources Publication 8149. Retrieved from http://anrcatalog.ucanr.edu/pdf/8149.pdf

Sykes, G. (1965). *Disinfection and Sterilization: Theory and Practice, Second Edition.* London: Chapman and Hall.

Timmons, M. B., & Ebeling, J. M. (2013). *Recirculating aquaculture.* Ithaca, NY: Ithaca publishing company.

ThermoFisher Scientific. (n.d.) *Aseptic Technique.* Retrieved from https://www.thermofisher .com/us/en/home/references/gibco-cell-culture-basics/aseptic-technique.htm

United Nations (2003). *Globally Harmonized System of Classification and Labelling of Chemicals (GHS). 1st ed.* New York: United Nations Publications.

United States Department of Energy. (n.d.). *Electric Power eTool: Glossary of Terms.* Retrieved from https://www1.eere.energy.gov/solar/pdfs/solar_timeline.pdf

United States Environmental Protection Agency [US EPA] (2014). *Laboratory Ethics and Data Integrity.* Retrieved from https://www.epa.gov/sites/production/files/2015-07/documents/ 2014aphllabethicstraining.pdf

United States Environmental Protection Agency [US EPA] (2017). *Volatile Organic Compounds' Impact on Indoor Air Quality.* Retrieved from https://www.epa.gov/indoor-air-quality-iaq/ volatile-organic-compounds-impact-indoor-air-quality

United States Environmental Protection Agency [US EPA](1986). *Ambient Water Quality Criteria for Bacteria.* EPA 440/5-84-002.

Volk, M. (2014). *Pump Characteristics and Applications.* Boca Raton, Florida: CRC Press.

Ward, N. B. (1852). *On the Growth of Plants in Closely Glazed Cases.* 2nd ed. London: J. Van Voorst.

Water Analytics (n.d.). *The Ten Things Everyone Should Know about pH and ORP.* Retrieved from http://www.wateranalytics.net/sites/default/files/Ten%20Things%20about%20pH%20&%2 0ORP.pdf

Weeks, N., Timmons, M., & Chen, S. (1992). *Feasibility of using foam fractionation for the removal of dissolved and suspended solids from fish culture water.* Aquacultural Engineering, 11(4), 251-265. doi:10.1016/0144-8609(92)90008-l

Wiesmann, U., Choi, I.S., & Dombrowski, E. M. (2007). *Fundamentals of Biological Wastewater Treatment.* New York: John Wiley & Sons.

World Health Organization [WHO] (2003). *Guidelines for Safe Recreational Water Environments* retrieved from http://www.who.int/water_sanitation_health/bathing/en/

World Health Organization [WHO] (2004). *Copper in Drinking-Water* retrieved from http://www.who.int/water_sanitation_health/dwq/chemicals/copper.pdf

Yanong, R. (2003). *Fish Health Management Considerations in Recirculating Aquaculture Systems – Part 2: Pathogens.* Retrieved from http://www.aces.edu/dept/fisheries/aquaculture/documents/fishhealth2.pdf

AALSO Periodic

Legend (color key):
- Actinides
- Alkali Metals
- Alkaline Earth Metals
- Lanthanides
- Metalloids
- Noble Gasses
- Non Metals
- Post Transition Metals
- Transition Metals

Hydrogen 1 **H** 1.01		

Lithium 3 **Li** 6.94	Beryllium 4 **Be** 9.01

Sodium 11 **Na** 22.99	Magnesium 12 **Mg** 24.31

Potassium 19 **K** 39.1 — Calcium 20 **Ca** 40.08 — Scandium 21 **Sc** 44.96 — Titanium 22 **Ti** 47.87 — Vanadium 23 **V** 50.94 — Chromium 24 **Cr** 52 — Manganese 25 **Mn** 54.94 — Iron 26 **Fe** 55.85 — Cobalt 27 **Co** 58.93

Rubidium 37 **Rb** 85.47 — Strontium 38 **Sr** 87.62 — Yttrium 39 **Y** 88.91 — Zirconium 40 **Zr** 91.22 — Niobium 41 **Nb** 92.91 — Molybdenum 42 **Mo** 95.94 — Technetium 43 **Tc** 98 — Ruthenium 44 **Ru** 101.07 — Rhodium 45 **Rh** 102.91

Cesium 55 **Cs** 132.91 — Barium 56 **Ba** 137.33 — Hafnium 72 **Hf** 178.49 — Tantalum 73 **Ta** 180.95 — Tungsten 74 **W** 183.84 — Rhenium 75 **Re** 186.21 — Osmium 76 **Os** 190.23 — Iridium 77 **Ir** 192.22

Francium 87 **Fr** [223.02] — Radium 88 **Ra** [226.03] — Rutherfordium 104 **Rf** [265.12] — Dubnium 105 **Db** [268.13] — Seaborgium 106 **Sg** [271.13] — Bohrium 107 **Bh** [270] — Hassium 108 **Hs** [277.15] — Meitnerium 109 **Mt** [276.15]

Lanthanum 57 **La** 138.91 — Cerium 58 **Ce** 140.12 — Praseodymium 59 **Pr** 140.91 — Neodymium 60 **Nd** 144.24 — Promethium 61 **Pm** 145 — Samarium 62 **Sm** 150.36 — Europium **E** 151

Actinium 89 **Ac** [227.03] — Thorium 90 **Th** 232.04 — Protactinium 91 **Pa** 231.04 — Uranium 92 **U** 238.03 — Neptunium 93 **Np** [237.05] — Plutonium 94 **Pu** [244.06] — Americium **A** [243]

Key box:
Element Name — Atomic Number
Atomic Mass
Legendum -1 **Le** 1.1 amu

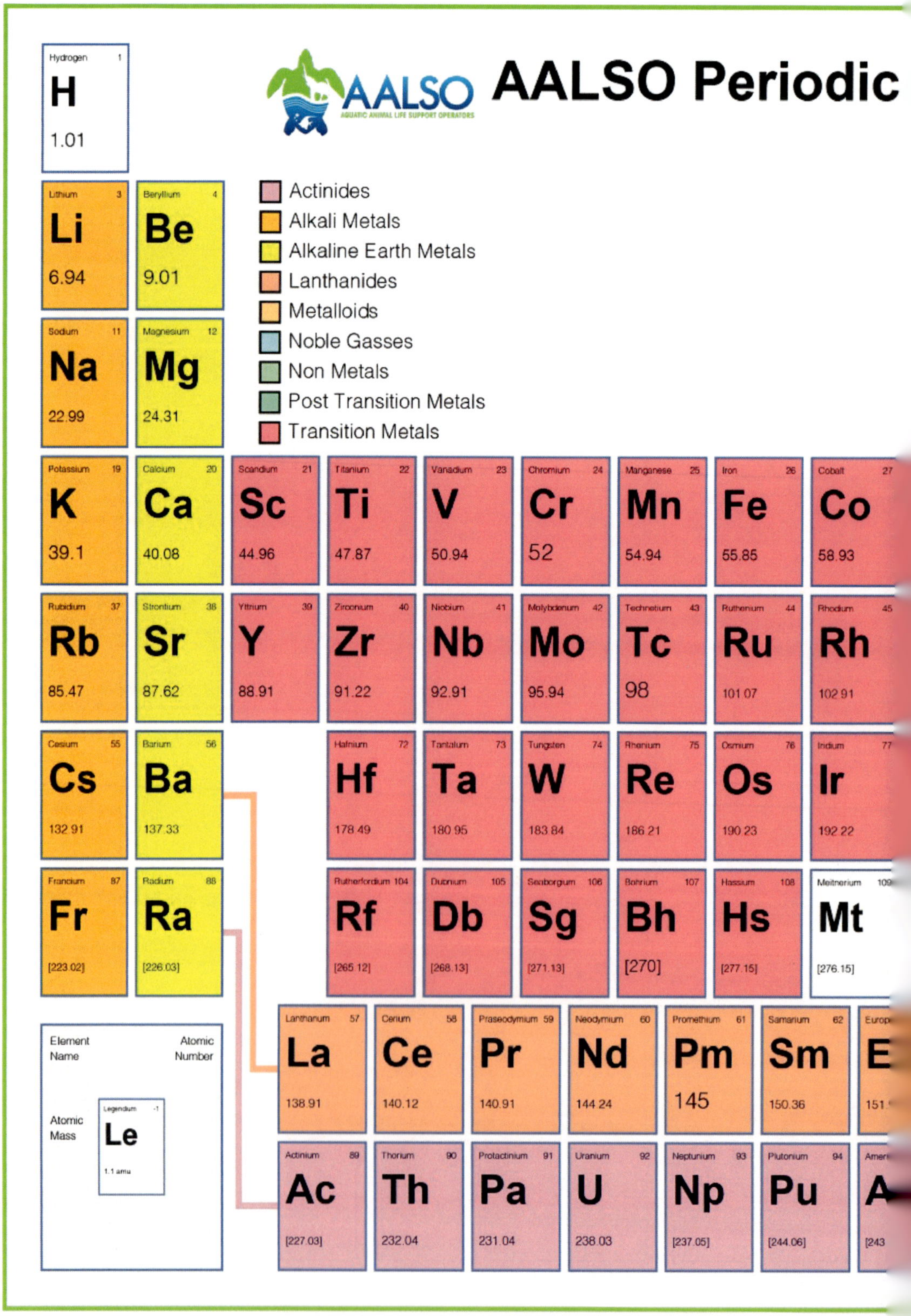

Table of the Elements

Helium 2
He
4

Boron 5	Carbon 6	Nitrogen 7	Oxygen 8	Fluorine 9	Neon 10
B	**C**	**N**	**O**	**F**	**Ne**
10.81	12.01	14.01	16	19	20.18

Aluminum 13	Silicon 14	Phosphorus 15	Sulfur 16	Chlorine 17	Argon 18
Al	**Si**	**P**	**S**	**Cl**	**Ar**
26.98	28.09	30.97	32.07	35.45	39.95

Nickel 28	Copper 29	Zinc 30	Gallium 31	Germanium 32	Arsenic 33	Selenium 34	Bromine 35	Krypton 36
Ni	**Cu**	**Zn**	**Ga**	**Ge**	**As**	**Se**	**Br**	**Kr**
58.69	63.55	65.39	69.72	72.64	74.92	78.96	79.9	83.8

Palladium 46	Silver 47	Cadmium 48	Indium 49	Tin 50	Antimony 51	Tellurium 52	Iodine 53	Xenon 54
Pd	**Ag**	**Cd**	**In**	**Sn**	**Sb**	**Te**	**I**	**Xe**
106.42	107.87	112.41	114.82	118.71	121.76	127.6	126.9	131.29

Platinum 78	Gold 79	Mercury 80	Thallium 81	Lead 82	Bismuth 83	Polonium 84	Astatine 85	Radon 86
Pt	**Au**	**Hg**	**Tl**	**Pb**	**Bi**	**Po**	**At**	**Rn**
195.08	196.97	200.59	204.38	207.2	208.98	[208.98]	[209.99]	[222.02]

Darmstadtium 110	Roentgenium 111	Copernicium 112	Nihonium 113	Flerovium 114	Moscovium 115	Livermorium 116	Tennessine 117	Oganesson 118
Ds	**Rg**	**Cn**	**Nh**	**Fl**	**Mc**	**Lv**	**Ts**	**Og**
[281.16]	[280.16]	[285.17]	[284.18]	[289.19]	[288.19]	[293]	[294]	[294]

63	Gadolinium 64	Terbium 65	Dysprosium 66	Holmium 67	Erbium 68	Thulium 69	Ytterbium 70	Lutetium 71
	Gd	**Tb**	**Dy**	**Ho**	**Er**	**Tm**	**Yb**	**Lu**
	157.25	158.93	162.5	164.93	167.26	168.93	173.04	174.97

95	Curium 96	Berkelium 97	Californium 98	Einsteinium 99	Fermium 100	Mendelevium 101	Nobelium 102	Lawrencium 103
	Cm	**Bk**	**Cf**	**Es**	**Fm**	**Md**	**No**	**Lr**
	[247.07]	[247.07]	[251.08]	[252.08]	[257.1]	[258.1]	[259.1]	[262.11]